The Unified Sta

An Agile and Resilient Approach to Data Warehouse and Analytics Design

Bill Inmon

Francesco Puppini

Technics Publications

Published by:

2 Lindsley Road
Basking Ridge, NJ 07920 USA
https://www.TechnicsPub.com

Edited by Sadie Hoberman
Cover design by Lorena Molinari

First Printing 2020

ISBN, print ed.	9781634628877
ISBN, Kindle ed.	9781634628884
ISBN, ePub ed.	9781634628891
ISBN, PDF ed.	9781634628907

Library of Congress Control Number: 2020946176

Acknowledgements

My first thanks go to Cindi Meyersohn, for the incredible support that she has given me throughout this adventure.

I also want to express my gratitude to all the people who have shared with me resources, contents, opinions and encouragements. Thank you, Steve Hoberman, Christian Kaul, Neil Strange, Kent Graziano, Mary Mink, Nols Ebersohn, Vincent McBurney, Julie Burroughs, Mike Lampa, Philip Lima, Aileen Sun, Christof Wenzeritt, Ersan Duran, Armin Gorgin, Antonio Viñé, Nico Fritz, Uli Waller, Carlos Aranibar, Chanakya Shah, Magda Murowańska, David Duchin, and Marcella Puppini.

A special mention goes to Giuseppe Boccuzzi for the endless hours of discussion and confrontation that we had on the topics that appear in this book. Dialogue is the foundation of knowledge.

But the biggest thanks go to Bill Inmon, for being the person who said: *Francesco, you need to write a book.*

Thanks to everyone,

Francesco Puppini

Contents at a Glance

Contents

Foreword

I had the pleasure of meeting and talking with Francesco Puppini a few years ago at the World Wide Data Vault Consortium. The WWDVC event draws data warehousing practitioners, Data Vault 2.0 practitioners and certified instructors, data analytics professionals, and industry thought leaders from all over the globe. It provides a rich, collaborative environment for forward-thinking professionals to share experiences, lessons learned, and future perspectives in our ever-changing data industry.

It was in this delightful petri dish that I was introduced to Francesco by my friend, Bill Inmon. I first met Bill in 2016 when he was introduced to me at the WWDVC 2016 consortium by Daniel Linstedt, the founder and inventor of the Data Vault (1.0 and 2.0); my dear friend and now business partner.

I was so amazed by Bill's humble and gentle presence. I cannot thank him enough for his wisdom and mentoring, not to mention the "doubled over in tears" laughter that he has gifted to me over the last four years from stories he has shared from his life experiences and our crazy industry. Bill is one of the funniest and best storytellers I have ever known. I consider him a national treasure. It is my honor and delight to be able to call him my friend. For those of you too young to know, much less remember, every single individual involved in data analytics and warehousing owes much to Bill (William H.) Inmon's extensive, lifetime contributions to the creation of our industry and livelihoods. Bill has been and remains to this day, one of our industry's most influential thought leaders.

Having been in IT for over 35 years, I was impressed that *the* "Father of Data Warehousing" was so intrigued by Francesco's concept that he wanted to co-author a book with this Italian innovator. Bill described Francesco as an energetic, passionate, bright, forward-thinking individual. My first encounter with Francesco confirmed Bill's description. I've had numerous opportunities to engage with Francesco and to listen to him wax eloquent regarding what I affectionately refer to as the "Puppini Bridge" – the central object around which the Unified Star Schema (USS) was conceived and developed.

Having read through Francesco's writings several times, the idea that he presents in the USS is an approach that complements the variety of consumable objects made available in the Data Vault 2.0 (DV2) Information Delivery layer. The concepts behind, and the implementation of, the Puppini Bridge, provide data analytics professionals with a set of keys from which rapid joins to the underlying data may be more easily assembled. Using this table of keys should render highly performant queries and deliver consistent results when adopted by the enterprise. Francesco has been extremely successful in solving his clients' analytics challenges through his development and refinement of the USS. He has fully embraced this construct and has implemented the USS across a variety of industries and data sets.

In my discussions with Francesco, he expressed his desire to "load test" the USS, and he has invited our community to actively participate in this endeavor, providing him with feedback on the results. His openness to having his approach critiqued speaks highly of his professionalism and passion for introducing effective solutions to some of our industry's tough analytics challenges. I hope to see the Puppini Bridge tested across a variety of industry verticals at increasing data volumes and velocity. As you read this book, I ask you to consider accepting this challenge and become active in proving the USS to be an effective tool in producing highly performant, consumable objects for your business's information delivery portfolio.

All the best, Francesco and Bill!

Cynthia Meyersohn, Founder & CEO, Authorized Data Vault 2.0 Instructor
DataRebels, LLC, www.datarebels.com, cindi@datarebels.com

Introduction

Master the most agile and resilient design for building analytics applications: the Unified Star Schema (USS) approach. The USS has many benefits over traditional dimensional modeling. Witness the power of the USS as a single star schema that serves as a foundation to be used for all present and future business requirements of your organization.

Data warehouse legend Bill Inmon and data warehouse expert Francesco Puppini explain step-by-step, why the USS approach is the preferred approach for business intelligence designs today, and how to use this approach through many examples.

This book contains two parts. Part I, Architecture, explains the benefits of data marts and data warehouses, covering how organizations progressed to their current state of analytics, and challenges that are faced as a result of current business intelligence architectures. There are eight chapters within Part I:

- **Chapter 1**, Data Marts and the Dimensional Model: Know the drivers behind, and the characteristics of, the data warehouse and data mart.

- **Chapter 2**, Dimensional Modeling Concepts: Master dimensional modeling concepts, including fact tables, dimensions, star joins, and snowflakes.

- **Chapter 3**, Data Mart Evolution: Appreciate the benefits of multiple data marts, and also the data quality, versioning, and credibility problems caused by improper data mart management.

- **Chapter 4**, Transformations: Understand the process of Extract, Transform, and Load (ETL), and the value ETL brings to reporting.

- **Chapter 5**, The Integrated Data Mart Approach: Know how a data warehouse benefits an organization's reporting efforts.

- **Chapter 6**, Monitoring the Data Mart Environment: Learn the motivations for monitoring data marts. Identify which data needs to be modified, distinguish actively used from inactively used data, and see how to purge dormant data.

- **Chapter 7**, Metadata and Documentation in the Data Mart Environment: Learn about the different types of metadata within the data warehouse environment, including table and element metadata, source metadata, load date metadata, combined metadata, and usage metadata.

- **Chapter 8**, The Evolution toward Integrated Data Marts: Progress through the evolution to our current modern data warehouse environment.

Part II, the Unified Star Schema, covers the Unified Star Schema (USS) approach and how it solves the challenges introduced in Part I. There are eight chapters within Part II:

- **Chapter 9**, Introduction to the Unified Star Schema: Become acquainted with the USS in this chapter. Learn about its architecture and use cases, as well as how the USS approach differs from the traditional approach. Analogies will reinforce key USS concepts, such as hunter and prey and houses connected with telephone lines. Also, this chapter will show you the dangers of denormalization.

- **Chapter 10**, Loss of Data: Learn about the loss of data and the reason why a full outer join in a data mart is not recommended. Witness that all the other joins (inner, left, and right), by definition, discard some data. For this reason, a data mart that has been prepared with these joins can only answer a subset of the possible questions. Understand that the USS approach does not create any join, and for this reason, it has no loss of data. Be introduced to the USS naming convention, which makes life easier for both developers and end-users. Also, learn about the Bridge and see how it connects to the other tables. Follow along with a practical implementation with Spotfire—it is so easy for the end-users to create a dashboard even without being data experts.

- **Chapter 11**, The Fan Trap: Get introduced to the Oriented Data Model convention, and learn the dangers of a fan trap through an example. Learn an alternative notation for the one-to-many relationship, which recalls the idea of "spreading". Differentiate join and association, and realize that an "in-memory association" is the preferred solution to the fan trap. Also, learn about the techniques of "splitting the measures" and "moving all the measures to the Bridge". Finally, see an example of the JSON fan trap and how it can be fixed.

- **Chapter 12**, The Chasm Trap: Become familiar with the Cartesian product, and then follow along with an example of a chasm trap based on LinkedIn, which illustrates that a chasm trap produces unwanted duplicates. Learn about how the chasm trap grows between linear and quadratic. Understand the method for the chasm trap row count, which helps to calculate the exact number of rows of the resulting table. See that the Bridge is based on a union, which does not create any duplicates. Finally, see an example of the JSON chasm trap and how it can be fixed.

- **Chapter 13**, Multi-Fact Queries: Distinguish between multiple facts "with direct connection" versus multiple facts "with no direct connection". See that a many-to-many relationship corresponds to a dangerous chasm trap with measures. Learn that although the best operation with a many-to-many relationship is the union, the union is difficult to create and can be confusing. Explore how BI tools are capable of building aggregated virtual rows, and how the USS approach is based on the Bridge, which naturally embeds the union. Follow along with an implementation in Spotfire to see how easy the end-users can build a valuable dashboard.

- **Chapter 14**, Loops: Learn more about loops and five traditional techniques to solve them. See that the USS approach is based on the Bridge, which naturally embeds the union. Consequently, the USS approach is a very good solution to the loops. Follow along with an SAP Business Objects implementation, which will illustrate that with the USS approach, the end-users can have a real "self-service experience".

- **Chapter 15**, Non-Conformed Granularities: Learn about non-conformed granularities through an example. See that creating a BI solution, when the dimensions are non-conformed, can present a number of challenges which have been traditionally solved by either creating ad-hoc queries, or by building dashboards that are not integrated. Learn that the Unified Star Schema introduces a solution called "re-normalization". Witness the benefits, including that the developers are only needed for the setup phase of the USS, and that the USS does not depend on the business requirements, so the end-users will be free to implement their personalized reports and dashboards.

- **Chapter 16**, Northwind Case Study. Witness how easy it is to detect the pitfalls of Northwind using the ODM convention. Verify that a join involving tables that form fan traps and chasm traps risks to produce incorrect totals. Become familiar with the concept of a "safe zone for a table", and that if we join all the tables together, not a single measure will have correct totals. Follow along with an implementation of the USS approach on the Northwind database with various BI tools. Understand that with the USS approach, all tables belong to a common safe zone: everything is compatible with everything.

Part I

Architecture

CHAPTER 1

Data Marts and the Dimensional Model

In the beginning, there were simple applications. These first applications were for human resources, inventory control, accounts payable, and a wide variety of subjects. The first applications gathered data, stored the data, and made the data available for reporting. Figure 1.1 depicts one of the first simple applications.

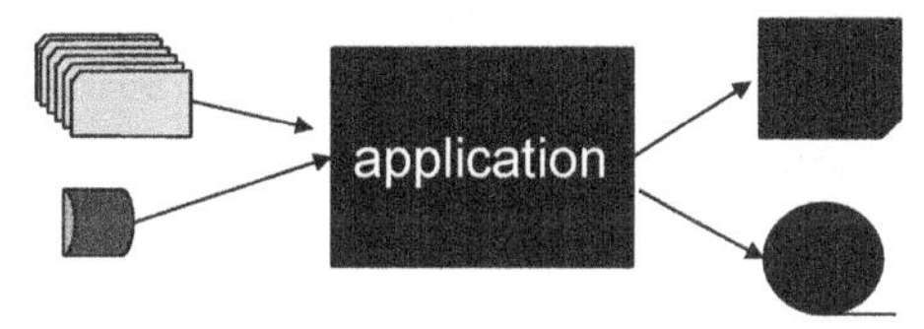

Figure 1.1: A simple application

These applications made use of master files. These applications grew in size and complexity. Soon very sophisticated, very large applications appeared. Then there were all sorts of interlocking applications. One application captured data and then fed it to another application. In short order, there was a proliferation of applications. Figure 1.2 shows the jungle of applications that appeared.

One of the features of the application-centric architecture was the existence of extract programs. The extract program was simple and innocent enough. An extract program merely moved data from one application to the next. The extract program appeared because the end-user using one application found that it would be useful to have data from another application. Rapidly, the same data element began to appear in many places throughout the architecture.

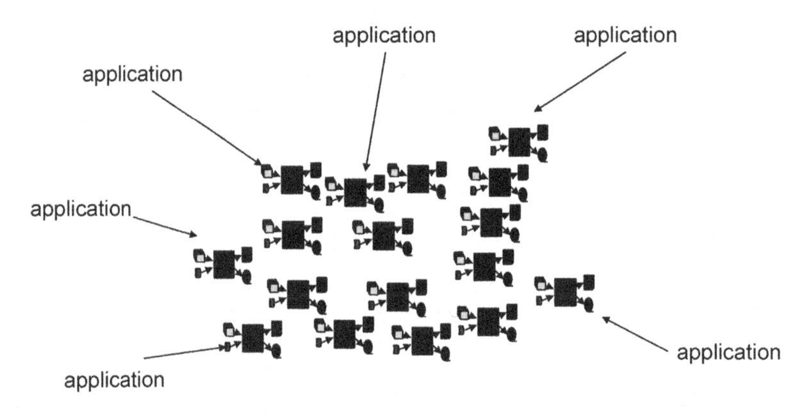

Figure 1.2: Soon there was a proliferation of applications

With this proliferation of data came even greater confusion. Not only was the same data element to be found in many places, but often due to timing issues or coding errors, there were different values for this data element throughout the architecture. There was chaos. It was a real challenge for management to make good decisions when no one knew what data was correct. Figure 1.3 shows the chaos.

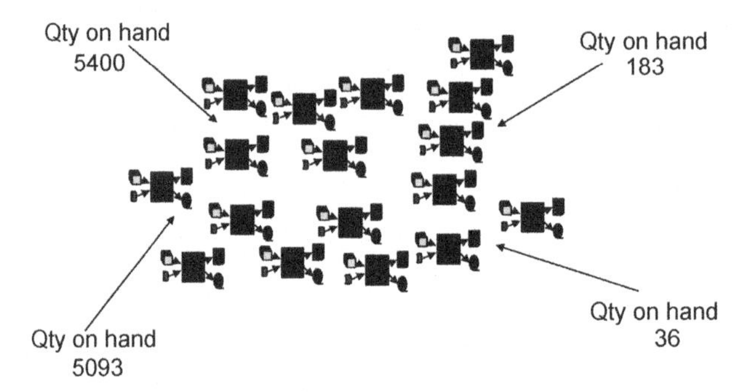

Figure 1.3: Data proliferation caused confusion as to the actual value and veracity of data

At the root of the problem was the approach to building applications. Applications were built to optimize information capture and storage, whereas requirements for the analysis of this data were ignored. Furthermore, applications had a narrow scope. The application focused on a small set of data that represented only a tiny portion of the business of the enterprise. Figure 1.4 shows the limited focus of each application.

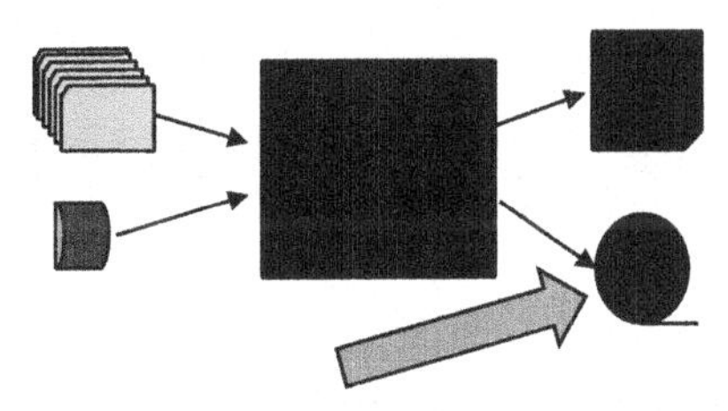

Figure 1.4: Data was optimized for capture and storage, not analysis

While each application may have solved a specific business problem, the applications did not work in harmony with each other.

The advent of the extract program created an environment where there was lots of data but no believable data.

In a word, the application-centric architecture had a major problem with data integrity. The problems of data integrity crept into the organization like a thief in the night. No loud bang or no trumpet announced the issues of data integrity. Instead, data integrity issues just appeared as the application-centric architecture grew and aged. An interesting observation is that trying to fix the problems of the application-centric architecture stymied most organizations. For years the way that organizations solved problems was to buy more technology and hire more consultants.

When confronted by the challenges of the application-centric architecture, buying more technology and hiring more people only made the problem worse, not better.

To use an analogy. Suppose a house is on fire. You take a bucket of liquid to try to douse the fire. The only problem is that your liquid is not water, but gasoline. Throwing gasoline on a fire to extinguish the fire has the opposite effect that you desire. And thus it was with the application-centric architecture. Buying more technology and adding more people made the problems of the application-centric architecture even worse, not better. Figure 1.5 shows this phenomenon.

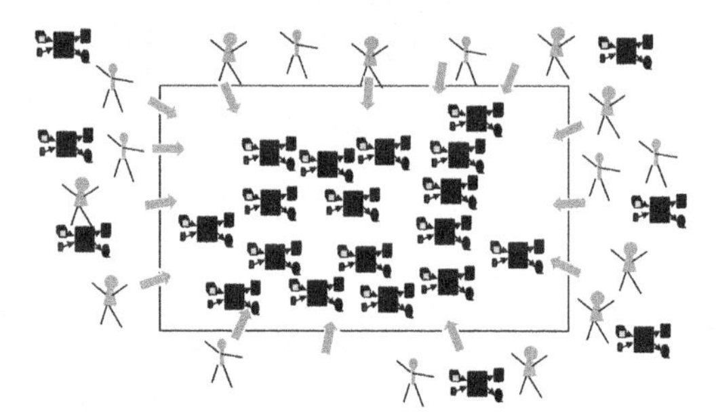

Figure 1.5: More people, machines, and technology only made matters worse

A profound change in architecture was needed. Enter the data warehouse. The emphasis on this new type of database was not on the capture and storage of information, but instead on organizing and preparing data for analytical processing. Features of the data warehouse included the need to have integrated data (corporate data) and to store data for a lengthy period. In addition, data was cast in the form of a series of snapshots in the data warehouse. Figure 1.6 shows the movement to the data warehouse.

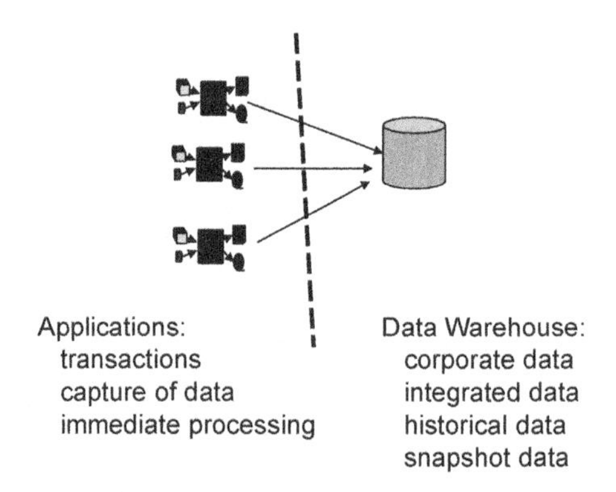

Figure 1.6: Movement to the data warehouse

As a simple example of the meaning of corporate data, suppose there are three applications. In one application, gender is signified by "m" or "f". In the next application, gender is signified by a "1" or a "0". In the third application, gender is signified by "male" or "female". When data is placed in the data warehouse, the data element gender is signified by only one representation. The applications that feed the data warehouse that do not specify gender the same way must be converted. When someone goes to read and interpret the data warehouse, there is a singular representation of gender. The simple example shown here is just that—simple. In reality, when data is loaded in the data warehouse, the transformation of data is almost always much more complex than the simple example shown here. Figure 1.7 shows the transformation of data from the application environment to the corporate environment.

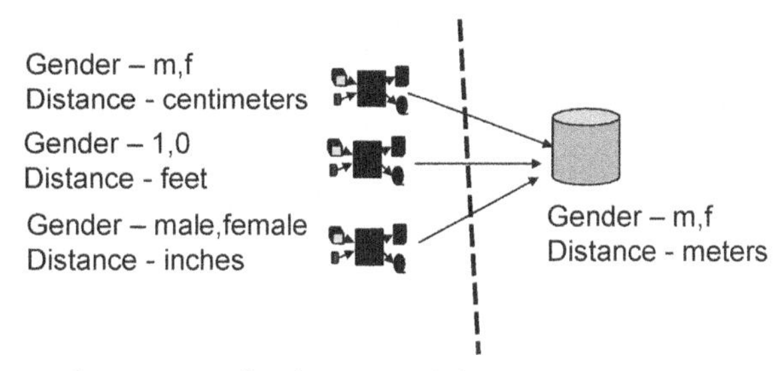

Figure 1.7: The data warehouse contains integrated data

Another feature of the data warehouse is the ability to hold lengthy amounts of data. In simple applications, there is often the desire to hold the minimum amount of data possible. This is because lengthy amounts of data slow down the application. For that reason, it is normal to find only a month's worth of data in the application. But in the data warehouse, it is normal to find five to ten years' worth of data. From the standpoint of timeliness, the data warehouse holds far more history than the applications. Figure 1.8 shows this difference.

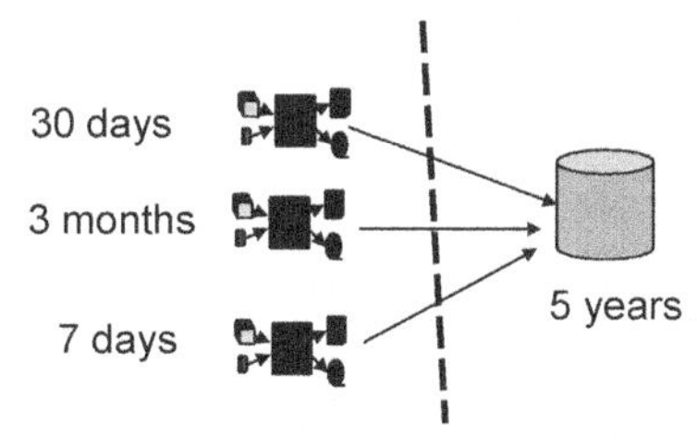

Figure 1.8: The data warehouse contains historical data

Yet another significant difference between the data warehouse and the application is the fact that data is frequently updated in the application. It is said of application data that data is current "up to the second". A simple example is your bank account balance. The bank works hard to make sure that when you access your account balance, the data found in the account is accurate. If it is 2:00 pm and your wife has made an ATM activity at 10:30 am, that ATM activity is reflected in your account when you go to access it at 2:00 pm.

Data in the data warehouse is fundamentally different. Data in the data warehouse is a series of snapshots. You can look out over the past month and find out every activity that has occurred against your account by looking in the data warehouse. Figure 1.9 shows the difference between the application database and the data warehouse database.

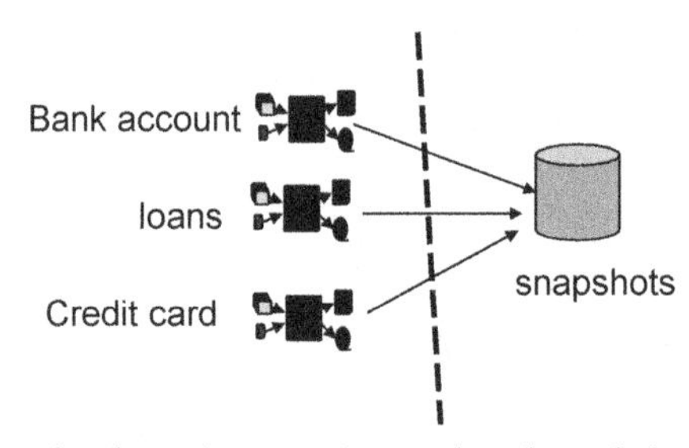

Figure 1.9: Applications contain data that can be updated, and data warehouses contain data that is a series of snapshots

While data warehousing represented an architectural solution to the problems of data integrity that plagued the application-centric environment, there were some problems with data warehousing. The primary problem with data warehousing came because the implementation of a data warehouse required an enterprise-wide effort. Many organizations had neither the will nor the vision to embark on a long term data warehouse development. To build a data warehouse successfully, there had to be an organization-wide effort led by top management. And getting that long term commitment and support from management was a difficult thing to do. Figure 1.10 shows that building a data warehouse was an enterprise-wide effort.

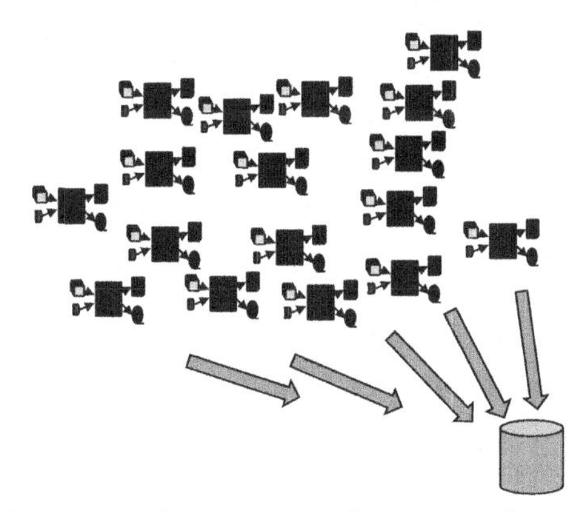

Figure 1.10: The data warehouse requires an enterprise approach

A more palatable approach to the problem was the approach of building a data mart. A data mart was very similar to a data warehouse in many respects. But the single largest difference was that a data mart required a much smaller scope of effort than the data warehouse. Because of the much smaller scale, a data mart could be built much more quickly. And a data mart did not require the cooperation and coordination across all entities in the enterprise. The data mart organized data so that the data was able to be easily analyzed. The data mart only looked across a single department, not across the entire organization. For these reasons (and more) the data mart required a much smaller scale of effort for development. Figure 1.11 shows the building of a data mart. To a very small extent, the data mart addressed the issue of data integrity. However, the data only addressed integrity from the standpoint of the view of a single department (out of potentially many departments).

When viewed on a smaller scale, the issues of data integrity across one or two departments is a much smaller problem than the issue of data integrity across the entire enterprise. Figure 1.12 shows the smaller scale of the data mart.

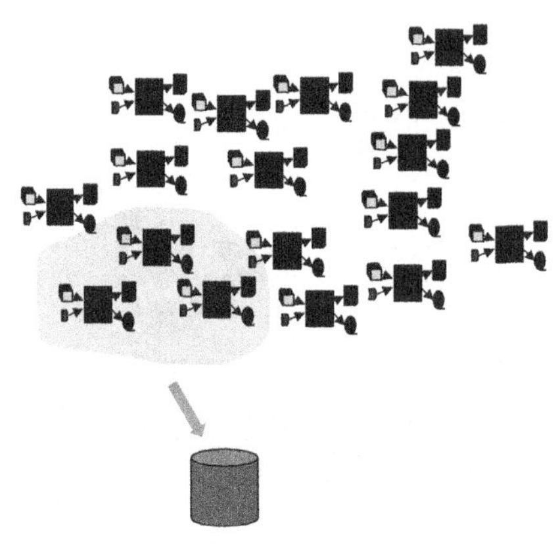

Figure 1.11: When the scope is narrowed, the task of building the structure is greatly lessened

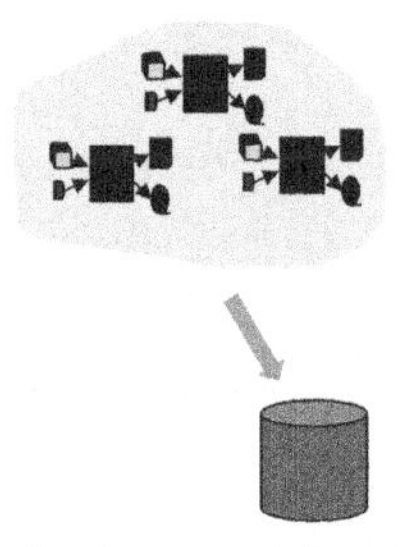

Figure 1.12: For a smaller organization, the issues of data integrity may not be as great

---

Because of the smaller scope of data that applies to data marts, the primary objective of database design for the data mart is the analysis of data (rather than the integrity of the data). The data mart lays data out so that it can be easily accessed and analyzed.

The data mart shares several characteristics with the data warehouse. Both the data warehouse and the data mart contain snapshot data. In that regard, they are very similar. But the data warehouse includes a lengthy amount of historical data, whereas the data mart contains only a fraction of historical data. Data is integrated across the enterprise before it enters the data warehouse. Usually, not much integration of data is needed when it is pulled from a single application. Because of the enterprise-wide nature of data in the data warehouse, there is usually a robust number of data elements in the data warehouse. But there are far fewer data elements in the data mart because it represents only departmental data. Figure 1.13 shows the difference between the two types of data structures.

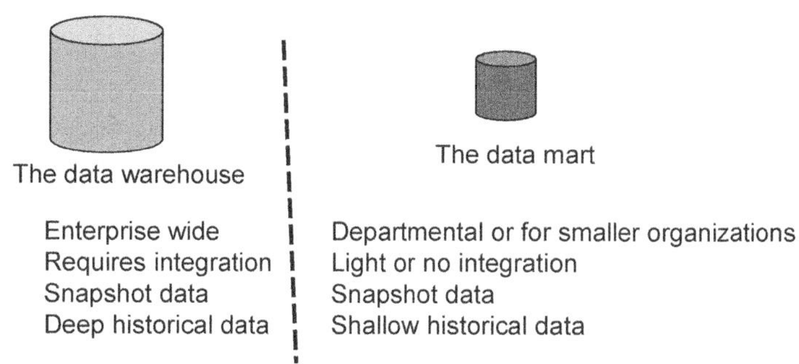

Figure 1.13: The difference between the data warehouse and data mart

The basic structuring of data in the data warehouse is the relational model. Figure 1.14 shows that the relational model provides a solid foundation for the data warehouse.

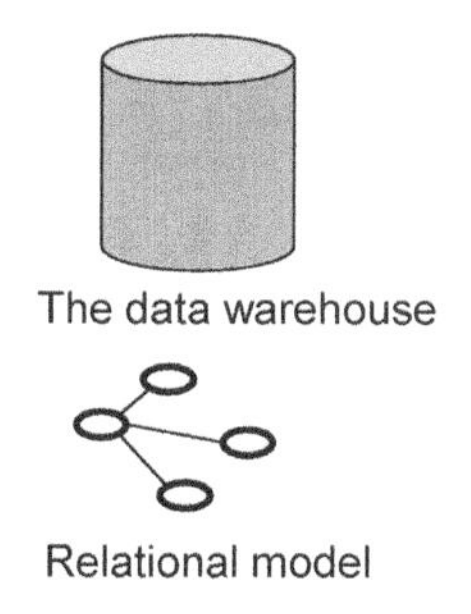

Figure 1.14: The standard foundation for the data warehouse is the relational model

The basic structuring for the data mart is the dimensional model. Figure 1.15 depicts the dimensional model.

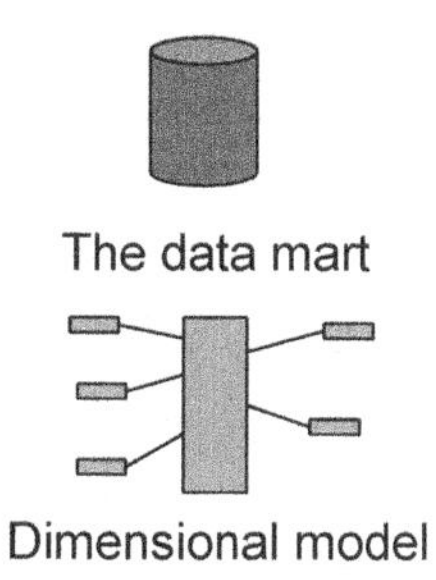

Figure 1.15: The dimensional model forms the basis for the data mart

CHAPTER 2

Dimensional Modeling Concepts

The dimensional model is designed to allow data to be accessed and analyzed easily. There are a minimal number of data relationships in the dimensional model. The fact that there are few relationships in the dimensional model means that the programmer does not have to do many (or any) complex joins to access the data. The dimensional model is portrayed in Figure 2.1.

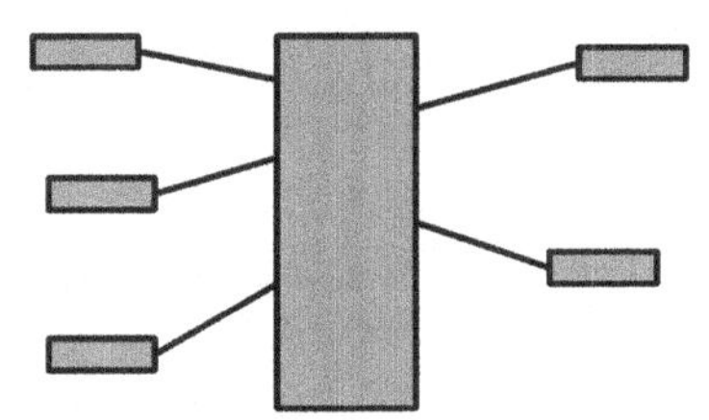

Figure 2.1: The dimensional model

There are two basic components to the dimensional model: fact and dimension tables. The fact table is the place where the bulk of the data is stored. Figure 2.2 depicts a fact table.

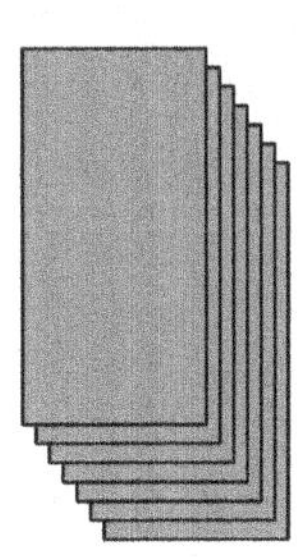

Figure 2.2: Fact tables

Typical fact tables are for things such as:

- The sales made by a retailer
- The telephone calls made by a sales organization
- The transactions made by a bank

A fact table includes many different types of data elements. A sales fact table might have data elements such as:

- Date of sale
- Item sold
- Sales price
- Taxes paid
- Location of sale
- Customer name
- Customer contact information
- Shipping information
- Condition of purchase

For a sales organization that makes telephone calls, the fact table may have information such as:

- Date of call
- Time of call
- Number called
- Length of call
- Call agent
- Action item from call
- Customer name
- Customer location

Typically, in a fact table, there are lots of different types of data that are combined into the table to allow for easy analysis. As such, the elements of data in the fact table are not highly normalized.

The other type of data found in a dimensional model is the dimension table. The dimension table expands information for the elements found in the fact table. Figure 2.3 depicts the positioning of the dimensions surrounding the fact table.

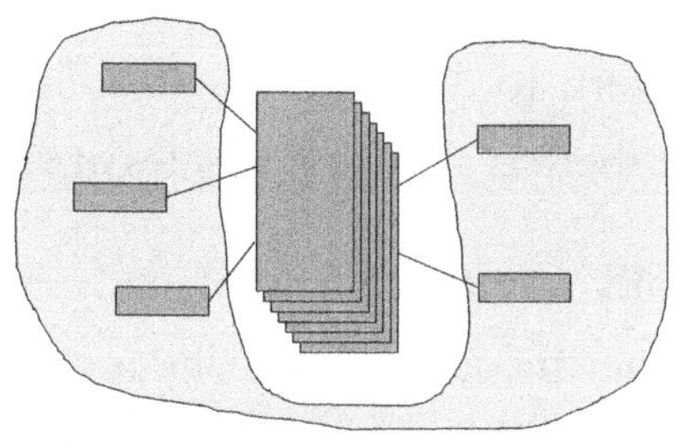

Figure 2.3: Dimensions surround fact tables

Typical dimensions might include:

- Time
- Date
- Product
- Customer
- Store

The dimensions link to the fact table by the existence of an element of data found in the fact table. Together the fact table and its dimensions form a structure referred to as the "star join". Figure 2.4 shows a simple star join.

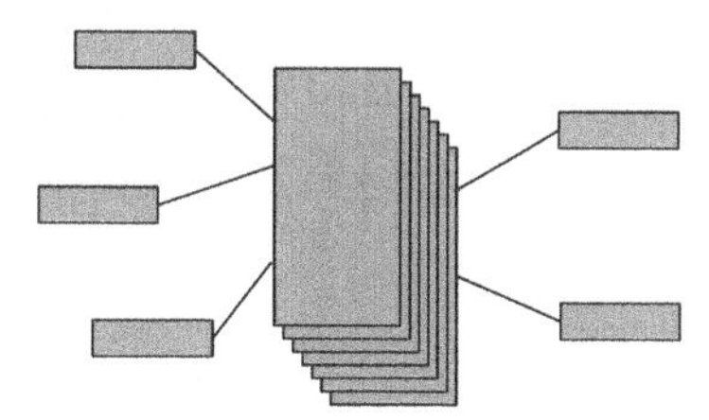

Figure 2.4: A "star join"

One of the most important aspects of the star join is the granularity of the data. The granularity of the data found in the fact table has great implications. The finer the granularity of the data, the more detailed the analysis that can be done.

For example, keeping a record of monthly sales does not allow the analyst to go more deeply into the days of the month. If all there is in the fact table is monthly sales, then the analyst cannot see if there are patterns on sales on a Friday, for example. Now suppose the analyst keeps track of data daily. The analyst can examine if there is a pattern to the sales on a Friday. But the analyst cannot examine the data to see if there is a pattern to sales at 9:00 am.

The granularity then greatly affects the kind of analysis that can be done against the data. As a rule, the finer the granularity, the more detailed the analysis can be. However, there is a practical limit as to how granular data can be. Data can be too finely granular. Take the stock market, for example. Suppose a record is written for every sale of stock. In a day, there would be billions of records that are written. There would be so many records written that important patterns would be hidden behind the many, many records of stock trades. A much more practical way, which reduces volume, is to keep track of stock records at the daily closing price. But by looking at the daily closing price, the analyst cannot do an analysis of the stock price at noon. So, there is a tradeoff in choosing the granularity of data in the fact table. The granularity should be low enough to accommodate normal analytical activities reasonably, but not so low as to create data that hides important trends and patterns. On occasion, it is desirable to have more than one fact table in the dimensional model. When multiple fact tables share the same dimension, that dimension is called a conformed dimension. Figure 2.5 shows a conformed dimension.

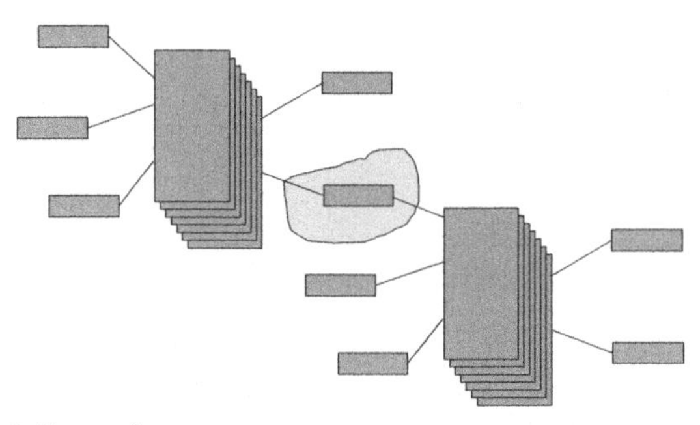

Figure 2.5: A conformed dimension

The only constraint with conformed dimensions is that they need to fit the granularity of the fact tables that are created. In some cases, the need to "normalize" the dimension table across multiple fact tables can present significant challenges to the designer.

Related to conformed dimensions is the snowflake structure. A snowflake structure is one where the different dimension tables can themselves have dimensions. Figure 2.6 shows a snowflake structure.

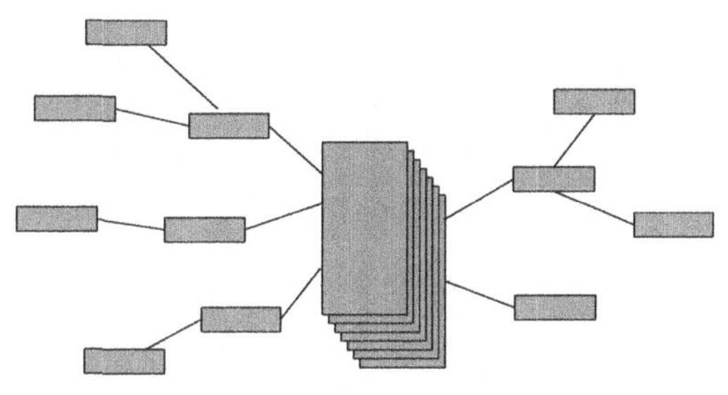

Figure 2.6: A snowflake structure

Once the first cut at design is made, it is a common practice to go into the star join and remove duplicate elements of data. The removal of duplicate elements of data is a crude form of the practice of normalization. Figure 2.7 shows the removal of duplicate elements of data that may have crept into the design of the star join.

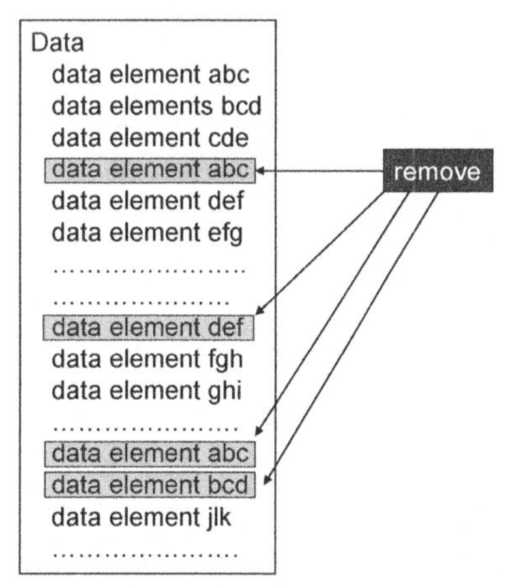

Figure 2.7: Data in the structure is "normalized"

Another feature of the dimensional model is the existence of views of data. Once the physical database has been created within the database management system, it is possible to define subsets of the physical model into a "view". The creation of a view can make it simpler for the end-user to access and interpret the data found in the dimensional model. Figure 2.8 shows a view that has been defined for the dimensional model.

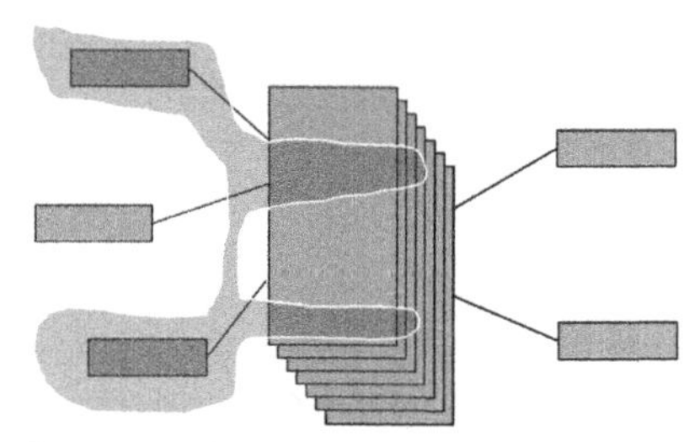

Figure 2.8: Internal "views" of data can be created

While there is no duplication of data elements in the dimensional model, on occasion, it makes sense to duplicate a few fields of data to enhance the performance of processing against the dimensional tables of data. See Figure 2.9.

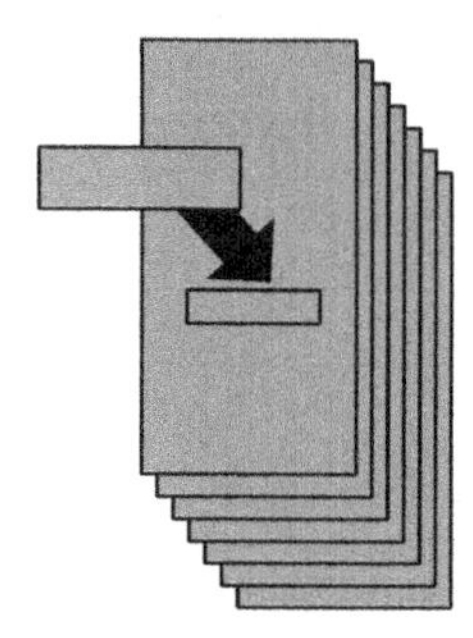

Figure 2.9: Occasionally, it makes sense to denormalize data for the sake of performance

CHAPTER 3

Data Mart Evolution

One day the organization wakes up to a world of applications. The applications were all designed for the capture and storage of data. The organization decides that it needs data from the applications. At that point, a data mart is sourced from one or more applications. Figure 3.1 shows the building of the first data mart.

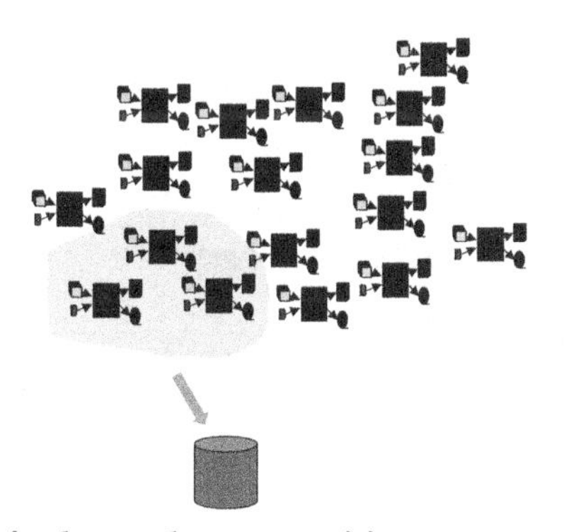

Figure 3.1: The first data mart is always the most exciting

The first data mart is the most exciting. The data mart was built cheaply and quickly. And once built, the data mart serves as an excellent base for analytical processing.

Success of the data mart spreads. Soon other departments within the organization decide that they want to build their own data marts. Figure 3.2 shows the advent of some new data marts.

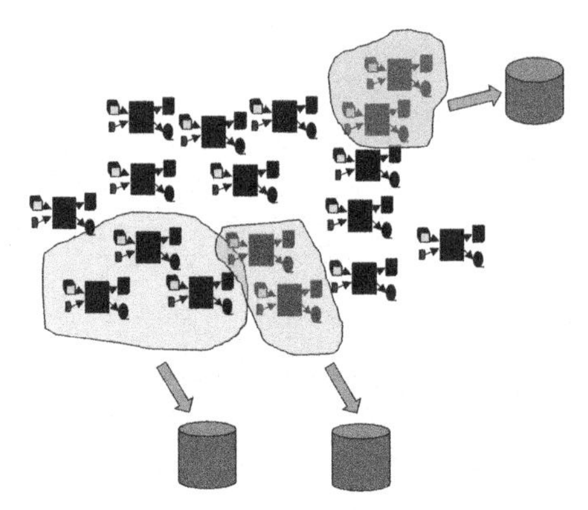

Figure 3.2: The next few data marts are soon built

Word continues to spread, and soon lots of other departments decide to build their own data marts. The building of lots of data marts is seen in Figure 3.3.

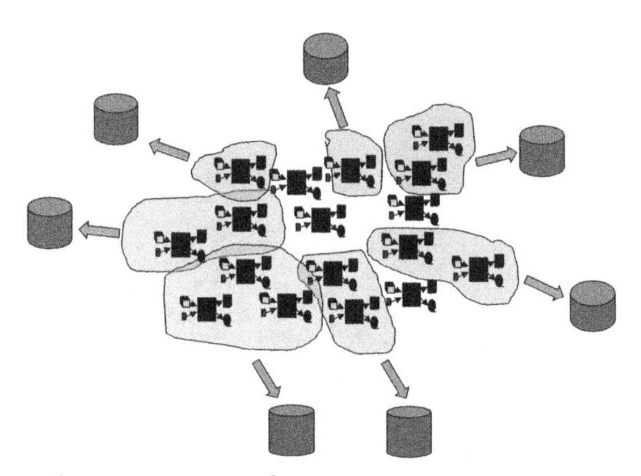

Figure 3.3: Soon there are data marts everywhere

These data marts are usually built around a single department. The departments that have their own data marts include marketing, sales, finance, human resources, and engineering. Figure 3.4 shows the affinity of the data marts for different departments.

Everything is fine. People are happy with their data marts. However, one day a top manager notices something curious. Top management asks each department for their cash projections for the next quarter. It is at this point that top management discovers that each department has its own set of numbers, and there's no agreement across the organization as to what set of numbers are correct.

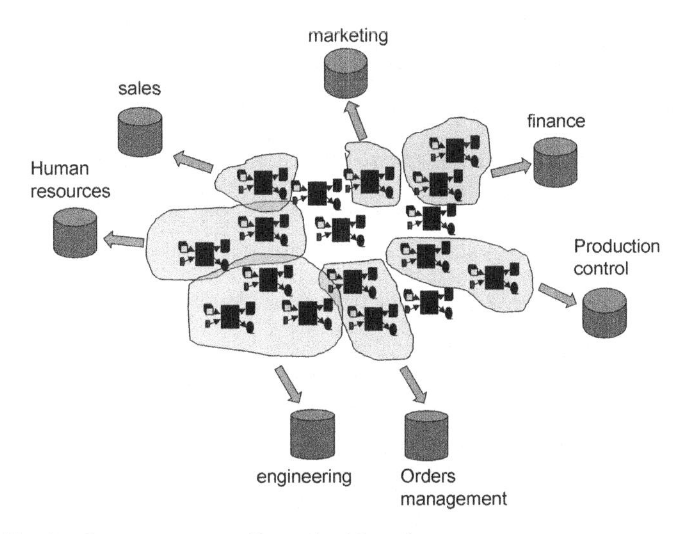

Figure 3.4: Usually the data marts are aligned with a department

Each department thinks that their set of numbers are correct. Figure 3.5 shows the dilemma of management.

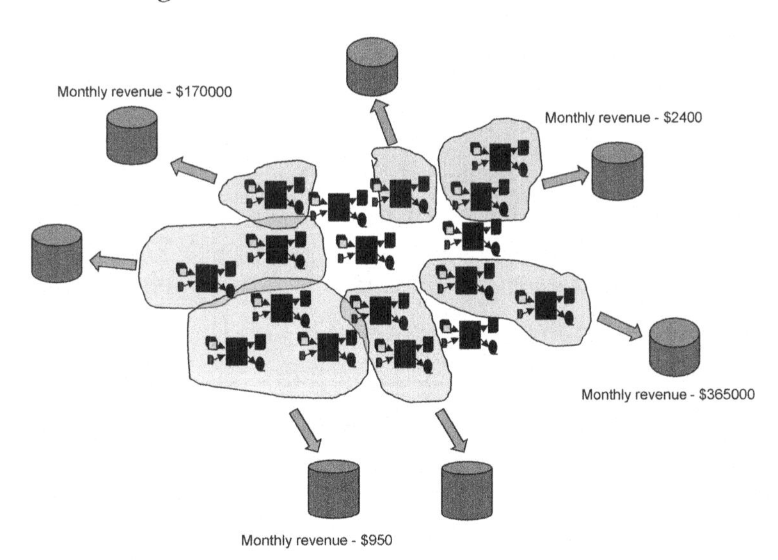

Figure 3.5: The same data appears in different data marts with a different value

---

How does management decide whose numbers are correct?
Furthermore, how does management untangle the mess that has been created?

Complicating matters is the fact that there are not just different data marts for different departments. Instead, there are different data marts for the same department! Organizations just create a new data mart instead of making changes to a data mart. Nothing happens to the old data mart once the new one is built, so now there are two data marts for the same data where once there was only one data mart. Figure 3.6 shows that over time the same department starts to accumulate multiple data marts.

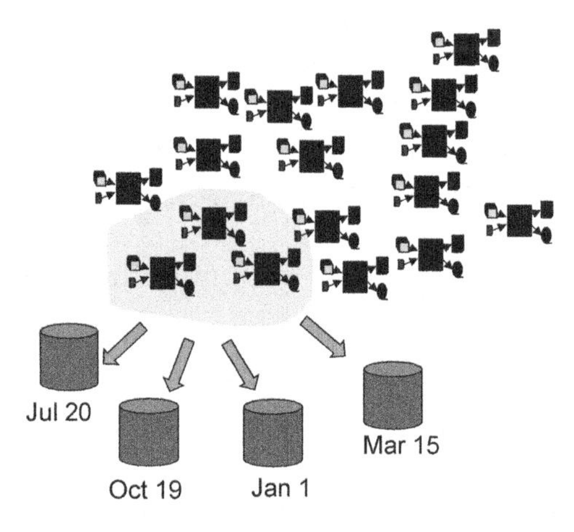

Figure 3.6: When the requirements for the data mart change, a new data mart is built, rather than doing maintenance on the existing data mart

In the face of conflicting data marts for different departments and multiple data marts for the same department, management is faced with a real dilemma as to who to believe. The building of data marts starts out with simple and honest intentions. As long as there are only a few applications, an architecture based on data marts works. But in the face of lots of applications, an architecture based on data marts leads to a quagmire. The basic problem with a data mart architecture based on lots of applications is the integrity of the data. Figure 3.7 shows the problems associated with such an architecture.

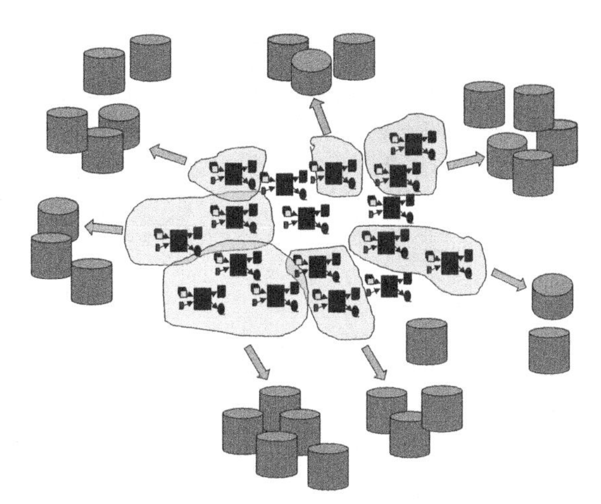

Figure 3.7: What happens to data marts over time...a big mess

The problems with the architecture seen in Figure 3.7 can be classified. The first problem is the creation and existence of duplicate data marts. Duplicate data marts are created as a by-product of the practice of never deleting a data mart once a new one is created. Figure 3.8 shows that there are duplicate data marts.

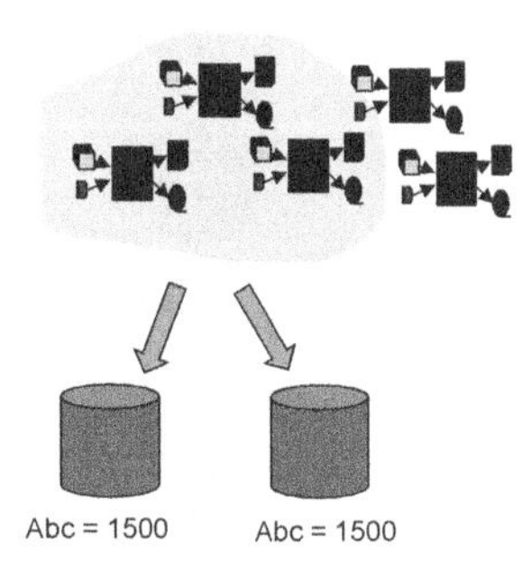

Figure 3.8: Duplicate data marts

The second kind of problem that arises is the creation of an "orphan" data mart. An orphan data mart is a data mart whose application is unconnected or unrelated to any other application. An orphan data mart is built from a totally disconnected application. The data from the orphan data mart has no connection or no relationship to the other data found in the organization. Figure 3.9 shows an orphan data mart.

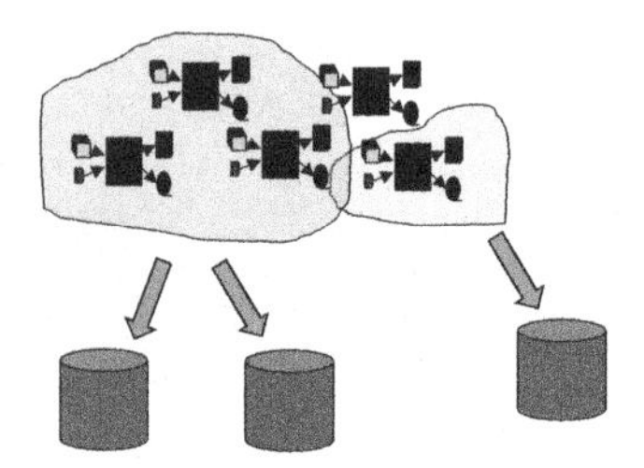

Figure 3.9: Orphan data marts

The third type of problem is the "bastard" data mart, which contains the same type of data as another data mart, but where the values presented to the user are different. Figure 3.10 shows a bastard data mart. Data mart abc has the monthly revenue for July at $10,871, whereas the next data mart, bcd, has the monthly revenue for July at $75,209. The bastard data marts purport to present the same data, but the data has widely divergent values.

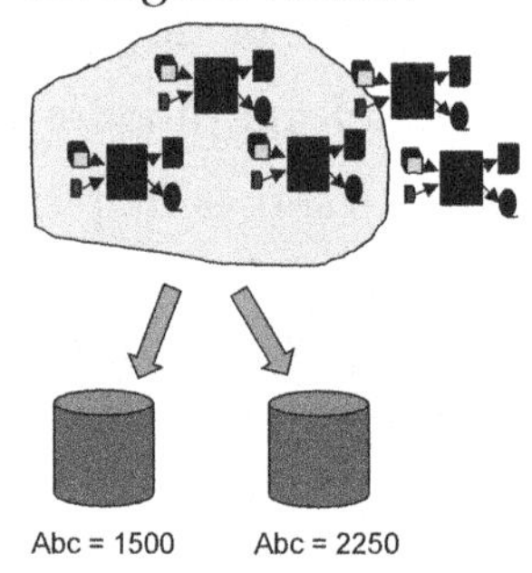

Figure 3.10: Bastard data marts

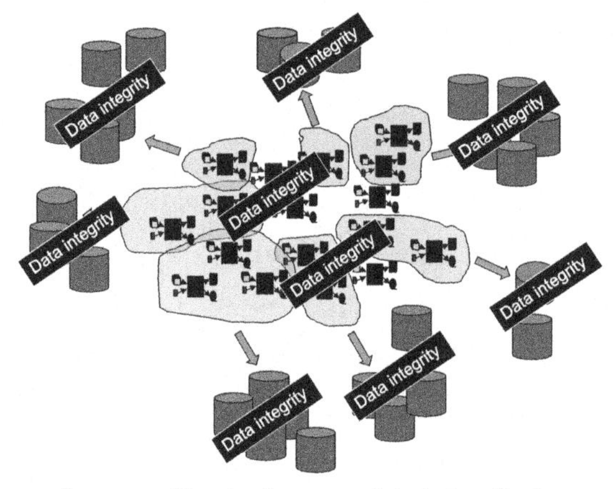

Figure 3.11: Duplicates, orphans, and bastards cause data integrity issues everywhere!

CHAPTER 4

Transformations

It seems that there is a lot of redundant data in the organization. There is data in the operational environment, and there appears to be the same data in the analytical and archival environment. And in the past, it has been observed that redundant data can lead to some very nasty difficulties. But there is a perfectly rational explanation for this apparent phenomenon of having redundant data in the databases of the organization. To explain why there is apparently a lot of data redundancy, consider the fact that the organization, at a high level, can be divided into several different modes of operation or intercourse:

- **Conversation**. The conversation mode is one where people have an interchange of words. The interchange can be between customers and representatives, between managers and employees, and between employees and people interviewing for a job. Conversations occur everywhere and for every reason imaginable.

- **Personal**. The personal mode of operation occurs when something happens on a personal level. A person may marry and change their name. A person may change addresses. A person may have a child that is born. There are many, many personal changes of states.

- **Operational**. The operational mode is where the organization does its business. In the operational mode, sales are made, contracts are signed, products are produced, installations of products are made, and so forth.

- **Litigation**. The litigation mode is where the organization engages in the court system to rectify a situation. Litigation may protect against a lawsuit, may prosecute a lawsuit, may advise on proper procedure, and so forth.

- **Analytical**. The analytical mode of operation is one where decisions are made. In the analytical mode it is decided to stop making a product, to start making a new product, to expand the market into a foreign country, to invest in research, and so forth.

- **Archival**. The archival mode is one where data is stored for lengthy periods of time. There may be lots of reasons why data needs to be stored for a lengthy period of time—statutory, market share analysis, historical curiosity, and so forth.

In one form or the other, every organization has some form of the modes that have been portrayed. It is absolutely normal for there to be an interchange of information from one mode to the next. Figure 4.1 shows that there is an interchange of information among the different modes of operation of the organization.

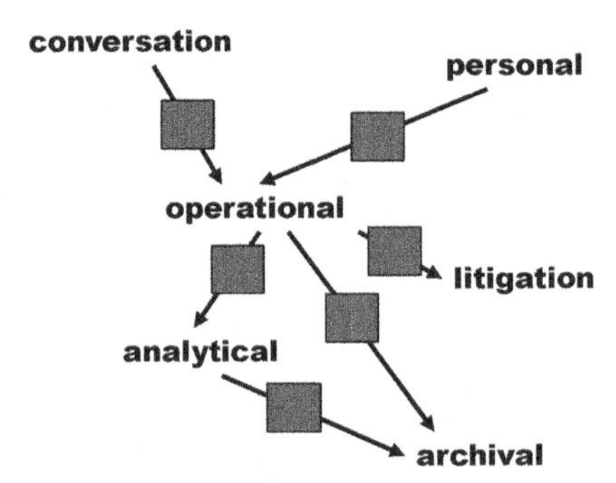

Figure 4.1: Transformations of data occur wherever data goes from one mode to the next

Over time data is transformed from one mode to the next. So it is true that there is redundant data across the organization. As long as the redundancy occurs as a result of the transformation of data from one mode to the next, the redundancy is perfectly acceptable and normal. Consider a very normal transformation. Consider how conversation passes to the operational environment, as seen in Figure 4.2.

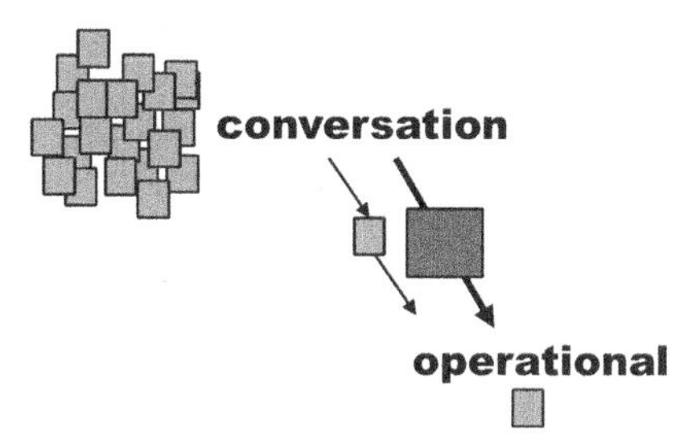

Figure 4.2: Very little data passes from one mode to the next

There are lots of ways that data passes from conversation to the operational environment. Consider the buying of a car. The salesperson shows the customers lots of cars for sale. The salesman discusses the merits of the cars, including the color, the miles per gallon, the air conditioner, and so on. After the customer has looked at many cars and asked many questions, the decision to purchase a car is made. At this point, a bill of sale (or a contract) is drawn up. The bill of sale is entered into the operational system as a sale.

There are many ways conversation is turned into operational data. Another way is through voice to text transcription. A conversation is recorded. The conversation is fed into voice to text transcription software. The conversation is then read by textual Extract, Transform, and Load (ETL) and turned into a standard database format. Figure 4.3 shows the transformation of conversation into operational data.

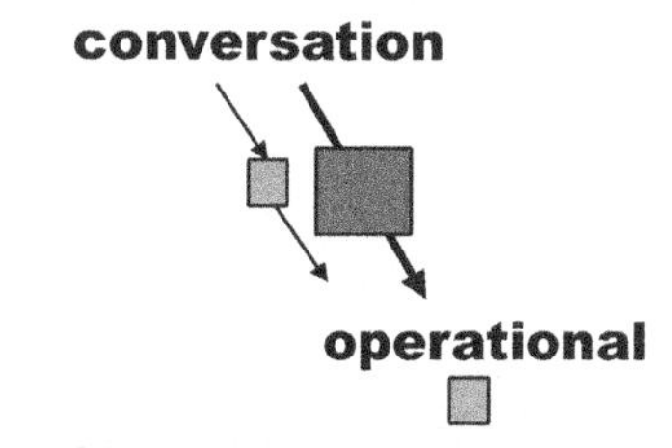

Figure 4.3: The kind of data that passes from conversation to operational

The transformation goes from a normal conversation between two or more people into a database. Once in a database, the conversation can be handled and managed by standard computer processing. Figure 4.4 shows the output of the transformation as it arrives in the operational environment.

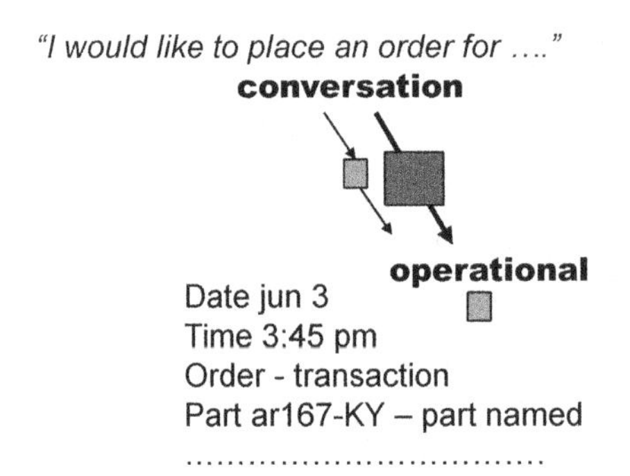

Figure 4.4: What the data looks like after the transformation

Another transformation occurs as data goes from personal data into operational data. One day a person changes his/her address. The person then alerts the company that a change of address has occurred. The change of address then goes from the person into the operational systems of the organization. Figure 4.5 shows the movement of data from a person to an operational system.

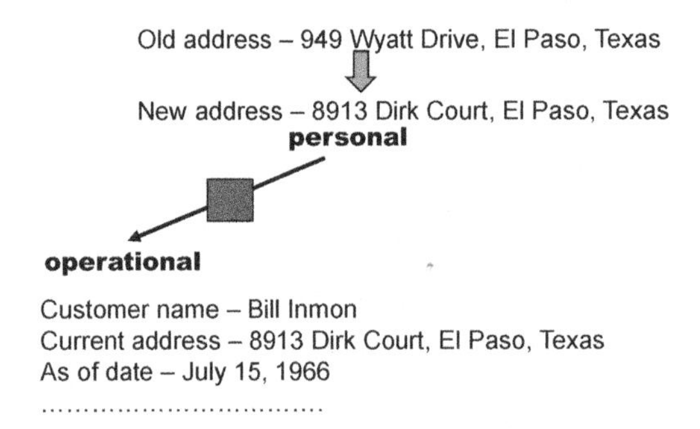

Figure 4.5: Personal data can be operationalized

Of course, there are many activities that are contained in the same mode. For example, suppose a banking transaction occurs. The banking transaction occurs entirely inside the same mode of operational processing. Figure 4.6 shows that a banking transaction occurs entirely inside of the operational mode of processing.

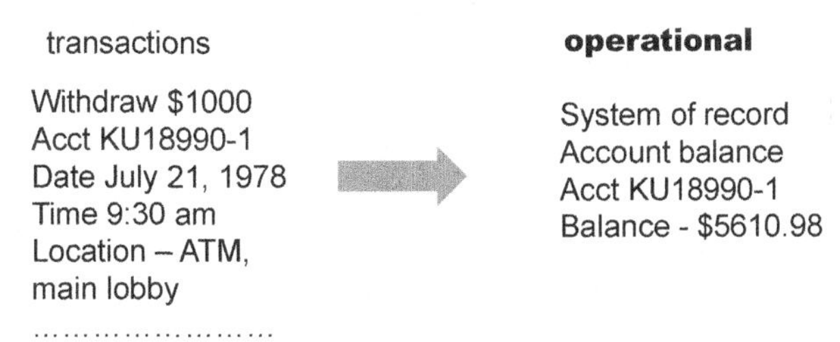

Figure 4.6: Transactions are run entirely within the domain of operational activity

The operational environment serves as the basis of many activities that happen in the world of litigation. Usually, litigation activities occur as a result of the filing of a lawsuit. Either a lawsuit has been filed against the company, or the company is preparing to file a lawsuit. The operational environment serves as a source for the records of what happened in the suit. Figure 4.7 shows that operational data flows into the litigation environment.

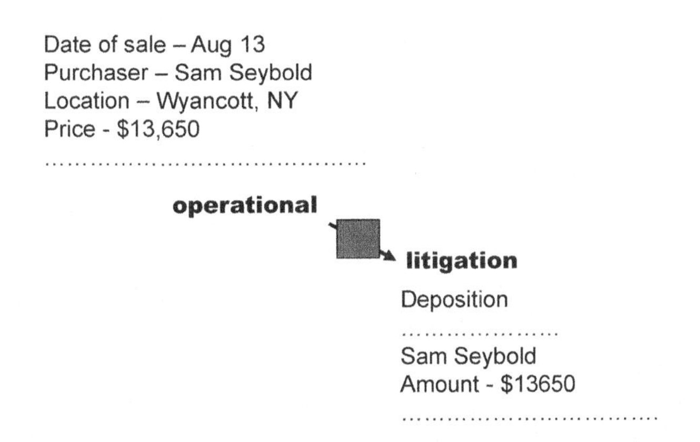

Figure 4.7: Data that goes to litigation has been vetted to an extreme degree

There is, of course, a flow of data into the analytic environment from the operational environment. As a rule, data flows when the usefulness of the data in the operational environment ceases to have great value. Figure 4.8 shows the flow of data from the operational to the analytic value.

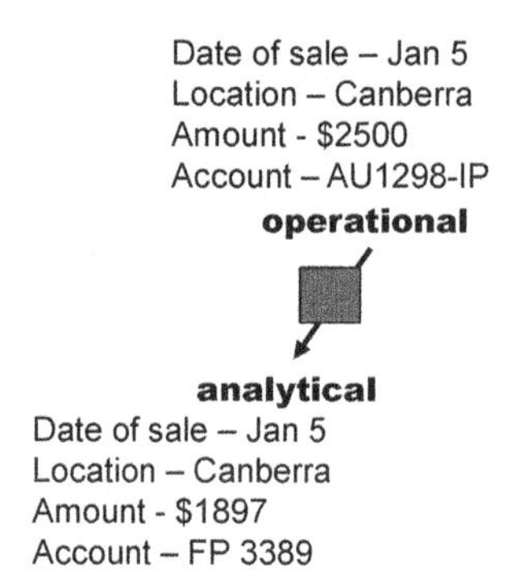

Figure 4.8: Operational data can be integrated as it passes from operational into analytical

Data flows into the archival environment when its active usefulness in the analytical environment diminishes. Figure 4.9 shows the flow of data into the archival environment.

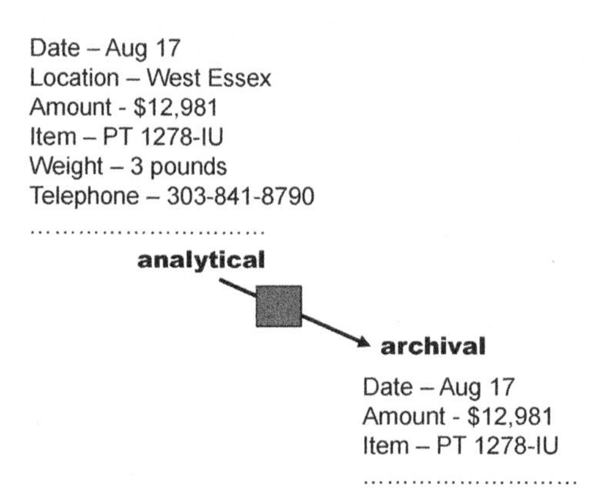

Figure 4.9: Only necessary data is passed during archival processing

In addition, data flows into the archival environment directly from the operational environment. Figure 4.10 shows this flow.

Different kinds of mechanisms are used for the transformations. Typically, personal data and litigation data are transformed manually. Textual ETL is used for the transformation of conversation data into operational data. And ETL technology is used for transformations elsewhere. Figure 4.11 shows that different means of transformation are used in different places.

Figure 4.10: Often times detailed data is summarized as it is archived

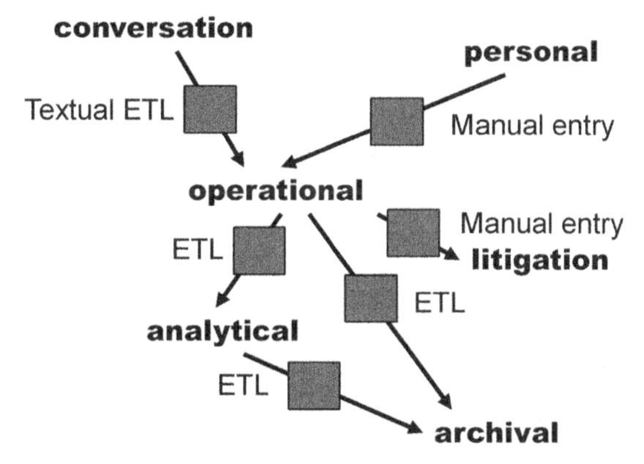

Figure 4.11: The different kinds of technologies that are used for transformation

When looking at Figure 4.11, it can be said that the same data appears redundantly. In a way, this is true. But when data is entered into a new mode, the usage of the data, the form of the data, and the users of the data change dramatically.

The application environment is built without discipline in most cases. Application designers define structures and element names in a free form fashion. The result is that there is little or no integration of data in the operational environment, especially where the application environment is made up of multiple applications. On the other hand, the integrated star schema environment is of necessity integrated. To create the integrated star schema environment, it is necessary to do integration somewhere. Figure 4.12 shows the dilemma. To integrate the data, gender must be converted to an "m,f" format, and money needs to be converted to US dollars.

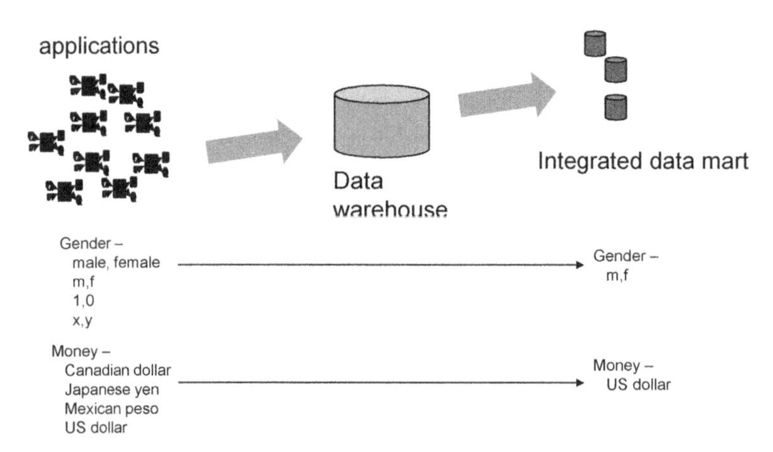

Figure 4.12: There is a lot of transformation that needs to be done in going from the applications to the integrated data mart

The question—where is it best to do this integration? The answer is that the basic integration that is being described here is best done as data passes into the data warehouse. It can be done as data passes into the data mart, but for many reasons, it makes sense to do the integration immediately after data passes out of the application environment and into the data warehouse. Figure 4.13 shows that integration is best done before data passes into the data warehouse.

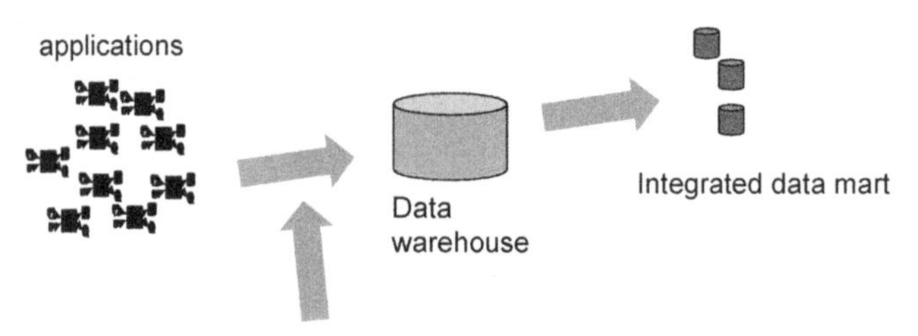

Figure 4.13: Integration is best done before data passes into the data warehouse

CHAPTER 5

The Integrated Data Mart Approach

In the face of a large application foundation, it becomes obvious that an architecture based on data marts and applications—an application-centric architecture—has major problems. The problems lie in the integrity of the data found in the architecture. Figure 5.1 shows the issues with the integrity of data.

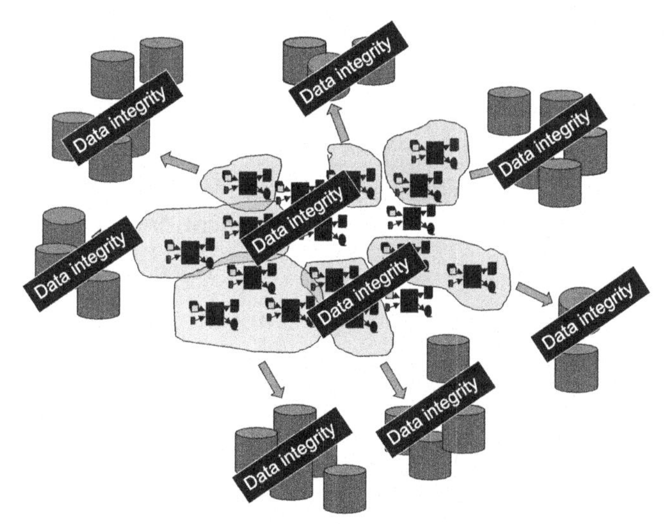

Figure 5.1: In the long run, an architecture based on data marts has fundamental integrity issues

There is a lack of data integrity within the applications. Then the issues of integrity continue into the data marts built upon these applications. In a way, building data marts on applications are like building skyscrapers on the sand. The first hurricane that comes along knocks the skyscrapers over, and much pain and suffering ensue.

Fortunately, there is an alternative. That alternative can be called the "integrated data mart" approach. The integrated data mart approach has many similarities to the application-centric approach with one major exception. In the integrated data mart approach, the source of data for the data marts is a data warehouse. Figure 5.2 shows the integrated data mart approach.

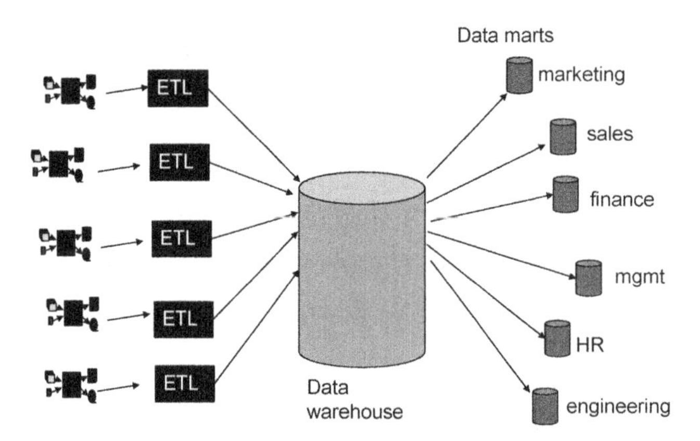

Figure 5.2: An architectural solution to the problem of data integrity that plagues data marts

In the integrated data mart approach, different applications feed the data warehouse. The data coming from the applications are integrated into a corporate format as it enters the data warehouse. The integration of the application data into a corporate format occurs by extracting the data from the applications into ETL technology. By the time the data arrives in the data warehouse, the data is now corporate data, as opposed to application data.

From the standpoint of the end-user, the data mart coming from an application, versus a data mart coming from a data warehouse, looks exactly the same. The only difference is that the data coming from the data warehouse is believable corporate data, whereas the data coming from the application is unintegrated application data.

A data mart that comes from an application is called an independent data mart.
A data mart coming from the data warehouse is called a dependent data mart.

The modeling foundation of the data warehouse is quite different from the data mart. The foundation for the data warehouse is the relational model, while the foundation for the data mart environment is the dimensional model. Figure 5.3 shows this significant difference.

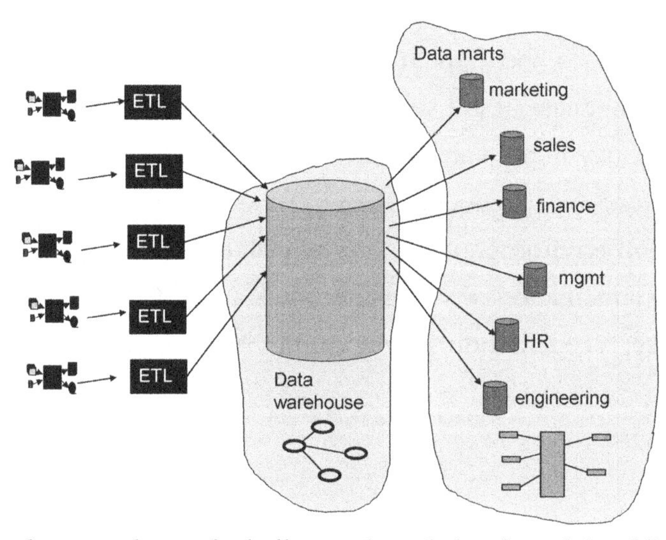

Figure 5.3: The data warehouse is built on the relational model, while the data mart environment is based on the dimensional model

When data marts are built from the data warehouse, the most obvious benefit is the integrity of the data found in the data mart. See Figure 5.4.

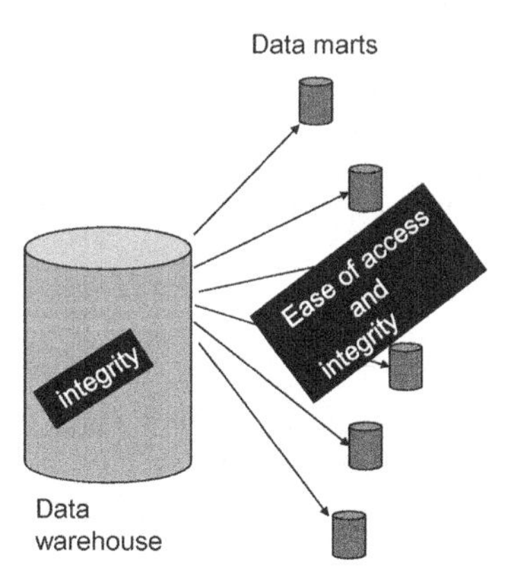

Figure 5.4: There are minimal data integrity issues when the data marts are based on a data warehouse

Reconciliation is another benefit. In Figure 5.5, two data marts have very different values for ostensibly the same data. This phenomenon can happen when data is fed from a data warehouse. However, when there is a dispute as to the values that are being calculated, it is a straightforward exercise to reconcile the discrepancy. One possibility is that there is a miscalculation in the data mart. Another possibility is the data has been incorrectly selected from the data warehouse. In either case, it is a straightforward exercise to determine why there is such a discrepancy in the values being reported in the data mart environment. Contrast this exercise of reconciliation with that of attempting to reconcile data in the application environment. When data marts are fed from the application environment, reconciliation of values becomes a much more complex operation. In the worst case, reconciliation simply cannot be done.

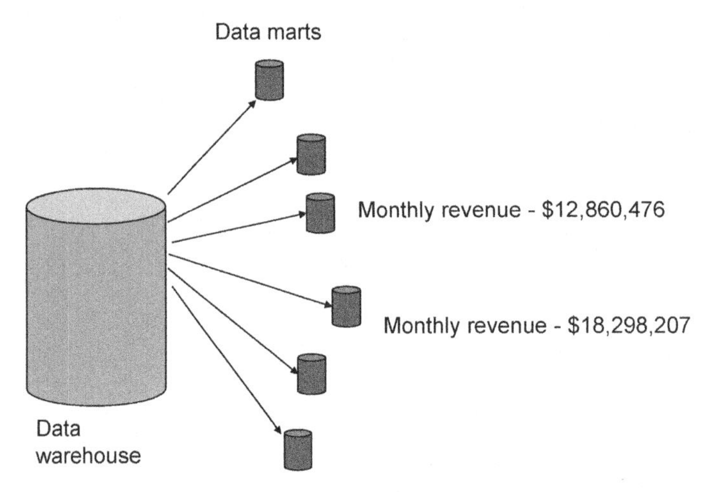

Figure 5.5: If discrepancies in data mart values occur, it is a very straightforward process to reconcile those calculations

Another benefit is extensibility. Once the data warehouse is populated, it becomes quite easy to build a new data mart. This is not true for the first few data marts that are built from the data warehouse. In truth, it takes a lot of work to build the data warehouse. So, building and populating the data warehouse is not a quick or easy thing to do at all. But, after the data warehouse has been built and after the first few data marts are up and running, building a new data mart becomes an easy thing to do. Figure 5.6 shows that there are other benefits to the building of data marts based on a data warehouse.

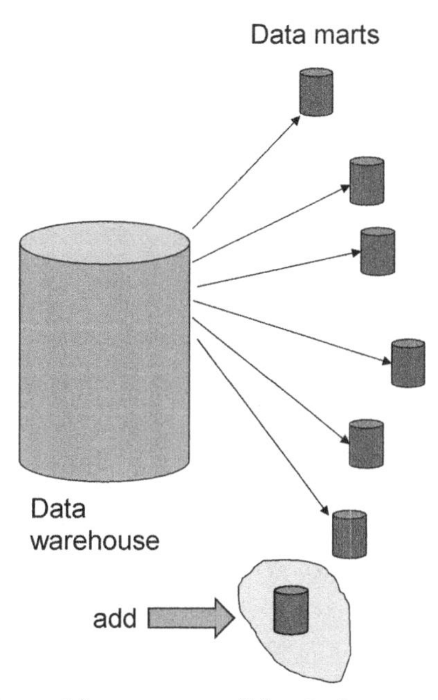

Figure 5.6: Adding a new data mart is a very easy thing to do

As appealing as the integrated data mart environment is, building the integrated data mart environment is a long term proposition. And it goes without saying that once you build the data warehouse-centric integrated data mart environment, there is no need to build independent data marts whose source is outside the data warehouse. Building an independent data mart is the first step to data disintegrity.

CHAPTER 6

Monitoring the Data Mart Environment

Most data marts are small enough and informal enough that they don't need to be formally monitored. However, some data marts are large enough and so widely used that it makes sense to monitor these types of data marts formally. There are several motivations for monitoring the data mart:

- **Cost**. The data mart costs money, and if the expenditure for the data mart is large enough, it makes sense to want to know how the data mart is being used.
- **Security**. Occasionally a data mart will be used by someone or some organization for purposes other than those intended. Knowing who is using a data mart is beneficial.
- **Future expansion**. Understanding what parts of the data mart are being used and what parts are not being used is a valuable piece of information that can help guide future expansions and enhancements of the data mart and analytical environment.

Figure 6.1 shows that on occasion, it makes sense to monitor the data mart environment. Monitoring the data mart environment can be a complex affair because queries can come into the data mart from a wide variety of sources. There is a wide audience of analysts who may need to access the data in the data mart. There are day to day clerks, financial analysts, data scientists, system administrators, and so forth, that all need to look at data in the data mart. Furthermore, these analysts and others can use a wide variety of tools for accessing the data found in the data mart. Figure 6.2 shows the wide variety of tools and the audience of users that need to look at data in the data mart.

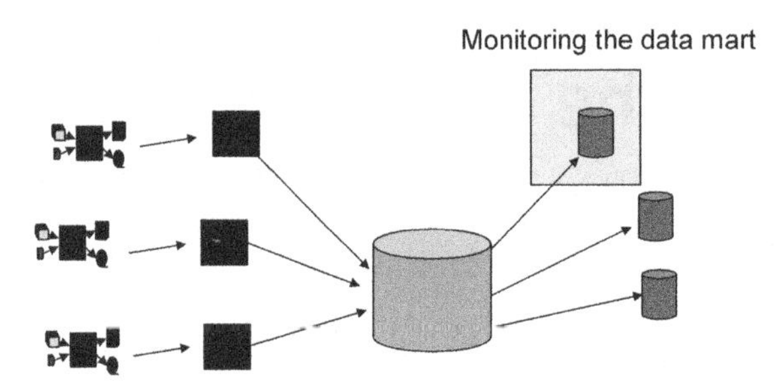

Figure 6.1: It is a good idea to monitor large and actively used data marts

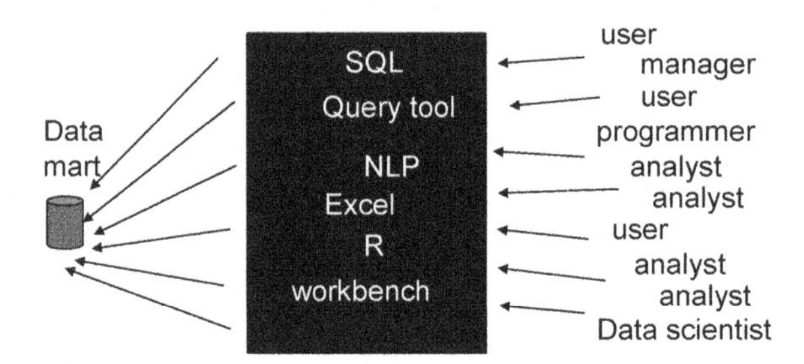

Figure 6.2: How the data mart is accessed

So what kind of data can be found by monitoring a data mart? Answers to questions like these:

- Who is writing queries?
- What query tool are they using?
- How often are they making queries?
- What data is being queried?
- What priority are the query requests?
- How long is the query taking?
- How much data is being accessed?
- How much data is being returned?

The calls that are made to the data mart are intercepted and read. The responses to those calls are also read. A log records the activity. From the analysis of the calls and responses, a record is made as to what data is being accessed and what data is being returned as a result of the access.

Actively used data vs. inactive data

A common phenomenon found when looking at the results of a monitor is that data fairly consistently divides itself into two classes—actively used data and inactively used data. As a rule, the fresher and newer data is inside the data monitor, the more likely it is to be accessed. Conversely, the older the data is inside the data mart, the less likely it is to be accessed. However, the age of the data is hardly the only criteria by which data can be classified. Many other criteria affect the popularity of data access inside the data mart. Figure 6.3 shows that data divides itself into actively used data and inactively used data.

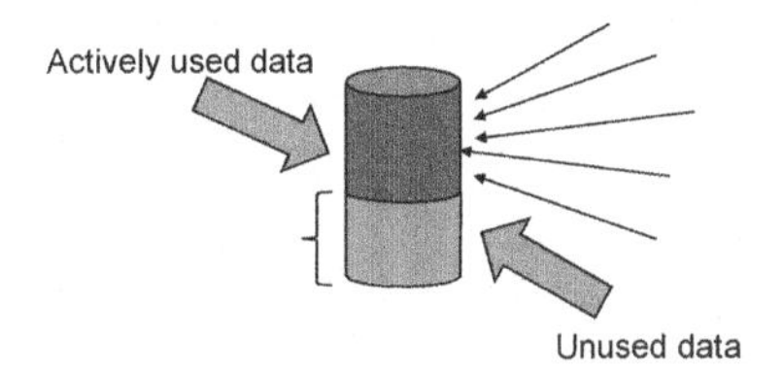

Figure 6.3: In a data mart, data divides itself into actively used data and inactively used data

There is a problem with inactively used data if there is a lot of it. Inactively used data costs money. It costs money to find data to put into the data mart that is not going to be used. And it costs money to store inactively used data.

The real problem with inactively used data is the confusion it causes. When an analyst goes to a data mart to find out what data is there, it helps if the data that can be potentially analyzed is actually useful data. Having data that is not used makes the job of the decision support analyst that much more difficult.

Removing dormant data

Figure 6.4 shows that data that is not used is best removed from the data mart.

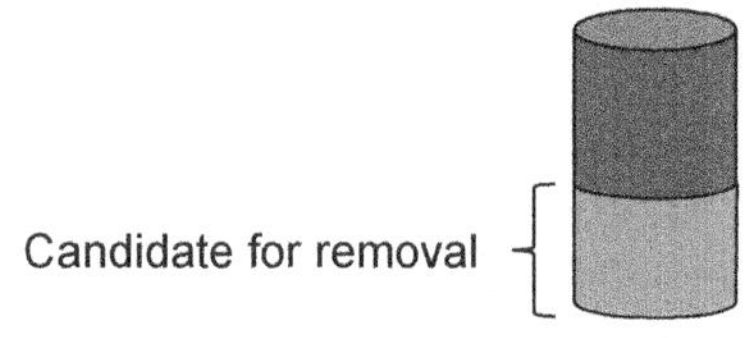

Figure 6.4: Data that is not used costs money, causes confusion, is a liability, and is a waste

In addition to the removal of unused data, another value of monitoring data is to tell the developer what types of data should be further extended. In other words, by looking at what people are using, future iterations of the data mart should include even more of that type of data.

Discarding older versions of the data mart

It is a sad fact that data marts are not discarded when their life is over. Because data marts are so easy to build, it is normal for an organization to simply build a new data mart rather than repair or do maintenance to an older mart. The result of this poor practice of data management is that the same data mart appears in different renditions. There is the data mart that was created last year. Then there is the same data mart that was created in January. Then we have the data mart that was completed in June, and so forth. Each time a new data mart is created, its predecessor(s) still exists. Figure 6.5 shows this phenomenon.

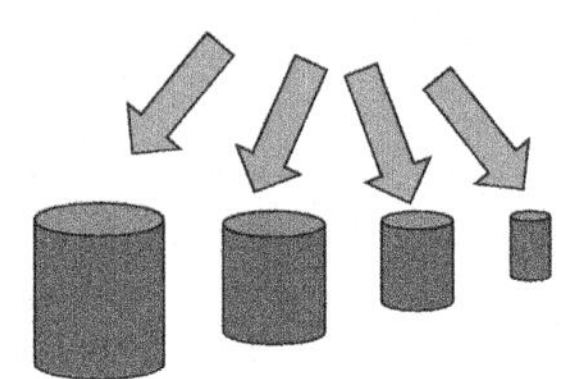

Figure 6.5: Instead of maintaining the data mart, a new data mart is created

The constant creation of new versions of data marts without the "dousing" of the previous versions of the data mart leads to a great deal of waste and confusion. The end-user simply does not know which version of the data mart to start to use for analysis. If the data mart environment is to be managed properly, it is necessary to delete all old versions of a data mart upon the creation of a new version.

CHAPTER 7

Metadata and Documentation in the Data Mart Environment

Even though it often does not get much attention, one of the most important components of the data mart environment is the metadata that describes what is in the data mart. The most important reason why metadata is important is that the data mart end-user needs metadata to describe what is in the data mart. Stated differently, the more the end-user can know about the data mart, the more effectively the end-user can be in doing his/her analysis. Figure 7.1 shows the architectural positioning of metadata for the data mart. Each data mart has its own metadata.

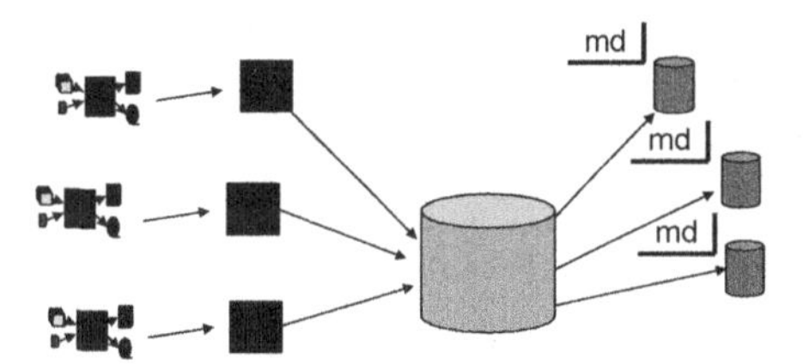

Figure 7.1: An important component of the data mart environment is the metadata component

Simple table and element metadata

There are lots of forms of metadata. The simplest form of metadata for the data mart environment is the documentation of the existence of the tables and the data elements in the table that are found in the data mart. Figure 7.2 shows this simple form of metadata.

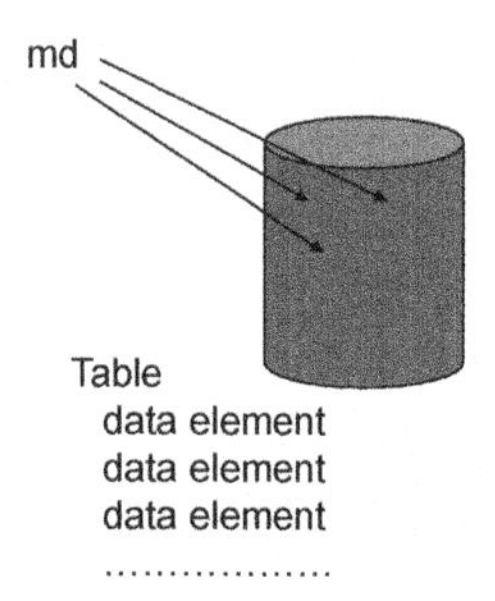

Figure 7.2: The metadata describes, among other things, the tables and data elements

As a simple example of the usage of this kind of metadata, suppose a data mart contains information about purchases made during the month. The end-user analyst looks in the metadata repository and sees that the description of the parts sold, the unit of measure, the parts per package, and other information has been captured in the data mart. The end-user analyst now knows how to start to query and analyze the data in the data mart.

Source metadata

Simple table and element descriptions are the most basic forms of metadata found in the data mart metadata repository. But other forms of metadata can be found in the metadata repository as well. Another form of metadata is the description of the source of data for the metadata. In other words, where did each table and each data element in each table come from? Figure 7.3 shows this form of metadata.

As an example of the usage of this form of metadata, suppose the analyst looks at a sales data mart. In the sales data mart are many kinds of sales—commercial sales, wholesale sales, residential sales, etc. The analyst decides to look at only wholesale sales. The analyst uses the metadata in the data mart repository to help determine how data should be qualified.

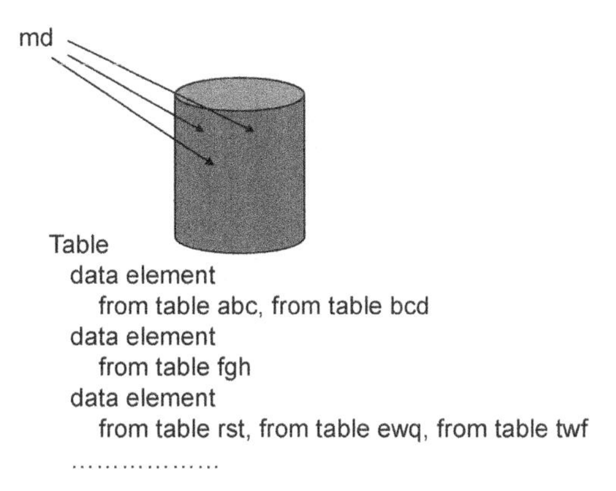

Figure 7.3: An important component of metadata is the lineage of each element in the data mart

Load date metadata

Yet another form of metadata is the date the data was loaded into the data mart. The date the data was loaded into the data mart and the source of the metadata can be important to the analyst doing analysis on carefully chosen elements of data. Yet another form of metadata that can sometimes be useful is a description of how data was selected to be in the data mart and—if applicable—how the data was calculated.

Combined metadata

Certainly, every data mart needs its own metadata. However, it is possible to create a combined metadata repository for more than one data mart. Figure 7.4 shows a combined metadata repository.

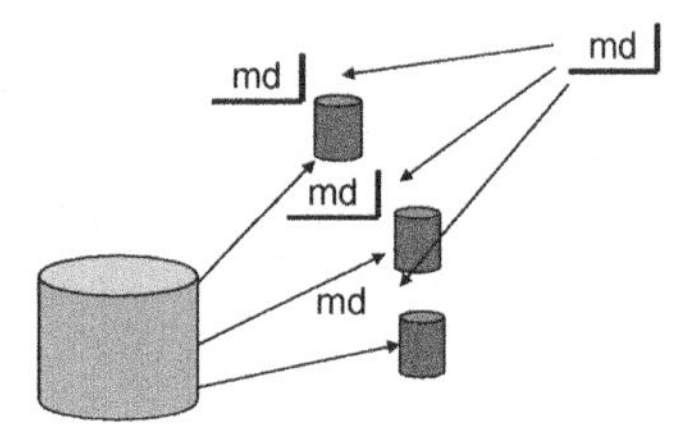

Figure 7.4: You can create an external metadata dictionary incorporating data mart features

A combined metadata repository might be useful where there are two or three widely used data marts. Of course, there may be numerous smaller data marts that do not participate in a combined metadata repository.

One of the issues with any data mart metadata repository—either combined or singular—is that of maintenance of the metadata. Over time the data mart and its contents change. In some cases, the change is gradual. In other cases, the change is sudden. The metadata needs to be changed in coordination with the changes to the data mart. Figure 7.5 shows that the metadata that reflects the contents of the data mart needs to be periodically maintained.

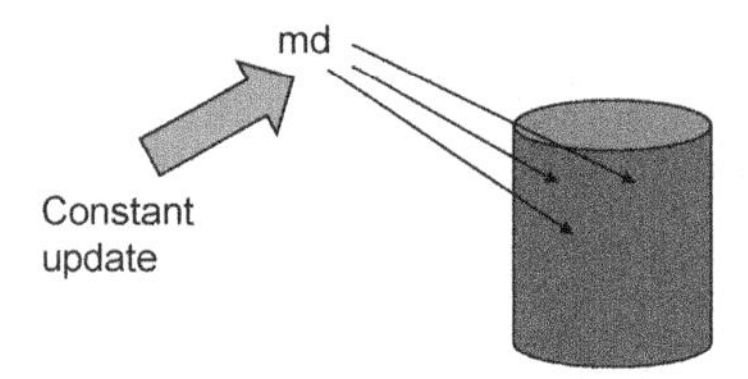

Figure 7.5: The metadata for the data mart requires constant update

Usage metadata

Another type of metadata is usage metadata. The usage metadata is a description of the types of access that occur against the data mart. The queries can come from anywhere and can come from a wide variety of tools. Furthermore, there is usually a very variable pattern of access. One day the data mart will have very few accesses. Another day the data mart will have a lot of accesses.

The usage metadata becomes useful in several ways. One way the usage metadata is useful is in determining how to expand the data mart. When it becomes apparent that one type of data is very popular, the next iteration of development of the data mart may contain even more data of that type.

Another way to use usage data is in answering the simple question—who is looking at the data? This is especially useful during audits or if it is suspected that unauthorized usage of the data in the data mart is occurring. Figure 7.6 shows that data mart usage data can be collected and placed in a metadata repository.

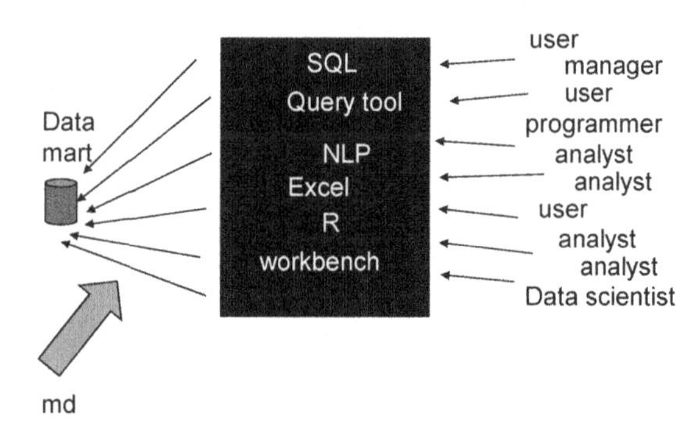

Figure 7.6: Another component of metadata is the usage of the data mart

CHAPTER 8

The Evolution toward Integrated Data Marts

Only very rarely does an organization suddenly decide to build integrated data marts. Much more ordinary is the evolution towards integrated data marts from the start of orphan data marts. Evolution occurs over time and at different rates for different companies. But the evolution is remarkably similar in the steps that occur. Figure 8.1 shows that there is an evolution from the orphan data mart to the integrated data mart environment.

Figure 8.1: The evolution from orphan data marts to integrated data marts

The typical first step in evolution is the creation of the first orphan data mart. As a rule, data marts are cheap to build, fast to build, and easy to build. So an organization—usually a department—decides to build a data mart.

If the organization is small there may be only a few applications. If there are only a few applications, it is unlikely that there will be a large problem (or any problem at all) with the pain of disintegrity of data. For very small organizations, a single data mart may suffice for all of their analytic needs, and therefore the evolution to the integrated data mart environment may never occur. However, there are many organizations where there are many applications. For those organizations, the evolution to the integrated data mart environment continues to occur. The typical next step in evolution is the creation of the second data mart. Word gets around the organization about the success of the first data mart, and soon another department (or group of people) wants to build their own data mart. Figure 8.2 shows the advent of the second data mart.

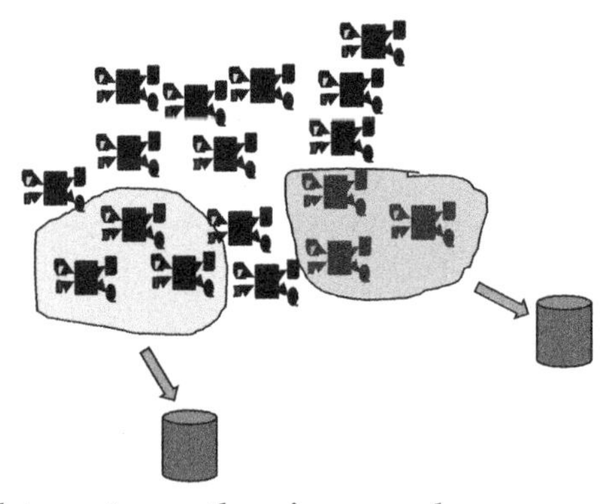

Figure 8.2: After the first data mart, soon there is a second

And like spontaneous combustion, there start to appear multiple data marts throughout the organization. Figure 8.3 shows the creation of multiple data marts in the organization.

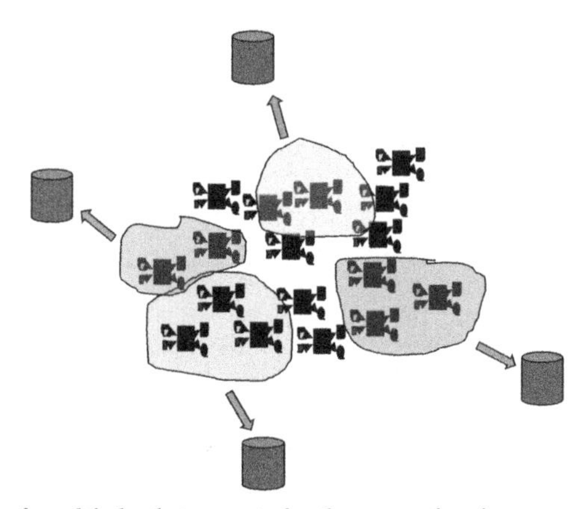

Figure 8.3: The creation of multiple data marts in the organization

Data out of harmony

Everything seems happy and in a state of order, until one day, a top manager discovers that the different data marts are not singing in harmony. One data mart is whistling the Beatles Yesterday. Another data mart is humming Bach. Another data mart is singing the national anthem. And another data mart is singing a Christmas carol. Together the voices do not form beautiful music.

When a closer examination is made, it seems that the different data marts are operating from diametrically different data. One data mart has the company heading into bankruptcy. Another data mart has the company going public next month. Another data mart sees terrific competition coming from a competitor. Another data mart desires to do an industry takeover of a large company. In a word, each of the organizations behind the data marts has a very different perspective for the company. Figure 8.4 shows this disparity of data among the different data marts.

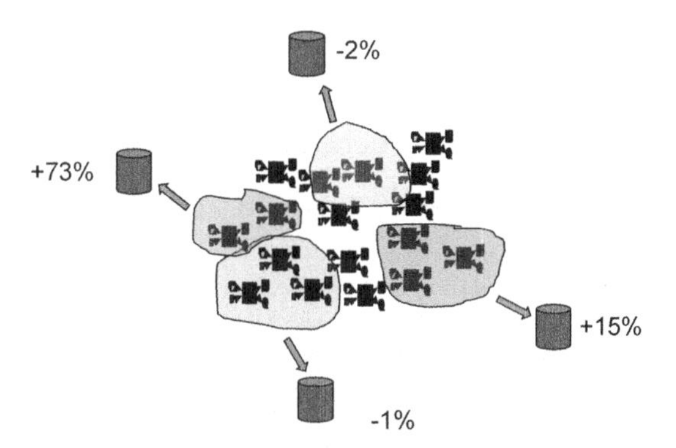

Figure 8.4: One day someone viewed the information across the enterprise and saw disunity

In some organizations, this disparity festers. Management chooses to believe whoever they want to believe. The subject of data validity becomes a political football.

Bad corporate decisions

When data starts not being used to make decisions, the organization is in real danger. Suddenly the organization starts to make some very bad decisions. And the marketplace punishes organizations who make bad decisions. Remember Ford's Edsel, IBM's Watson, DeLorean, Enron, Sharper Image, British Petroleum oil exploration, and Pan Am airlines. So it makes sense for organizations to harvest real data and to take care of that data.

Once the organization has captured real data, then the organization needs to make sense of the data and to turn the data into good corporate decisions.

Building more data marts, stacking on more data, and hiring more consultants does not solve the problem. What is needed is a change in architecture. Merely trying to do what was done in the past is not a solution.

It is at this point that the organization faces the reality that what is needed is a single version of the truth for the data for the organization. What is needed is not data but believable data. And when the organization finally comes to terms with this realization, the road to building a data warehouse begins.

There is no question that building a data warehouse is a long term proposition. Too much data needs to be rectified, too many applications represent yesterday's data, and too many people cling to their data marts regardless of the fact that the data mart does not have the correct data in it on which to make sound decisions.

Yet the pain of making bad decisions is such that eventually, organizations commit to clean up the mess that has been made by having unintegrated applications.

Enter the data warehouse: The single version of the truth

Slowly the data warehouse starts to take shape. Figure 8.5 shows the first steps in the migration to the integrated data mart environment.

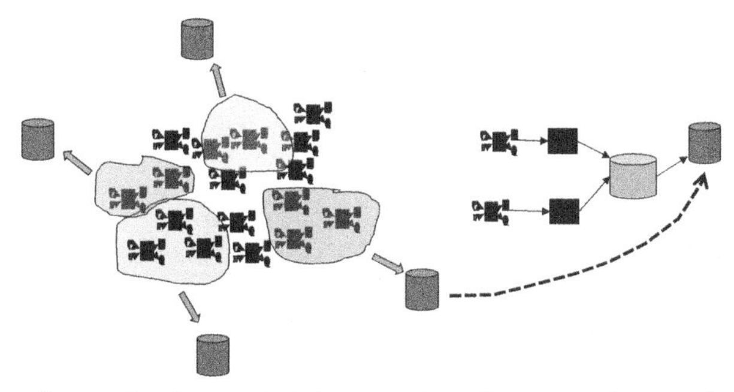

Figure 8.5: The migration to the integrated data mart environment began slowly at first

But as time passes and more corporate data starts to collect in the data warehouse, more and more end-users are attracted to it. At some point, a tipping point is reached and the organization starts to use the corporate data found in the data warehouse as a basis for the data marts that have been built.

Figure 8.6 shows the migration of many data marts to the foundation offered by the data warehouse.

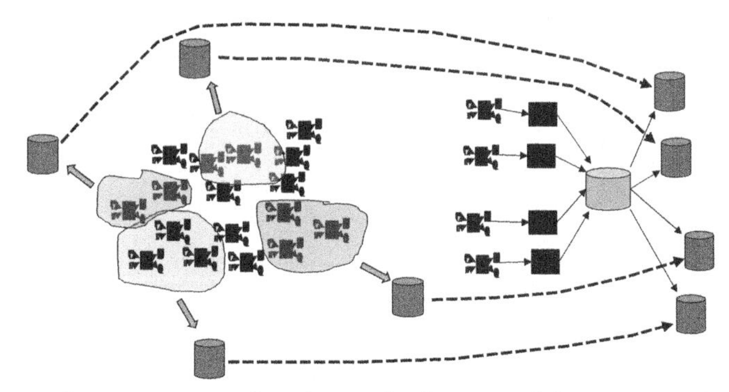

Figure 8.6: But soon there was an acceleration to the integrated data mart environment

The migration that has been described is one that is gradual, taking six months to six years. Different organizations have their own rate to which they adhere.

After a period of time, the organization ends up in the position seen in Figure 8.7.

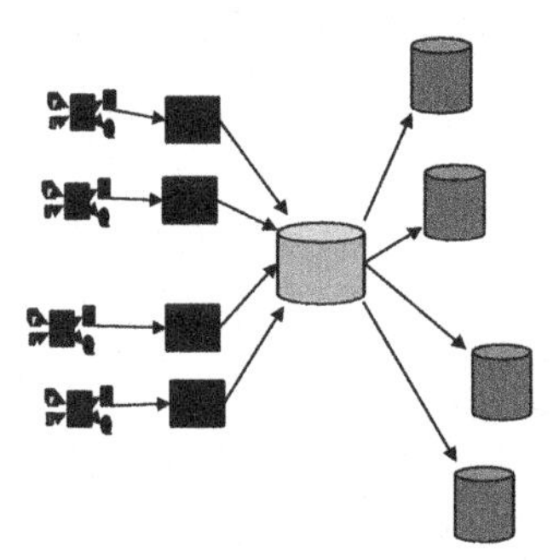

Figure 8.7: And after a while integrated data mart environment was all that was left

The different steps in the migration to the integrated data mart environment are seen in Figure 8.8.

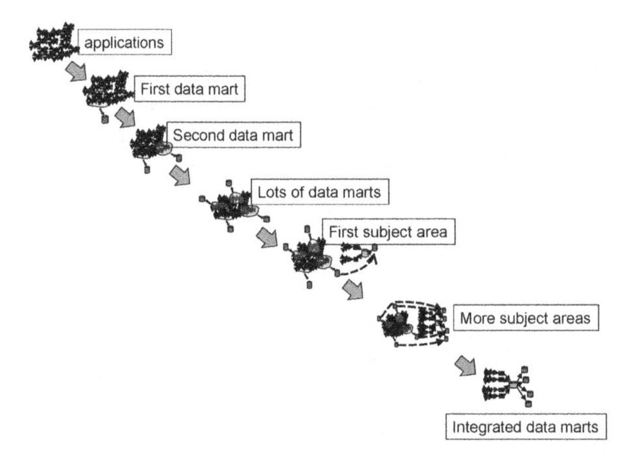

Figure 8.8: The typical progression in many shops

Part II

The Unified Star Schema

CHAPTER 9

Introduction to the Unified Star Schema

In Part I, we reviewed the history of the data warehouse from the early days until now. Across the chapters, we have learned that integrated data marts are the most recommended solution for an enterprise. However, we have also learned that enterprises today tend to accumulate too many data marts, which leads to confusion. This problem needs to be solved.

The Unified Star Schema (USS) solves this problem.

We introduce the USS in this chapter. Learn about its architecture and use cases, as well as how the USS approach differs from the traditional approach. Analogies will reinforce key USS concepts, such as hunter and prey and houses connected with telephone lines. Also, this chapter will show you the dangers of denormalization.

The Unified Star Schema is a star schema centered on a table called the "Bridge". See Figure 9.1.

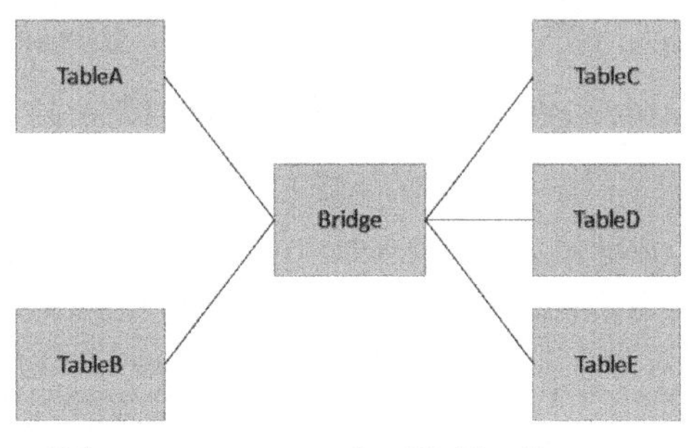

Figure 9.1: The Unified Star Schema centers on the "Bridge"

The Bridge handles the connections among all the tables, such as Sales, Products, Clients, Shipments, Invoices, Purchases, Suppliers, Targets, and Stock. If you create a normal join involving all of these tables, you will end up having duplicates. Instead, with the Bridge, you will have no duplicates at all. This book will show you how this is possible.

Please note that, with traditional dimensional modeling, every star schema (or snowflake schema) centers on a single fact table at a time. For example, if you have six fact tables, you will need to build at least six star schemas. In some cases, the same fact tables may need to be used in multiple ways, at different levels of granularity. For this reason, a project of business intelligence normally has a very large number of star schemas (or snowflake schemas). With this approach, instead, there is one single star schema. Even if you have many facts and dimensions at different levels of granularity and a complex set of business requirements, you will always have one single star schema that serves as a foundation for every possible business requirement.

Although, during the next few chapters, we will frequently use the terms "fact" and "dimension", the methodology to build the Unified Star Schema does not need to make this distinction. The only relevant distinction is whether or not a table contains "measures".

Measures in literature have been defined in many different ways, and we like to give our own definition. Imagine that a business intelligence report contains a bar chart: this will have an "X" axis and a "Y" axis. Measures are those numeric columns that can be displayed in the "Y" axis of a bar chart, and they are usually aggregated by sum or by average. On the "X" axis, instead, you will have the dimensions: these can be columns containing textual descriptions, dates, or numbers that should not be aggregated. In the next chapters, you will find many examples of measures.

According to traditional dimensional modeling, measures belong to the fact tables. But in reality, measures can be anywhere. In the chapter of Northwind, for example, we will see that the table "Products" contains information about the units in stock and the units in order. Therefore, we can say that Products contains measures, but it is certainly not a fact table. The Unified Star Schema goes beyond the assumption that measures belong to fact tables, and it treats all the tables the same way.

The ultimate goal of the USS approach is to reduce the data transformations drastically. With traditional dimensional modeling, each data mart is created "ad-hoc" for a particular set of business requirements. The USS approach is different.

With the USS approach, one single data mart serves as a foundation for every possible business requirement.

When the business requirements are very complex, you may need to build additional transformations and views on top of the foundation. In all the other cases, there will be no need for transformations at all: the Unified Star Schema will be your ready-to-use data source.

The architecture

The Unified Star Schema is a data mart, and it is positioned in the presentation layer of a data warehouse. See Figure 9.2. The traditional data marts typically consist of multiple star schemas or snowflake schemas. The USS, instead, consists of one single star schema.

The design process of the Unified Star Schema is extremely simple.

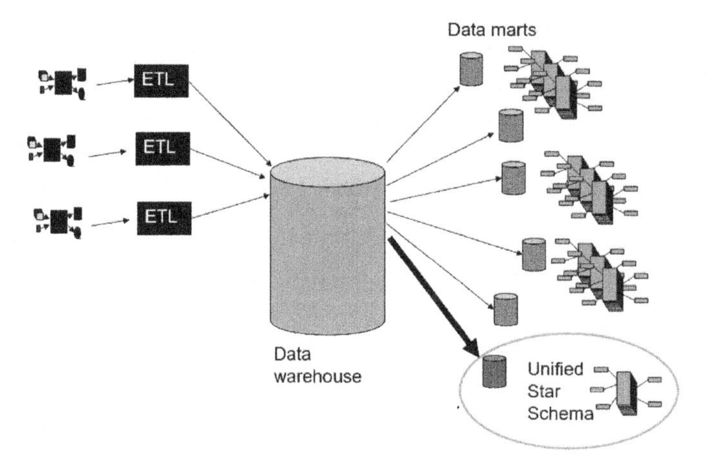

Figure 9.2: The USS is a new data mart to be added to the existing ones

---

For the creation of the USS, we do not need to go through the classic exercise of conceptual, logical, and physical data modeling. The Unified Star Schema is built entirely based on data, and it does not depend on the business requirements.

The business requirements play an important role in the design of a data warehouse, because they define first of all the "scope" of a project. An organization may have thousands of tables, but only a few of them need to be loaded into the data warehouse. The "core layer" of the data warehouse contains all the data that is "in scope". This data is called "raw data" because it is not yet prepared for the end-users. Only later, in the presentation layer, the data marts will implement the detail of what the end-users want to see in the final reports and dashboards.

The Unified Star Schema introduces a change to this paradigm: the presentation layer of the data warehouse is also "unbiased", like the core layer. It is prepared to be consumed by the end-users, but it is built independently from the business requirements. The business requirements are pushed outside of the data warehouse: they will be implemented in the BI tools because that's the place where they belong.

The business requirements belong to the BI tools.

The BI tools are the right place to implement the business requirements, and we say this for a few good reasons. First of all, BI tools are very powerful: their libraries of functions are usually much richer and smarter than the SQL language. Second, BI tools are much easier to use: most have a graphical interface, and they have been designed to be used by an audience of end-users with no data expertise. Last but not least, Key Performance Indicators (KPIs) often contain ratios of numbers that typically need to be implemented in BI tools, because in the data marts they would not be "additive". This deserves an explanation.

Imagine that you need to implement a KPI that calculates the ratio of sales versus target, in percentage. If you calculate this ratio row by row in a data mart, you will not be able to perform aggregations because the sum of ratios does not make any sense. Conversely, if you do it inside a BI tool, all the numbers will be aggregated first, and then the ratio will happen later. The calculation of a KPI inside a BI tool executes the steps in the correct order.

Pushing the business requirements to the BI tool sounds like "postponing the problem", but it is not. In today's reality, business requirements are implemented both in the data mart and in the BI tool. They are happening "a bit here, and a bit there". This is not a good way to implement a solution. Shifting the whole business logic to the BI tool makes the maintenance much easier, because it needs to be done in one place instead of two.

It has to be said, however, that every project has its own peculiarities, and the ultimate decision needs to be made by a data architect, based on a set of specific needs and challenges. In some cases, a part of the business logic may need to be implemented in the data warehouse for performance reasons, or for reasons of "re-usability". Our recommendation is to push the business requirements to the BI tool as much as possible, unless you have a good reason to do otherwise.

It is not easy to build a data mart that serves as a foundation for every possible business requirement. The next chapters will explain how the Unified Star Schema is able to achieve this result.

The USS approach

The Unified Star Schema can be implemented whenever the data sources are in a tabular format, such as in database tables, Excel files, and CSV files.

But the USS can also be built in the cases when data is not organized in tables—as long as it's possible to convert this data into tables. This is the case of XML files, JSON files, Avro format, Parquet data storage, and any other data format that can be converted into a tabular format. This makes the Unified Star Schema easy to integrate also with the cloud technologies and with the APIs.

The guiding principle of the USS approach is that two tables are never connected directly to each other—they are always connected through the Bridge.

With the USS approach, all the tables are always connected through the Bridge.

Figure 9.3 shows the main difference between the traditional approach and the USS approach.

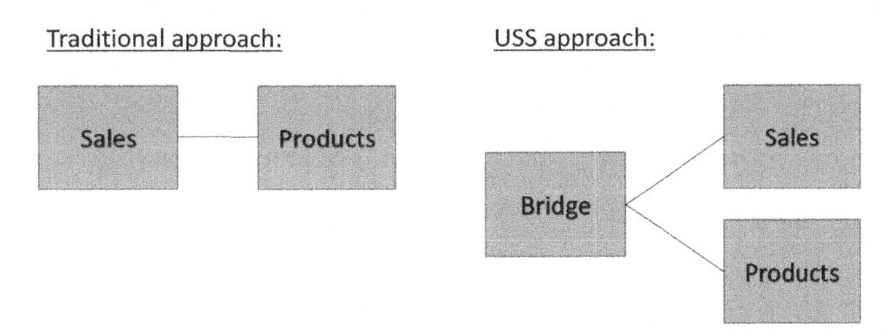

Figure 9.3: Sales and Products with the USS approach are connected through the Bridge

It is worth clarifying this concept with an example. Please note that all the examples in the next chapters will have very few rows. There is no need to work on millions of rows: ten or fifteen rows are more than enough to illustrate the concepts that we want to share. Figure 9.4 shows Sales and Products.

Sales:

SalesID	Date	Client	Product	Quantity	Amount
1	01-Jan	Bill	PR01	1	100
2	02-Jan	Bill	PR02	1	70
3	02-Jan	Francesco	PR02	2	140
4	03-Jan	Francesco	PR03	1	300

Products:

ProductID	ProductName	UnitPrice
PR01	Hard Disk Drive	100
PR02	Keyboard	70
PR03	Tablet	300
PR04	Laptop	400

Figure 9.4: Sales and Products

These two tables are connected through the product ID, which is called "Product" in Sales and "ProductID" in Products. Figure 9.5 contains an example of an SQL query, based on the traditional approach.

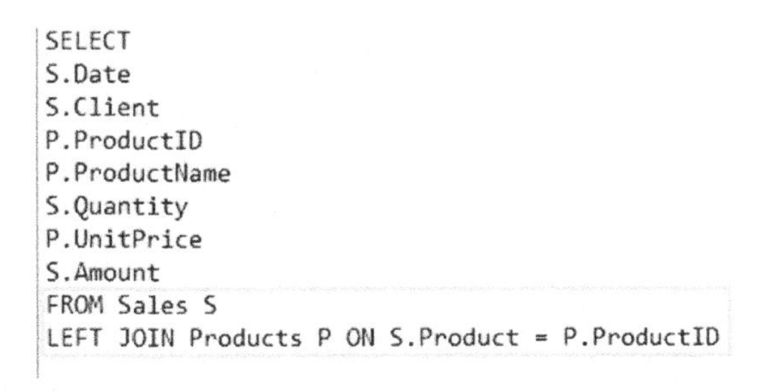

```
SELECT
S.Date
S.Client
P.ProductID
P.ProductName
S.Quantity
P.UnitPrice
S.Amount
FROM Sales S
LEFT JOIN Products P ON S.Product = P.ProductID
```

Figure 9.5: An SQL query based on the traditional approach

When we create an SQL query, we typically read from multiple tables. With the traditional approach, we need to choose what table to mention first (in this case, the query starts with Sales), and then we need to add all the other tables, one by one. In a traditional SQL query, the order that we choose for the tables is particularly relevant: starting with a different table or swapping the order of two tables may produce different results. Figure 9.6 contains the results of this query.

Date	Client	ProductID	ProductName	Quantity	UnitPrice	Amount
01-Jan	Bill	PR01	Hard Disk Drive	1	100	100
02-Jan	Bill	PR02	Keyboard	1	70	70
02-Jan	Francesco	PR02	Keyboard	2	70	140
03-Jan	Francesco	PR03	Tablet	1	300	300

Figure 9.6: Result of the query, based on the traditional approach

Now let's introduce a simple example of the Bridge table, as shown in Figure 9.7. The Bridge is a table that only contains IDs. This is a very simplified version. In the next chapters, we will give a proper definition of the Bridge and a set of rules and conventions to build it.

SalesID	ProductID
1	PR01
2	PR02
3	PR02
4	PR03

Figure 9.7: The Bridge in its simplest form

Figure 9.8 contains an example of an SQL query, based on the USS approach.

```
SELECT
S.Date
S.Client
P.ProductID
P.ProductName
S.Quantity
P.UnitPrice
S.Amount
FROM Bridge B
LEFT JOIN Sales S ON B.SalesID = S.SalesID
LEFT JOIN Products P ON B.ProductID = P.ProductID
```

Figure 9.8: An SQL query based on the USS approach. The Bridge must always be mentioned first

An SQL query based on the USS approach must always start with the Bridge, and then all of the other tables must be joined with a "left join". With the USS approach, the order that we choose for the other tables in the query will not affect the results.

The result of the query in Figure 9.8 will look identical to the results from the previous query, shown earlier in Figure 9.6. The advantages of using this approach will be explained throughout the next chapters.

The USS approach requires every table to have a "unique identifier": a column that uniquely defines each row of that table. When the unique identifier consists of multiple columns, it is recommended to concatenate (or hash) them into one single column. This unique identifier will be used as a connection between each table and the Bridge. If such an identifier is not available, it is always possible to create a "surrogate key": a "system-generated unique identifier" with no business meaning.

Throughout the book, we will use the term "Primary Key" (PK) to indicate the unique identifier for a table. A table, in general, may have multiple unique identifiers, but only one must be chosen as the "primary".

The term "Primary Key" may generate a bit of confusion because, in the world of relational databases, it may have a specific meaning of "enforced Primary Key": a mechanism that produces an error when the uniqueness of the key is violated. But this is not what we mean: by PK we simply mean the unique identifier for a table. Other authors call it a "Business Key" or "Natural Key".

Likewise, throughout the book, we will use the term "Foreign Key" (FK) to indicate a column referencing the PK of another table. This term may also generate a bit of confusion because, in the world of relational databases, the term "Foreign Key" may have a specific meaning of "enforced Foreign Key": a mechanism that produces an error when a particular value is unreferenced. But this is not what we mean: by FK we simply mean a column that references a PK.

In our example based on Sales and Products, shown in Figure 9.4, the column "Product ID" is a PK for Products. The column "Product" in the Sales table is a FK that references the Products table.

Now that we know what we mean by PK and FK, we can give a preliminary definition of the Bridge.

The Bridge is a table that absorbs all the PKs and FKs from all the tables.

Hunter and prey

The tables of a database need to be connected to each other.

It is important to understand that this connection is always "oriented": one table points to the other, and not vice versa. For this reason, it is represented as an arrow, as seen in Figure 9.9.

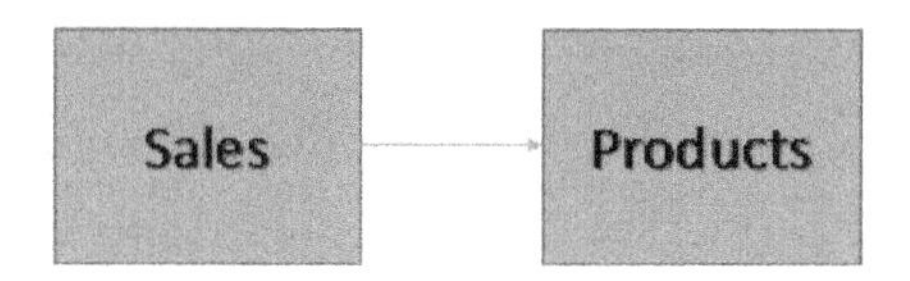

Figure 9.9: Sales points to Products, and not vice versa

The connection between two tables is always oriented.

The concept of "oriented connection" is the foundation of the USS approach. Starting from this concept, it will be possible to introduce our own concept of an "Oriented Data Model" (ODM), which is a graphical convention for drawing data models. Based on the ODM convention, we will be able to give some straightforward and simplified definitions of "fan trap" and "chasm trap", which are two scenarios that occur very often in business intelligence. These traps generate duplicates, and duplicates are a problem. Based on our simplified definitions, we will be able to detect these problems and prevent them.

Solving problems is great. Preventing them is even better.

To better explain the concept of oriented connection, let's make an analogy with the world of wild animals, as in Figure 9.10. Let's compare the tables of a database with hunter and prey, like the lion and the gazelle. The Sales table contains a Foreign Key (FK) that references the Primary Key (PK) of Products. By this key, Sales "grabs" some information from Products. So, we can say that Sales is the hunter, and Products is the prey. Sales is the lion, and Products is the gazelle. In the spoken language, we often say that "Sales points to Products".

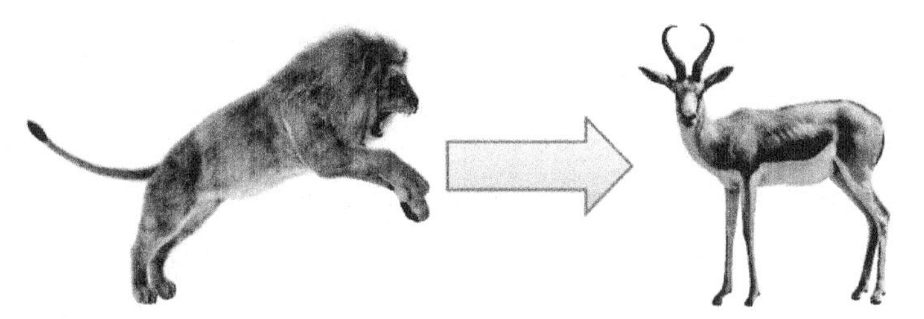

Figure 9.10: Sales points to Products the same way as the lion points to the gazelle

The analogy with hunter and prey helps to fix in mind that a connection between two tables is always oriented: one table points to the other, and not vice versa. The gazelle will never hunt the lion. Likewise, Products will never have a FK pointing to Sales.

This first example is easy because it deals with only two subjects, and it is very easy to determine which one is the hunter and which one is the prey. But the real world is much more complex than this. Sometimes more hunters may aim at the same prey. The lion hunts the gazelle, but the leopard also hunts the gazelle. And the lion may hunt the leopard. See Figure 9.11.

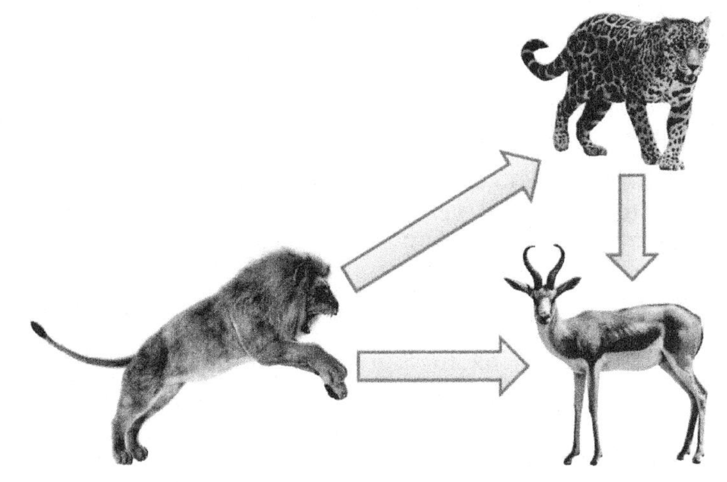

Figure 9.11: The food chain is actually more complex than a simple chain

---

The food chain, despite its name, does not look like a chain at all: it is actually a complex tangle of relations.

The tables of a database are even more complex than the food chain of wild animals. Traditional dimensional modeling is based on a simplified assumption: facts point to dimensions. Or, in the case of the snowflake schema, dimensions point to other dimensions, within the same hierarchy. But these two scenarios only represent a partial picture of reality. Sometimes a fact points to another fact. Sometimes a dimension points to a dimension that is not within the same hierarchy. Sometimes multiple facts point to the same dimension but on a different level of granularity. Sometimes it is not easy to determine whether a table is a fact or a dimension. Sometimes tables form a closed circle, also known as a "circular reference" or "loop". Sometimes we need information from multiple tables, but we cannot find an easy way to connect them together.

Sometimes two tables point to each other. Sometimes a table points to itself. And the list goes on.

We need a data structure that is able to handle all these scenarios in an easy way. And that's where the Unified Star Schema comes into play.

Loops

Loops are another problem that occurs very often in business intelligence. For this reason, they deserve our attention in this chapter.

Let's start from the previous example based on Sales and Products, and add a new table, "Shipments". Shipments is a fact table.

In our daily life, when we make a large purchase, it may happen that the vendor does not have enough units in stock. Let's imagine that a client wants to buy 40 hard disks, and the shop only has ten of them in stock. A first shipment should be made immediately with the ten available hard disks, and then a second shipment should be made as soon as possible with the remaining 30.

In the underlying database, the Shipments table contains a FK that points to the PK of Sales. In this case, we can say that Shipments is the hunter, and Sales is the prey. This is an example of a fact pointing to another fact. See Figure 9.12 for how we represent the oriented connection between Sales and Shipments.

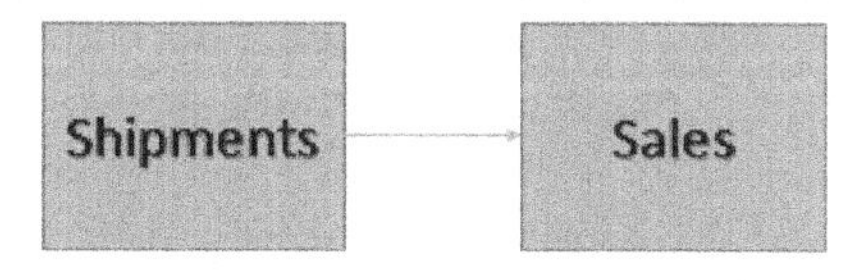

Figure 9.12: One fact (Shipments) pointing to another fact (Sales)

Thanks to this connection, we are able to identify, for each row of Shipments, the "one and only" row of Sales that it references. This may be useful, for example, if we want to retrieve, for each shipment, the information of the sales date. Based on this, we can calculate the "fulfilment latency", row by row. This allows us to build a KPI that shows the average latency per country, per product category, per month, and so on.

This is a "one-to-many" relationship. One row of Sales is potentially associated with multiple rows of Shipments, but each row of Shipments is associated with "one and only one" row of Sales.

Figure 9.13 shows that two rows of Shipments reference the same row of Sales.

Shipments:

ShipmentID	SalesID	ShipmentDate	ShipmentQuantity	ShipmentAmount
1	1	01-Jan	1	100
2	2	02-Jan	1	70
3	3	02-Jan	2	140
4	4	03-Jan	1	300
5	5	04-Jan	10	1000
6	5	31-Jan	30	3000

Sales:

SalesID	Date	Client	Product	Quantity	Amount
1	01-Jan	Bill	PR01	1	100
2	02-Jan	Bill	PR02	1	70
3	02-Jan	Francesco	PR02	2	140
4	03-Jan	Francesco	PR03	1	300
5	04-Jan	Francesco	PR01	40	4000

Figure 9.13: There are two rows of Shipments referencing one row of Sales

But Sales, in turn, points to Products. This forms a chain. Figure 9.14 shows that Shipments, Sales, and Products are connected as a chain.

Figure 9.14: Shipments, Sales, and Products form a chain

In the above schema, we can see that Sales is in the middle. Sales is, at the same time, hunter and prey.

But what happens now if Shipments contains a Product ID that points to Products directly? By adding one more connection, we produce a "loop", as shown in Figure 9.15.

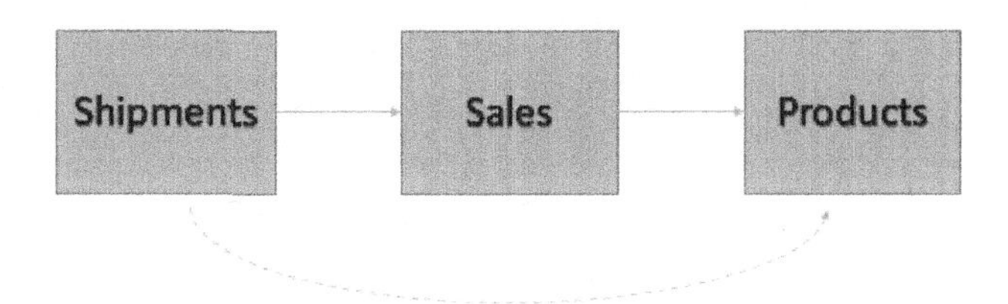

Figure 9.15: If we add one more connection between Shipments and Products, we produce a "loop"

A loop is a topology of entities where we have multiple possible paths to go from one entity to another. See a loop in Figure 9.16. To go from A to C, you can go either directly, or via B. This is a loop.

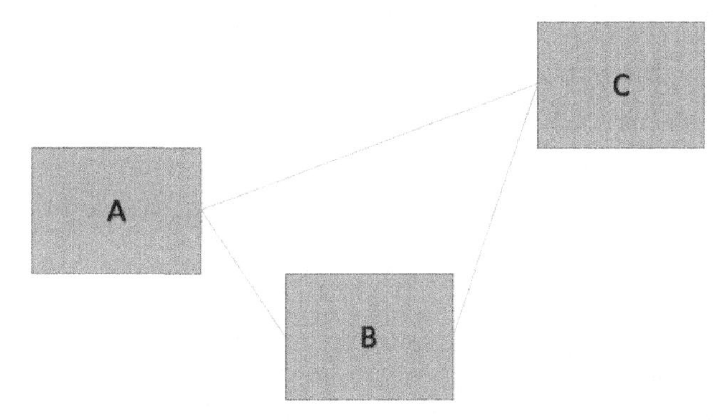

Figure 9.16: Schema of a loop

In the particular loop that we have seen earlier in Figure 9.15, the problem could be solved by "disregarding" the direct connection from Shipments to Products, assuming that the same information is available also in Sales. This assumption is supposed to be true when everything in the process goes fine, but this is not always the case. The direct connection from Shipments to Products is a piece of information that may be helpful at some point, for example, for troubleshooting. In general, disregarding Foreign Keys should be avoided.

Loops are a big problem in SQL because they introduce "ambiguity", and this ambiguity produces an error in the execution of the SQL query. Loops also produce an error in business intelligence tools.

To better explain loops, let's make another analogy—this time with a village of houses connected with telephone lines. See Figure 9.17.

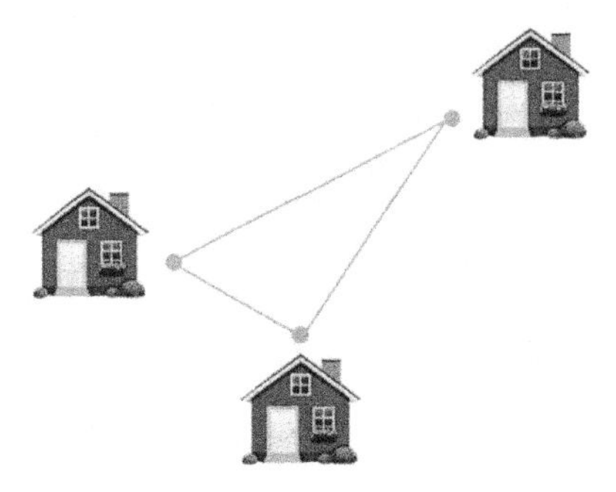

Figure 9.17: Tables and connections can be compared with houses and telephone lines

We can compare the tables of a database with houses, and we can see the connection between two tables like the telephone line that connects two houses.

If we have three houses and we want to avoid a loop, we can build at most two lines. The third line will inevitably create a loop. See Figure 9.18.

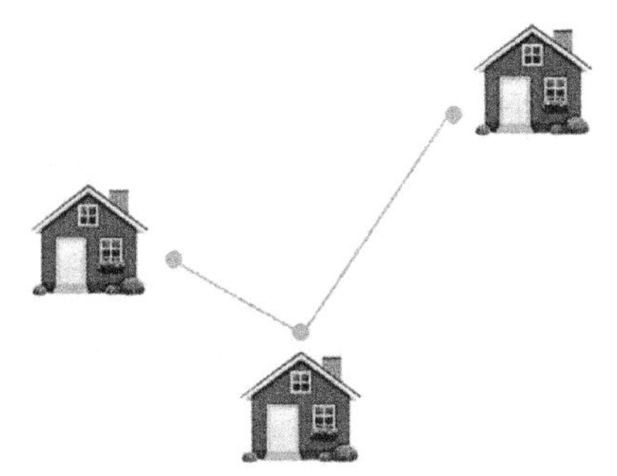

Figure 9.18: With three houses we can build at most two lines. The third line will inevitably create a loop

If we have five houses and we want to avoid loops, we can build at most four lines. The fifth line will inevitably create a loop. You can easily verify this with pen and paper: you will never manage to build more than four lines without creating a loop. See Figure 9.19.

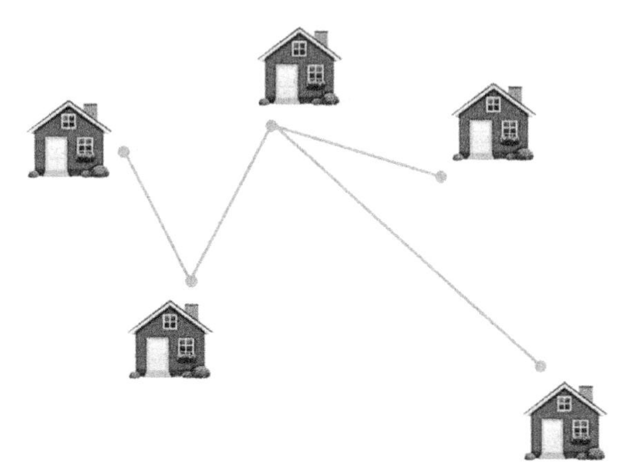

Figure 9.19: With five houses we can build at most four lines. The fifth line will inevitably create a loop

We can now generalize:

If we have (n) houses and we want to avoid loops, we can build at most (n-1) lines. Likewise, if we have (n) tables and we want to avoid loops, we can build at most (n-1) connections.

In a typical database, when we have (n) tables, we usually have more than (n-1) connections. This means that, if we want to avoid loops, we need to "disregard" some of the connections. In other words, we have to disregard some of the FK columns. But disregarding columns means losing information, and we don't want that.

There is one more question that we should ask ourselves at this point: "If we were OK with creating loops, how many lines could we possibly build?" In the example of five houses, we could build ten lines, as you can see in Figure 9.20. Where does this number 10 come from? It comes from the formula [n * (n-1) / 2]. We have five houses (n = 5): the possible connections are [5 * 4 / 2] = 10. If we had 100 houses (n = 100), then the possible connections would be [100 * 99 / 2] = 4950.

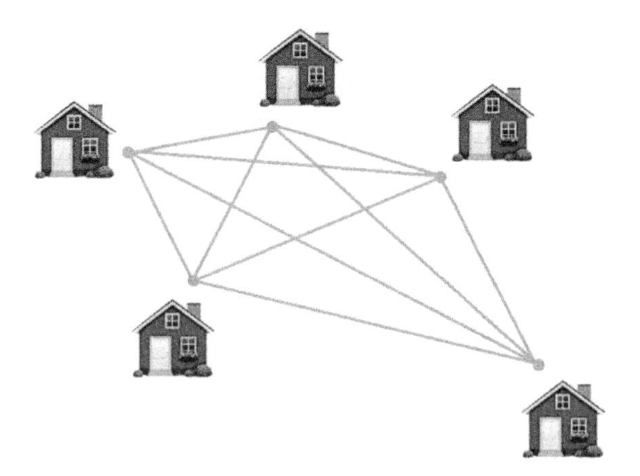

Figure 9.20: With five houses, the possible connections are ten

These lines are clearly creating multiple loops, but they are all needed. How can we solve this problem?

The central table

If we want to have all the houses connected and we want to avoid loops, we can add one central switchboard, as shown in Figure 9.21.

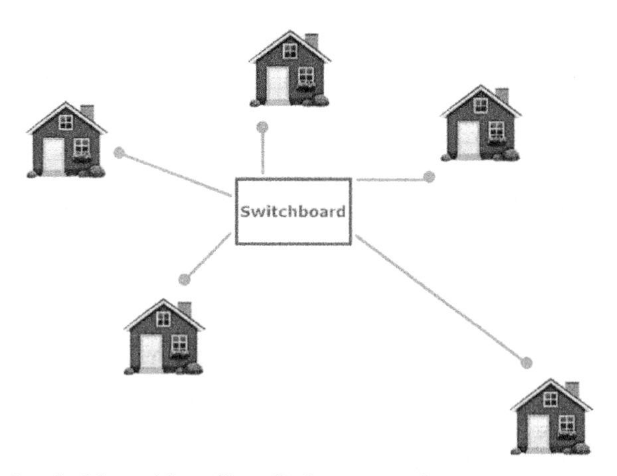

Figure 9.21: A central switchboard handles all the connections

A switchboard is a device that handles all the possible connections. Figure 9.22 shows an old switchboard.

Figure 9.22: An old switchboard

The Bridge that we use in the Unified Star Schema is very similar to a telephone switchboard.

If we have a database with 100 tables, they will all connect to the Bridge. The drawing of the data model will show 100 connections. But in reality, the Bridge will be able to handle all the possible connections, which are 4950. See Figure 9.23.

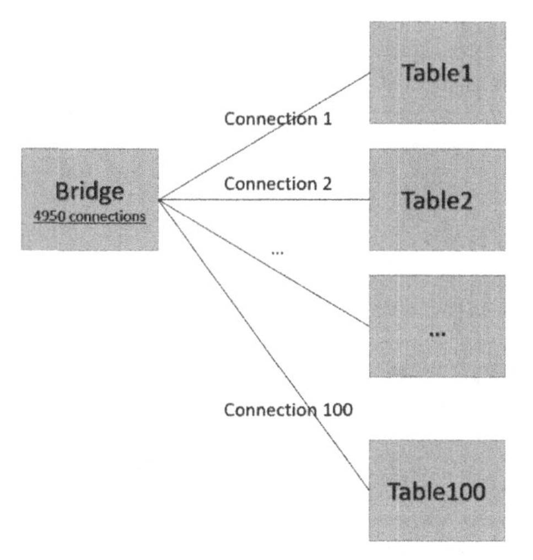

Figure 9.23: The Bridge handles many more connections than the drawing shows

In reality, with 100 tables, the Bridge can handle even more than 4950 connections, using the technique of "multiple stages per table". But this is an advanced topic that goes beyond the scope of this book.

Earlier in this chapter, in Figure 9.15, we saw a loop based on Shipments, Sales, and Products. Instead of discarding one of the three connections, thanks to the Bridge, we can keep them all. Figure 9.24 shows the USS approach applied to that example.

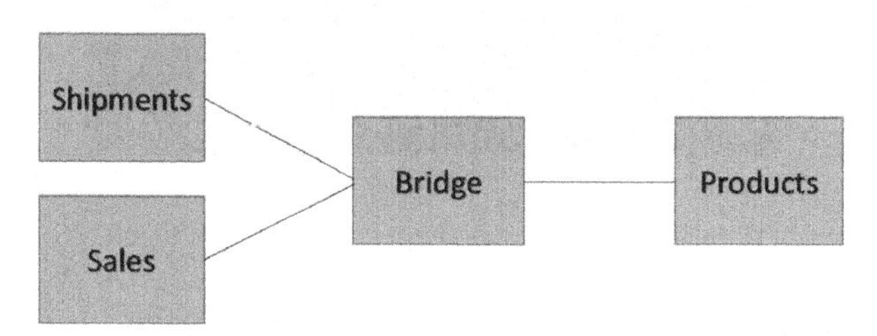

Figure 9.24: The Bridge solves the loop

Although the model in Figure 9.24 appears simplistic, it is actually magical! The three lines that you see in this figure are just the connections of the tables to the Bridge. We can call them the "trivial connections". But the real information about "who points to what" is embedded "inside" the Bridge.

All the connections are now handled inside the "magic box".

The next chapters will clarify in detail how this works.

The dangers of denormalization

Before proceeding with the next chapters, let's go through some thoughts about denormalization, also known as the process of "flattening" tables.

Data is usually created in the applications. The basic structuring of data in the applications is the relational model. This has been considered for decades the best way to handle operations, and today it is still the most common and recommended industry standard.

The data warehouse is also structured as a relational model. However, to make the analysis easier, the standard structuring for the data marts is the dimensional model. This allows data to be accessed and analyzed easily because the data relationships in the data mart have been minimized. The dimensional model is organized in a way that the developer does not need to create complex joins to access the data. In some cases, the data can be denormalized into one single table (or view), which means that the developer does not need to create any join at all.

But then, let's go a bit beyond now. If denormalization is so good, why don't we build a fully denormalized table that joins all the tables together? Why don't we build a "big table with everything inside"?

The most common answers to this question would mention "size", "performance", and "security". Someone else would also say that too many columns in the same table would confuse the end-users.

But these are not the real reasons. The real reason is that a fully denormalized table would create two families of problems:

1. Losses
2. Duplicates

Let's take the example of "Northwind", a well-known sample database from Microsoft. It contains only 13 tables, and it has a total of 3308 rows and 86 columns. We can definitely say that size, performance, and security cannot be a problem with such a small database containing sample data. So, does this mean that we can join all 13 tables together, denormalizing them all into one single table?

No, we cannot do it. If we do it, we will have losses and duplicates.

Denormalization causes losses and duplicates

Losing data is not a good thing, and duplicating data is even worse because it can produce incorrect numbers.

By "incorrect numbers", we mean numbers that are different from the ones that we see in the data source.

The next chapters will describe in detail those scenarios that produce losses and duplicates. You will understand why these phenomena happen, and you will learn how to prevent them.

CHAPTER 10

Loss of Data

In this chapter, learn about the loss of data and the reason why a full outer join in a data mart is not recommended. Witness that all the other joins (inner, left, and right), by definition, discard some data. For this reason, a data mart that has been prepared with these joins can only answer a subset of the possible questions. Understand that the USS approach does not create any join, and for this reason, it has no loss of data. Be introduced to the USS naming convention, which makes life easier for both developers and end-users. Also, learn about the Bridge and see how it connects to the other tables. Follow along with a practical implementation with Spotfire—it is so easy for the end-users to create a dashboard even without being data experts.

The loss of data is a phenomenon that we observe during the transformation of our data. Let's imagine a scenario where, starting from a set of original tables (A, B, C, etc.), we produce a new table T (the letter "T" stands for "Transformed"), as shown in Figure 10.1.

We say that the transformation has introduced a "loss of data" when the new table "T" contains less information than the original tables.

The loss of data can be observed in different scenarios. It happens in a query against a single table A, in the obvious case when we retrieve a subset of the rows (using the WHERE clause) or a subset of the columns. It also happens when we retrieve an aggregation of the rows of A (using the GROUP BY clause).

All these cases are obvious because we are intentionally extracting a particular portion of the table A for a particular use case.

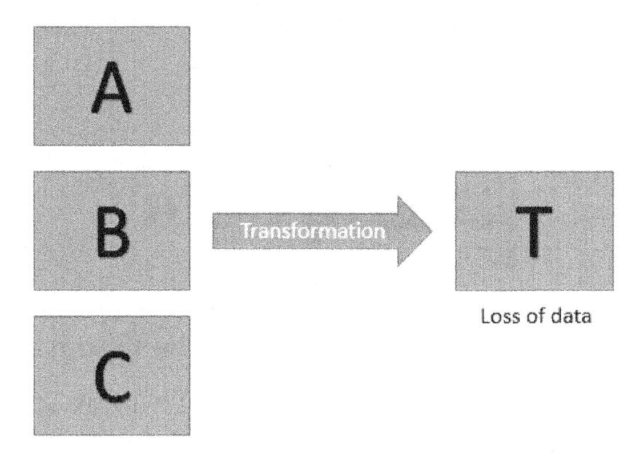

Figure 10.1: We have "loss of data" when the T table contains less information than the original tables A, B, and C

But the phenomenon of loss of data can also be observed when we denormalize a set of tables (A, B, C, etc.) by joining them together. We usually do not think about it, but in most cases, the join introduces a loss of data.

This chapter is focusing on the scenario of loss of data resulting from a join. However, the loss of data is a wider concept, as defined here above. In general, the loss of data is a problem, and it needs to be solved.

The loss of data is one of the key reasons why today we have a big redundancy of data marts. Why? Because the new table T is usually built ad-hoc for a particular business requirement, but it is not always usable for other business requirements. Every new business requirement will produce more and more copies of the same information. All similar, but all different.

If we manage to eliminate the loss of data, we will have a good chance to reduce the redundancy of data marts.

Example based on sales and products

Let's introduce the loss of data with the example based on Sales and Products from the previous chapter. To make an exhaustive example, this time we have added to the Sales table a new row that contains a product with product ID "PR99", which does not exist in the Products table. This is called a "non-referenced ID", or an "orphan key".

SalesID	Date	Client	Product	Quantity	Amount
1	01-Jan	Bill	PR01	1	100
2	02-Jan	Bill	PR02	1	70
3	02-Jan	Francesco	PR02	2	140
4	03-Jan	Francesco	PR03	1	300
5	04-Jan	Francesco	PR99	3	600

Figure 10.2: The Sales table has now a row with a non-referenced product ID: PR99

The row with the orphan key is a valid row of sales, and we do not want to lose it. Figure 10.3 shows again the Products table from the previous chapter.

ProductID	ProductName	UnitPrice
PR01	Hard Disk Drive	100
PR02	Keyboard	70
PR03	Tablet	300
PR04	Laptop	400

Figure 10.3: The Products table

Please note that also the Products table has an ID, PR04, which does not appear in Sales. This is not an orphan key, because we do not expect all the existing products to appear in the Sales table. However, the row of PR04 contains some useful information: we can see that it is a laptop, and we can see that the unit price is 400. This is also a row that we do not want to lose.

So, now that we have seen the two tables, let's join them together.

When we create a join between two tables, we always need to make a decision: should we create an inner join, a left join, a right join, or a full outer join?

Please note that the words "left" and "right" in SQL have nothing to do with the drawing of the data model. The word "left" simply indicates the table that was mentioned first in the SQL query, while "right" indicates the one that was mentioned second. Let's work in the case of an SQL query where Sales is mentioned first: this means that a "left" join will keep all the rows of Sales, and it will discard all the non-matching rows of Products.

Before looking at the four types of joins, let's draw a Venn diagram of this relationship. This will help us to better visualize our example. The two tables connect through the Product ID. For this reason, the Venn diagram needs to be based on this common element. Figure 10.4 shows the Venn diagram.

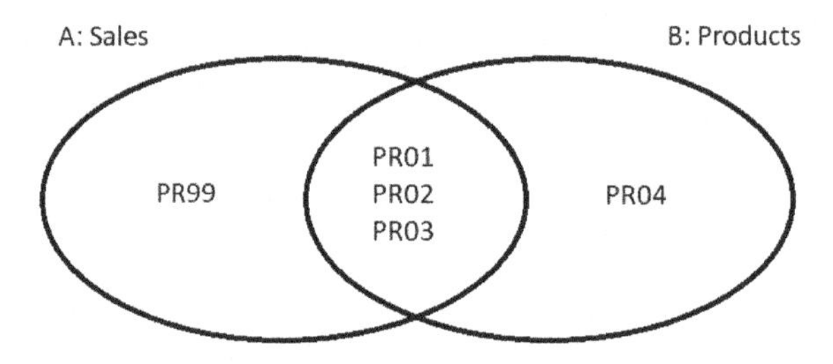

Figure 10.4: The Venn diagram shows what Product IDs are in common and what Product IDs are not

For the sole purpose of coherence, we have positioned Sales on the left side of the Venn diagram, and Products on the right side. By doing so, the word "left" will consistently refer to Sales, both in the SQL query and in the Venn diagram.

Please note that in Venn diagrams, the elements must never be repeated. PR02, for example, appears twice in Sales, as seen in Figure 10.2, but it appears only once in the Venn diagram.

If we create an **inner join** between the two tables, this will keep only the rows containing the IDs that appear in both tables: PR01, PR02, and PR03. The result of the query looks like Figure 10.5.

SalesID	Date	Client	Product	Quantity	Amount	ProductID	ProductName	UnitPrice
1	01-Jan	Bill	PR01	1	100	PR01	Hard Disk Drive	100
2	02-Jan	Bill	PR02	1	70	PR02	Keyboard	70
3	02-Jan	Francesco	PR02	2	140	PR02	Keyboard	70
4	03-Jan	Francesco	PR03	1	300	PR03	Tablet	300

Figure 10.5: The inner join keeps only the rows with the common IDs

In this query, one row from Products has been discarded, with product ID PR04. In addition, also one row from Sales has been discarded, with product ID PR99 and amount 600. As a consequence, the total of Sales Amount will be incorrect. This is an example of loss of data.

Please note, there is nothing wrong with the inner join in general. It is actually very common in business intelligence. But the developer needs to be aware of the risk of loss of data. When the query is created ad-hoc for a particular need, the inner join can be a sensible choice. But when we are preparing data for a data mart that needs to be used to satisfy multiple business requirements, both present and future, we recommend not to use the inner join.

Let's see now in Figure 10.6, a **full outer join**.

SalesID	Date	Client	Product	Quantity	Amount	ProductID	ProductName	UnitPrice
1	01-Jan	Bill	PR01	1	100	PR01	Hard Disk Drive	100
2	02-Jan	Bill	PR02	1	70	PR02	Keyboard	70
3	02-Jan	Francesco	PR02	2	140	PR02	Keyboard	70
4	03-Jan	Francesco	PR03	1	300	PR03	Tablet	300
5	04-Jan	Francesco	PR99	3	600			
						PR04	Laptop	400

Figure 10.6: The full outer join has no loss of data, but the resulting table is a strange mix

If we create a full outer join, we have no loss of data. However, the result looks a bit awkward because it contains a mix of things that do not really make sense together. It does not represent a list of Sales, and it does not represent a list of Products. You cannot even give a name to this table: it is neither Sales nor Products. It is just a mix.

This is also a query that we would not recommend. It has no loss of data, which is a good thing, but it is a strange mix.

The **right join** is also an inconvenient choice, because the row of Sales with product ID PR99 and amount 600, again, gets discarded. As a consequence, the total of Sales Amount will be incorrect.

The **left join** is probably the most sensible choice, because it shows all the rows of Sales, as shown in Figure 10.7.

SalesID	Date	Client	Product	Quantity	Amount	ProductID	ProductName	UnitPrice
1	01-Jan	Bill	PR01	1	100	PR01	Hard Disk Drive	100
2	02-Jan	Bill	PR02	1	70	PR02	Keyboard	70
3	02-Jan	Francesco	PR02	2	140	PR02	Keyboard	70
4	03-Jan	Francesco	PR03	1	300	PR03	Tablet	300
5	04-Jan	Francesco	PR99	3	600			

Figure 10.7: The left join shows all the rows of Sales

The last row in the figure does not show the name of the product nor the unit price, but at least we are not losing the amount of 600 and the rest of the information that comes from Sales, such as the date, the client, and the quantity. We have only lost PR04: from this table, we cannot see that PR04 is a laptop with unit price 400.

Let's draw some conclusions now. What is the best type of join to use? Well, it depends! The left join seems to be the best choice because it shows all the data about Sales. However, it has lost the information about product PR04. If at some point, we want to get the list of Products that have never been sold, we cannot derive such information from this query: we will rather need to create a new query that combines the original tables Sales and Products in a different way.

The conclusion is that the choice of what join to use depends on the information that we want to get from the tables. In other words, the query depends on the business requirements. This is how business intelligence works today.

With the Unified Star Schema, things are different: the way how we connect the tables does not depend on the business requirements.

With the USS approach, the way we connect the tables does not depend on the business requirements.

We will see in this chapter how this is possible.

Postponing the join

When we create a join between two tables, A and B, the result is a new table T. If we use a left join, as we have done in the previous example, we will have a loss of data.

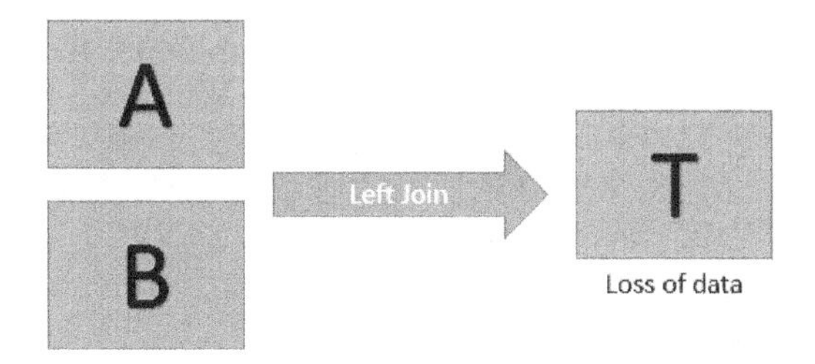

Figure 10.8: The left join between A and B produces a new table T, which has lost some data

It is very important to understand that it is impossible, starting from T, to restore all the information that was in the original tables A and B. When we have a new question that cannot be answered by T, we must go back and get the answer from the original tables A and B. The T table is useful, but it cannot replace A and B.

If we create a data mart in our data warehouse, and that data mart creates a left join between A and B, sooner or later, we will receive a new requirement that needs the creation of a different data mart, based again on A and B. The data coming from A and B will appear in multiple data marts. This will introduce redundancy because the same information will be stored on disk multiple times. This will also produce redundancy of code and much confusion.

So, it appears that the solution for avoiding the loss of data and consequently, the redundancy of data marts, is simply to avoid creating joins.

The USS approach does not create any join. It only prepares the tables to be joined later. By doing so, we can say that the USS has no loss of data.

The USS approach has no loss of data because it does not create any join.

The join should be created only at the moment when data is consumed by the end-users, and not before.

The Unified Star Schema does not create any join, but it organizes data in a way that makes life very easy for the end-users. This is possible thanks to the Bridge and to the USS naming convention.

The heart of the USS: The Bridge

Figure 10.9 shows the tables A, B, and the Bridge.

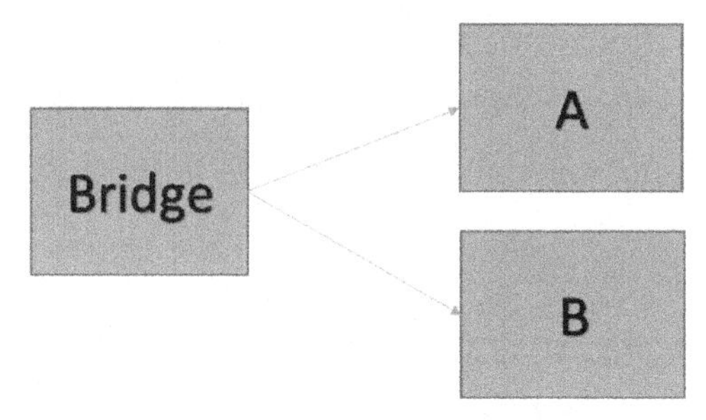

Figure 10.9: The USS approach does not create any join. It only prepares the tables to be joined to the Bridge, in the moment of data consumption

Tables A and B contain all the original data. They have no loss of data because no join was created yet. They will be joined to the Bridge only in the moment of data consumption. Let's take the example based on Sales and Products, and see how the Bridge is built.

Stage	_KEY_Sales	_KEY_Products
Sales	1	PR01
Sales	2	PR02
Sales	3	PR02
Sales	4	PR03
Sales	5	PR99
Products	NULL	PR01
Products	NULL	PR02
Products	NULL	PR03
Products	NULL	PR04

Figure 10.10: The Bridge is a matrix of Foreign Keys organized as a union of stages

The "Bridge" is a matrix of Foreign Keys. It is actually a union of matrices called "stages". Each stage has the same number of rows as the table that it originates from.

It is very important to clarify the meanings of the words "join" and "union" because, in the spoken language, they have similar meanings. Yet, in the SQL language, they are two completely different operations.

Let's start by saying that a table contains rows and columns, and each column has a header. Figure 10.11 shows the high-level difference between a join and a union.

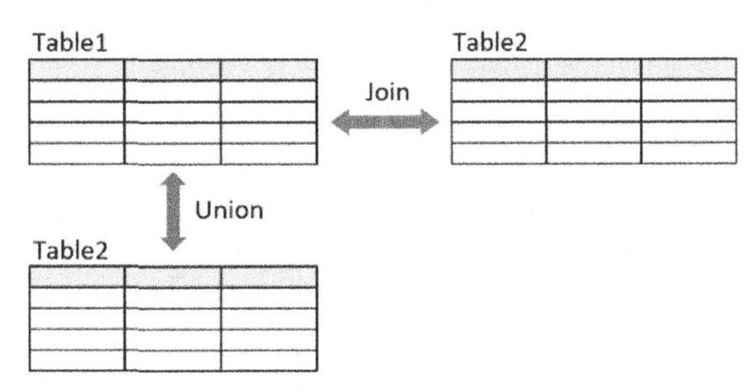

Figure 10.11: The high-level difference between a join and a union

We can summarize the difference in one sentence:

A join between two tables puts their columns next to each other, while a union between two tables puts their rows underneath each other.

Join and union are quite easy to create when the two tables have an identical structure because they appear as two identical rectangles. But what happens when the two rectangles are not identical?

In the real world, the two tables rarely have an identical structure. When you have to merge two tables, they typically appear as two rectangles with a different shape, as shown in Figure 10.12.

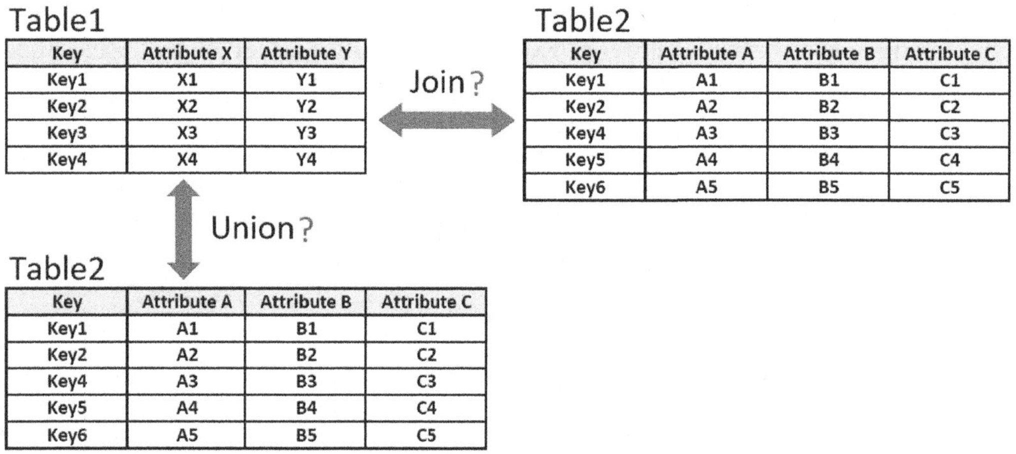

Table1

Key	Attribute X	Attribute Y
Key1	X1	Y1
Key2	X2	Y2
Key3	X3	Y3
Key4	X4	Y4

Join?

Table2

Key	Attribute A	Attribute B	Attribute C
Key1	A1	B1	C1
Key2	A2	B2	C2
Key4	A3	B3	C3
Key5	A4	B4	C4
Key6	A5	B5	C5

Union?

Table2

Key	Attribute A	Attribute B	Attribute C
Key1	A1	B1	C1
Key2	A2	B2	C2
Key4	A3	B3	C3
Key5	A4	B4	C4
Key6	A5	B5	C5

Figure 10.12: How to create a join and a union between tables that are not identical?

The problem of how to merge these two rectangles has nothing to do with technology and computers: it is a problem that anyone can try to solve with pen and paper. The only constraint is that the result must be a table, hence a rectangle.

You can close this book for a moment and try to draw yourself the join and the union between Table1 and Table2. It will help you to understand the magic ingredient of the Unified Star Schema.

In this modern world, very often, we are intrigued by the challenge of a very large data set, a distributed system, a security firewall, a constraint of memory, a high demand for computational power, and so on. We tend to forget, however, the power of a few minutes spent with a white piece of paper and a pen. You should draw the two tables first, and then you should try to merge them. The join will come quite easy, while the union will probably make you think a bit more. Those few minutes will be very valuable. Figure 10.13 shows the merge of Table1 and Table2 by a join.

Key	Attribute X	Attribute Y	Attribute A	Attribute B	Attribute C
Key1	X1	Y1	A1	B1	C1
Key2	X2	Y2	A2	B2	C2
Key3	X3	Y3			
Key4	X4	Y4	A3	B3	C3
Key5			A4	B4	C4
Key6			A5	B5	C5

Figure 10.13: The two tables are merged by a join

The join aligns the rows with the matching keys, and it keeps the cells empty (NULL value) where the keys are not matching. Most developers and analysts are very familiar with the join. Figure 10.14 shows the merge of Table1 and Table2 by a union.

Key	Attribute X	Attribute Y	Attribute A	Attribute B	Attribute C
Key1	X1	Y1			
Key1			A1	B1	C1
Key2	X2	Y2			
Key2			A2	B2	C2
Key3	X3	Y3			
Key4	X4	Y4			
Key4			A3	B3	C3
Key5			A4	B4	C4
Key6			A5	B5	C5

Figure 10.14: The two tables are merged by a union

The union does not align the rows. It never does. Also, there is no concept of matching keys. To be fair, there is no concept of "key" at all: the union, in general, has nothing to do with the concept of key. The union, however, tries to "pile up" the columns that represent "the same thing". By "pile up", we mean "share the same column". In this example, only the column named "Key" is common between the two tables, and for this reason, it has been piled up. But if there was, in both tables, a column with the employee name, or with the creation date, those columns would need to be piled up too, because they represent the same thing. The names of the columns do not need to be identical. For example, if it turns out that the two columns "Attribute Y" and "Attribute C" represent the same thing, then they should be piled up with an appropriate name chosen by the developer. This is why the choice of how to create the union between two tables cannot be done by a computer. It needs to be done by a human who understands the meaning of all the columns.

Please note, if your drawing has the rows sorted in a different way, it does not matter. As long as you have drawn the same nine rows as in Figure 10.14, you have done right.

Most people, based on this example, would find the join better than the union: with the join, the values of the attributes are all displayed in the same row, and for this reason, they can be compared and computed together. With the union, instead, the values from the two original tables are always displayed in different rows. So, why would we need the union then? Here follows the answer.

The real world is one tiny step more complex than this example: when we merge two tables, they usually do not have the "same unique identifier". The scenario that we have seen in this example is known as "one-to-one" (some would call it "one-to-zero", because the two sets of keys are not identical). It exists, but it is quite rare. The most common scenario is when the two tables have one element in common that is unique in only one of them. This is known as "one-to-many". The most challenging and interesting scenario, however, is when the two tables have a few elements in common, but none of them is a unique identifier. This is known as "many-to-many", and that's where the union becomes an incredibly powerful solution.

Now that we have a good understanding of the word "union", we can look back at Figure 10.10. We will notice that the Bridge was built with an operation of union, because the values of the Products stage are listed underneath the values of the Sales stage. In the column "_KEY_Products" we can see that the values from the two tables have been piled up, because they represent the same thing.

The Sales stage has five rows, exactly like the Sales table. The Products stage has four rows, exactly like the Products table. Each column of the Bridge contains a FK that points to the PK of some table. The Sales stage points to Sales (the originating table) and to Products, while the Products stage points only to Products (the originating table), and nothing else. This stage, despite not pointing to any other table, is useful because it contains the ID PR04, which we cannot see anywhere else. The Bridge has a stage for each table, even when a table does not point to anything. Thanks to this method, we obtain a "full outer join effect": every unit of information is available to the end-user. The end-user is creating a left join, but this time the left join has no loss of data.

The USS approach organizes the tables in a way that is much better than the traditional approach, for several reasons.

First of all, each business entity here is available as a self-standing table. The number of rows of each table has a precise business meaning: for example, if the Products table has four rows, it means that we have four products. With a denormalized data mart, this information would not be available.

Second, and more importantly, data is not repeated. If you think about it, Products is usually pointed not only by Sales but also by many other tables. If we would "embed" Products into Sales, then we would need to embed another "copy of Products" into Purchases, and another copy into Stock, and so on. This would generate many copies of the same information, producing redundancy on disk and a lot of confusion. Instead, with the USS approach, Products is only one table, available in only one place. It can be used in many ways, but it's only one.

With the USS approach, data is not repeated. Every table represents one specific business entity. All tables can be easily combined by the end-users in the moment of data consumption.

In the next examples, you will notice that that the Bridge is a very large table, but it is mostly empty. As we have seen earlier in Figure 10.10, the Products stage contains some NULLs because it does not point to Sales. The Bridge is populated only when a table points to another table. It is populated only when the hunter aims at the prey. The stage of the lion is densely populated because the lion is a big hunter. The stage of the gazelle, on the other hand, will have only one column populated because the gazelle does not aim at any other animal. The stage of the leopard will be populated, but less than the one of the lion.

The Bridge is conceptually one single large table, but in some cases, it is convenient to implement it physically as a set of multiple tables: one for each stage. The stages will be merged together at the moment when a query is generated, and the end-user will retrieve only the stages that are needed. The merge operation must be done with a union. This will not be difficult for the end-users because many BI tools allow the creation of a union quite easily, especially when the column names have been prepared with a good naming convention.

The USS naming convention

With the USS approach, the names of tables and columns must follow a very simple, strict, and logical naming convention.

The first column of the Bridge is always called "Stage" (or "Bridge Stage"). Then, each column is called "_KEY_TableName", where "TableName" is the name of the table that the column points to.

The preceding underscore "_" is recommended because many systems and tools automatically sort names alphabetically, and this allows having all the keys shown at the beginning. Some systems (like Oracle) do not allow the preceding underscore in column names: in that case, it is up to the developer to choose between omitting the underscore and finding an alternative. The choice of the case is also up the developer: it can be Capitalized ("_Key_") or UPPERCASE ("_KEY_"). What really matters is coherence.

In our example, we have two tables: Sales and Products. This means that the Bridge will have three columns: Stage, _KEY_ Sales, and _KEY_ Products. If our project has 100 tables, the Bridge will have 101 columns. If our project has (n) tables, the Bridge will have (n + 1) columns.

When two tables of your data set have the same name, it is necessary to do a renaming exercise, also known as "data dictionary". If your data source is an integrated data warehouse, the renaming exercise has probably been done by the data warehouse team. But if this is not the case, then it must be done by the developer who builds the Unified Star Schema.

For example, you may have a set of tables that comes from two different sources, such as a banking system and a CRM. In this case, the table "Accounts" from the banking system probably represents the bank accounts, while the table "Accounts" from the CRM probably represents the Customers. This means that we have two tables named "Accounts", but they represent two completely different business entities, and they must not be confused. When this ambiguity happens, it is necessary to make a decision about the renaming. Ideally, this should be done with the help of one or more end-users from the business departments. An easy solution, in this case, is to rename the CRM table "Accounts" as "Customers". The final table names must be unique, sensible and intuitive.

The same principle also applies to the column names. If you have a column "ZIP Code" in the Customers table and a column "ZIP Code" in the Suppliers table, these columns must be renamed. A good renaming could be as "Customer ZIP Code" and "Supplier ZIP Code". Each column must be fully understandable regardless of the context. You must imagine that every column name is written on a piece of paper, and then all the pieces of paper are mixed together in a bucket. If you pick a piece of paper from the bucket, you must know what that name represents. The final column names must be unique, sensible, and intuitive.

The names of tables and columns do not necessarily need to match the ones that will appear in the final reports and dashboards, because it's always possible to apply a further renaming inside the BI tool. The aim of this renaming exercise, both for tables and for columns, is to eliminate synonyms and to create a sensible and intuitive data dictionary.

How the USS solves the loss of data

Now that we have seen the Bridge, let's focus on the two other tables of our example, and see in detail how this solution solves the problem of the loss of data.

With the USS approach, all the tables remain pretty much identical to the original. However, each of them must have one additional column named "_KEY_TableName". This column must be a Primary Key for that table, and it is recommended to put it in the very first position. Figure 10.15 shows the Products table with the USS approach.

_KEY_Products	ProductID	ProductName	UnitPrice
PR01	PR01	Hard Disk Drive	100
PR02	PR02	Keyboard	70
PR03	PR03	Tablet	300
PR04	PR04	Laptop	400

Figure 10.15: The Products table with the USS approach has one additional KEY column

Please note that the additional column _KEY_Products is identical to ProductID. This may appear redundant, but it is not: the first one is a "technical column", to be used for the joins, while the second is a "business column", to be potentially displayed in the final reports and dashboards.

Figure 10.16 shows the Sales table with the USS approach.

_KEY_Sales	SalesID	Date	Client	Product	Quantity	Amount
1	1	01-Jan	Bill	PR01	1	100
2	2	02-Jan	Bill	PR02	1	70
3	3	02-Jan	Francesco	PR02	2	140
4	4	03-Jan	Francesco	PR03	1	300
5	5	04-Jan	Francesco	PR99	3	600

Figure 10.16: The Sales table with the USS approach has one additional KEY column

Again, the columns _KEY_Sales and SalesID are identical. As before, the first one is a "technical column", to be used for the joins, while the second is a "business column", to be potentially displayed in the final reports and dashboards. In this case, SalesID is a surrogate key, and it's quite unlikely that anybody will want to see it in a report: if this is the case, it could be in theory removed. However, it is recommended to keep it during development, and maybe hide it later.

Now that we have described Bridge, Sales, and Products, we can put these three pieces together, as shown in Figure 10.17.

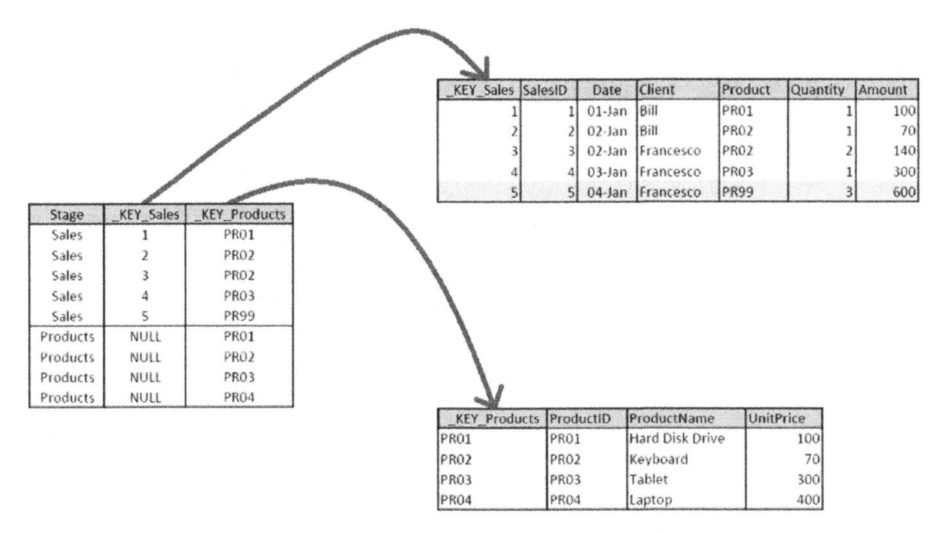

_KEY_Sales	SalesID	Date	Client	Product	Quantity	Amount
1	1	01-Jan	Bill	PR01	1	100
2	2	02-Jan	Bill	PR02	1	70
3	3	02-Jan	Francesco	PR02	2	140
4	4	03-Jan	Francesco	PR03	1	300
5	5	04-Jan	Francesco	PR99	3	600

Stage	_KEY_Sales	_KEY_Products
Sales	1	PR01
Sales	2	PR02
Sales	3	PR02
Sales	4	PR03
Sales	5	PR99
Products	NULL	PR01
Products	NULL	PR02
Products	NULL	PR03
Products	NULL	PR04

_KEY_Products	ProductID	ProductName	UnitPrice
PR01	PR01	Hard Disk Drive	100
PR02	PR02	Keyboard	70
PR03	PR03	Tablet	300
PR04	PR04	Laptop	400

Figure 10.17: The Bridge, Sales and Products are now ready to be joined

Please remember that the USS does not create any join. It only prepares the tables to be joined to the Bridge, in the moment of data consumption. This will typically happen in a BI tool.

The result of the join, as it will appear inside the BI tool, is shown in Figure 10.18.

Stage	_KEY_Sales	_KEY_Products	SalesID	Date	Client	Product	Quantity	Amount	ProductID	ProductName	UnitPrice
Sales	1	PR01	1	01-Jan	Bill	PR01	1	100	PR01	Hard Disk Drive	100
Sales	2	PR02	2	02-Jan	Bill	PR02	1	70	PR02	Keyboard	70
Sales	3	PR02	3	02-Jan	Francesco	PR02	2	140	PR02	Keyboard	70
Sales	4	PR03	4	03-Jan	Francesco	PR03	1	300	PR03	Tablet	300
Sales	5	PR99	5	04-Jan	Francesco	PR99	3	600	NULL because PR99 is unreferenced		
Products	NULL	PR01	NULL because _KEY_Sales is NULL						PR01	Hard Disk Drive	100
Products	NULL	PR02							PR02	Keyboard	70
Products	NULL	PR03							PR03	Tablet	300
Products	NULL	PR04							PR04	Laptop	400

Figure 10.18: The result of the join

Please spend a moment watching the figure. The first three columns come from the Bridge. The six central columns come from Sales, and the last three columns come from Products.

When the IDs in the Bridge are either unreferenced or NULL, the corresponding joined columns will also be NULL. This can be seen very clearly in Figure 10.18.

So, now that we have seen the result of the join, it's time to understand why we say that the USS solves the problem of the loss of data.

If we focus on the upper half of Figure 10.18 (the Sales stage), we can notice that it is identical to the "left join" between Sales and Products that we have seen earlier in this chapter, in Figure 10.7. The row of Sales with amount 600 is visible, the attributes of the product PR99 are not available, and the product PR04 is not visible. However, in addition to that, the lower half of the figure (the Products stage) shows the full list of all the existing products, regardless of whether or not they appear in Sales.

With the USS approach, the resulting table contains every single unit of information. We can find all the products, together with their name and their unit price: this is true also for PR04, even though it was unsold. We can also find all the sales, with all the details about the date, the client, and so on. The only information that we do not find is the name and the unit price of PR99, but this information was not given in the original data source. Therefore, we can safely say that this solution has no loss of data.

But there is more! With the USS approach, we achieve not only "zero loss", but also "zero redundancy". Please look at Figure 10.19.

Stage	_KEY_Sales	_KEY_Products	SalesID	Date	Client	Product	Quantity	Amount	ProductID	ProductName	UnitPrice
Sales	1	PR01	1	01-Jan	Bill	PR01	1	100	PR01	Hard Disk Drive	100
Sales	2	PR02	2	02-Jan	Bill	PR02	1	70	PR02	Keyboard	70
Sales	3	PR02	3	02-Jan	Francesco	PR02	2	140	PR02	Keyboard	70
Sales	4	PR03	4	03-Jan	Francesco	PR03	1	300	PR03	Tablet	300
Sales	5	PR99	5	04-Jan	Francesco	PR99	3	600			
Products	NULL	PR01							PR01	Hard Disk Drive	100
Products	NULL	PR02							PR02	Keyboard	70
Products	NULL	PR03							PR03	Tablet	300
Products	NULL	PR04							PR04	Laptop	400

Figure 10.19: Some units of information appear to be repeated, but they are actually stored on disk only once

The repetitions that you see in the figure only occur in the moment when the join is created. But as we know, the USS does not create any join. It only prepares the tables to be joined in the moment of data consumption.

For example, the Products table in the USS data mart is stored as a self-standing table. The word "Keyboard" is stored on disk only once and not three times, as you may think by watching Figure 10.19. In a traditional data mart, the word "Keyboard" would be stored three times because data is stored in a denormalized form, with the aim to make life easier for the end-users. With the USS approach, we help the end-users through the naming convention, and we keep data normalized, achieving zero redundancy. Knowing that the data volumes will keep growing in the coming years, it's good to know that we are able to build a business intelligence solution that minimizes the storage effort.

With the USS approach, there is zero redundancy in data storage.

Saving space on disk is good. However, the main reason why we like normalization is that data is organized in a more logical way. If the end-users need some information about products, it is more intuitive for them to find it in a table called "Products" rather than embedded into Sales. With normalization, everything is more logical, more intuitive, and much tidier.

Implementation with Tibco Spotfire

Let's make a practical implementation with Tibco Spotfire. The examples in this book are based on Spotfire Analyst, v7.10.0. It has to be said that Tibco has produced several new versions after this one: they are cloud-based, and they have been enriched with many new modern features. However, we have chosen to use this version for our tests simply because it was available for an unlimited trial period. We have also tested the cloud version, and we have observed that the way how data gets merged has not changed anyway. It is very easy to create a query against the USS with Spotfire. When two tables have two columns with identical names, Spotfire, by default, suggests to connect them based on those two columns. The end-users need to follow these three basic steps:

- Start by loading the Bridge
- Add all the tables that are relevant to their needs (in this case, Sales and Products)
- Make sure that the join is a left join (it is normally the case, by default)

The query is shown in Figure 10.20.

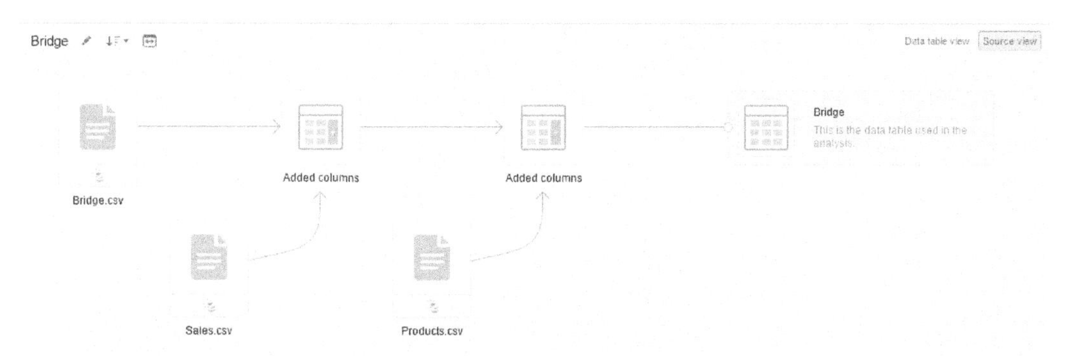

Figure 10.20: Thanks to the USS naming convention, Spotfire automatically recognizes what columns to use to connect the tables

The result of the query is shown in Figure 10.21.

Stage	_Key_Sales	_Key_Products	SalesID	Date	Client	Product	Quantity	Amount	ProductID	ProductName	UnitPrice
Sales	1	PR01	1	01/01/2019	Bill	PR01	1	100	PR01	Hard Disk Drive	100
Sales	2	PR02	2	02/01/2019	Bill	PR02	1	70	PR02	Keyboard	70
Sales	3	PR02	3	02/01/2019	Francesco	PR02	2	140	PR02	Keyboard	70
Sales	4	PR03	4	03/01/2019	Francesco	PR03	1	300	PR03	Tablet	300
Sales	5	PR99	5	04/01/2019	Francesco	PR99	3	600			
Products		PR01							PR01	Hard Disk Drive	100
Products		PR02							PR02	Keyboard	70
Products		PR03							PR03	Tablet	300
Products		PR04							PR04	Laptop	400

Add rows

Add calculated column

Figure 10.21: The result of the query in Spotfire

Now that the query has retrieved the needed data, the end-users can perform their analysis directly with Spotfire.

From one single query, it is possible to see the "Sales by Product", but it's also possible to expose the "Unsold Products".

With traditional dimensional modeling, this would require two separate queries. With this solution, instead, we have both answers integrated into one single query, coming from one single star schema. This makes the user experience easier and more natural.

Figure 10.22 shows the report "Sales by Product".

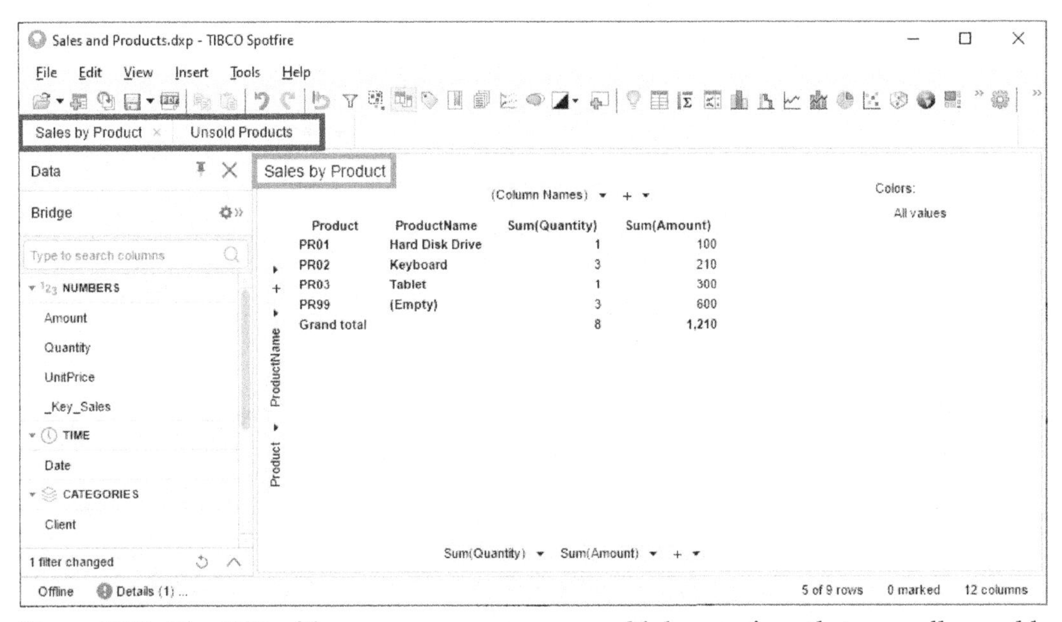

Figure 10.22: The USS with one query can answer multiple questions that normally would require multiple queries

Figure 10.23 shows this is the report "Unsold Products".

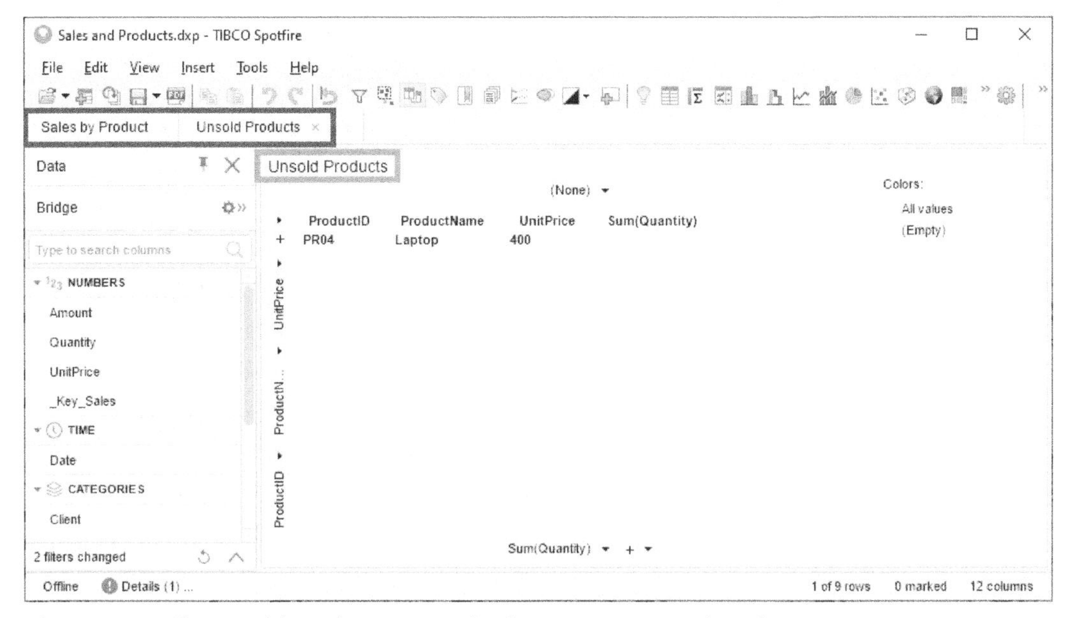

Figure 10.23: The unsold products appear in the same query as the sales

In this example, we have seen that the end-user can build, with a simple drag and drop, a dashboard that can answer multiple questions that would normally require multiple SQL queries or even separate dashboards. This is possible because the USS is a general-purpose star schema, with all the data available in one place.

The end-user experience becomes much easier this way because all the answers can be found in one place. Every unit of information is located in the place where the end-user expects it to be, and the connections between tables are made very easy. Thanks to this new approach, every end-user becomes pretty much independent. This is our idea of self-service business intelligence.

The USS approach introduces a different way of making "self-service BI": not anymore based on technology, but rather based on a different way of organizing the information.

CHAPTER 11

The Fan Trap

In this chapter, receive an introduction to the Oriented Data Model convention, and learn the dangers of a fan trap through an example. Learn an alternative notation for the one-to-many relationship, which recalls the idea of "spreading". Differentiate join and association, and realize that an "in-memory association" is the preferred solution to the fan trap. Also, learn about the techniques of "splitting the measures" and "moving all the measures to the Bridge". Finally, see an example of the JSON fan trap and how it can be fixed.

The fan trap is a problem that occurs in the vast majority of business intelligence projects today. If you look up "fan trap" on the Internet, you will find a series of articles giving a definition, an explanation, and a rich set of examples. But these articles are sometimes a bit difficult to read, and they also conflict with each other to a certain extent. However, they all share the same core principle: a fan trap is a particular combination of tables that produces a duplication of measures. But before giving our definition of fan trap, let's introduce the Oriented Data Model convention.

The Oriented Data Model convention

In chapter 9, we learned that the tables of a database can be seen as hunter and prey. The connection between the two tables is always "oriented". The relationship between the two tables is, in most cases, one-to-many. This means that two tables can be connected by a "key" that is unique on one table (PK) and not unique on the other table (FK).

"Oriented Data Model" (ODM) is a graphical convention for data models where the table with the FK stays on the left, and the table with the PK stays on the right. See Figure 11.1.

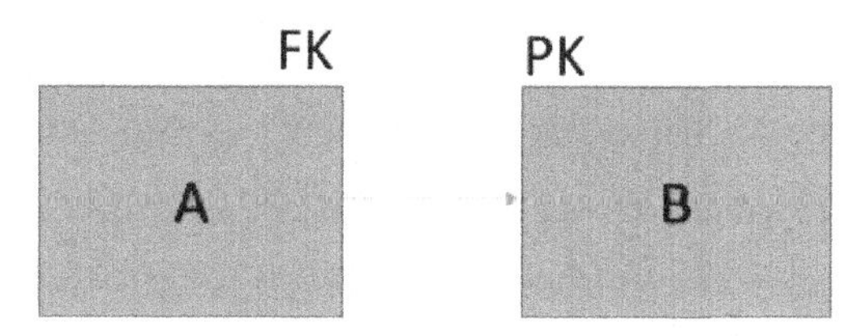

Figure 11.1: The table with the FK stays on the left, and the table with the PK stays on the right

According to the ODM convention, the arrow is always oriented from left to right. Let's look at Sales and Products in Figure 11.2.

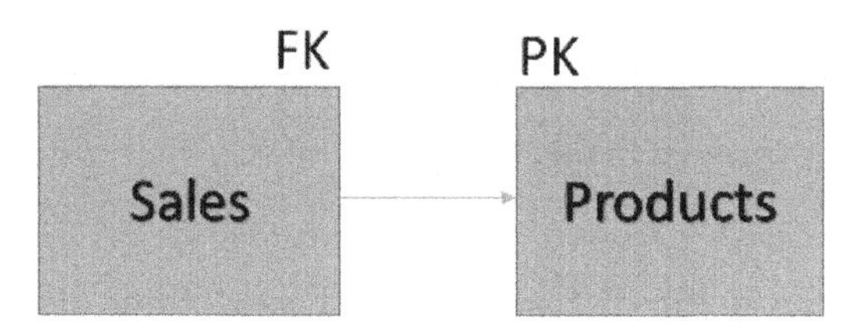

Figure 11.2: Sales stays on the left and Products stays on the right

Sales and Products are joined by the product ID. This is a PK in Products and a FK in Sales. For this reason, Sales stays on the left, and Products stays on the right. Sales points to Products, from left to right.

Not all relationships, however, are one-to-many. There are some cases when two tables A and B have a many-to-many relationship. This means it is impossible to find a key that is unique in A and available in B, or vice versa. They may have one or more keys in common, but these keys are never unique, neither on the left nor on the right. When this is the case, according to the ODM convention, the two tables must not be connected by any direct line. Despite not being directly connected, the two tables can still be compared and computed together, and they can appear merged in end-user reports and dashboards. Chapter 13 on multi-fact queries will explain how.

There are also cases when the relationships are one-to-one, which means that the common key is unique in both tables. In these cases, the relative position is good either way.

The ODM is a graphical convention that can simplify our understanding of complex data models. The example in chapter 16 on Northwind will show you in practical terms how to use the ODM convention. Besides simplifying the understanding of data models, the ODM convention can also simplify our language. When we say that "A is on the left of B", we mean that A has a FK that points to the PK of B. This is equivalent to saying that A is the hunter and B is the prey, and that A points to B. The definition of fan trap is based on these words "left" and "right".

Definition of the fan trap

A fan trap is a particular combination of two tables where the table "on the right" contains at least one measure.

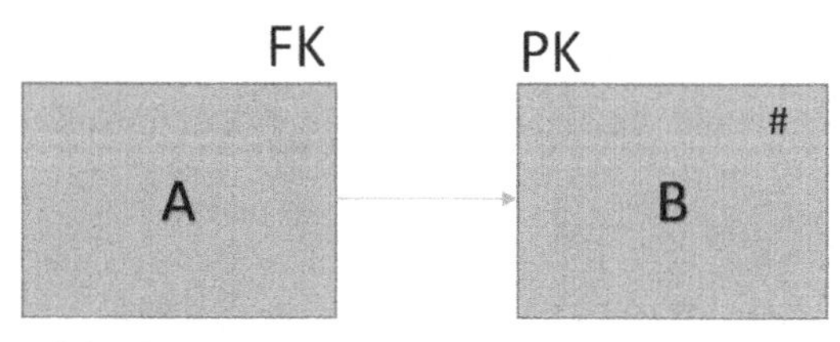

Figure 11.3: The schema of the fan trap

The small symbol "#" in Figure 11.3 indicates that table B contains at least one measure.

Examples of measures are sales amount, sales quantity, shipment amount, shipment quantity, and stock count. A year is a number, but it is not a measure. You will never make the sum or the average of two years, and you will never show the year as a value in the "Y" axis of a chart. For this reason, the year cannot be relevant in the definition of a fan trap.

The arrow from A to B, as usual, indicates that A points to B. This means that one row of B is potentially pointed by multiple rows of A. When a fan trap occurs, we say that "B gets duplicated by A". Or, even better, "B gets exploded by A".

The core principle of the fan trap is very simple: one row of B, containing a measure, gets exploded by A. And when measures are duplicated, the totals become incorrect.

Please note that our definition of a fan trap is based on two tables. If you look it up on the Internet, you will find several definitions based on three tables. Our definition is more general. For this reason, you will easily find in your data a combination of tables that is not a fan trap based on other definitions, but is a fan trap based on ours.

Example based on sales and shipments

Let's see this in an example based on Sales and Shipments.

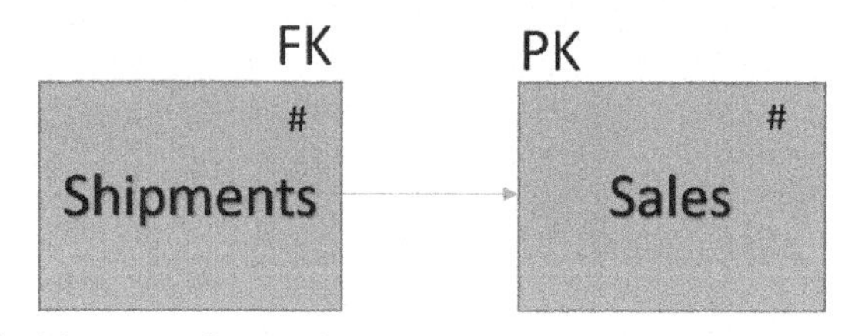

Figure 11.4: Sales and Shipments form a fan trap

Both tables, Sales and Shipments, contain measures. The measures in Shipments are not a problem because Shipments does not have any table on the left. But the measures in Sales cause a fan trap because Shipments is on the left of Sales.

Figure 11.5 contains Sales data.

SalesID	Date	Client	Product	Quantity	Amount
1	01-Jan	Bill	PR01	1	100
2	02-Jan	Bill	PR02	1	70
3	02-Jan	Francesco	PR02	2	140
4	03-Jan	Francesco	PR03	1	300
5	04-Jan	Francesco	PR01	40	4,000
				45	**4,610**

Figure 11.5: Sales has two measures, and the totals are 45 and 4610

The total quantity is 45 and the total amount is 4610.

Figure 11.6 contains Shipments data.

ShipmentID	SalesID	ShipmentDate	ShipmentQuantity	ShipmentAmount
1	1	01-Jan	1	100
2	2	02-Jan	1	70
3	3	02-Jan	2	140
4	4	03-Jan	1	300
5	5	04-Jan	10	1,000
6	5	31-Jan	30	3,000
			45	**4,610**

Figure 11.6: Shipments has two measures. The totals are 45 and 4610, like in Sales

The totals of Shipments are identical to the totals of Sales. This is because all the orders have been successfully fulfilled. The row number 5 of Sales got split up into two separate shipments because only a part of the ordered quantity was immediately available in stock, and the rest was shipped later.

Please note that Sales and Shipments do not have the same identical granularity: the Sales table has five rows, while the Shipments table has six rows. For this reason, they cannot line up perfectly when joined. Figure 11.7 shows what happens if we join them together.

Shipment ID	Sales ID	Shipment Date	Shipment Quantity	Shipment Amount	Sales Date	Client	Product	Sales Quantity	Sales Amount
1	1	01-Jan	1	100	01-Jan	Bill	PR01	1	100
2	2	02-Jan	1	70	02-Jan	Bill	PR02	1	70
3	3	02-Jan	2	140	02-Jan	Francesco	PR02	2	140
4	4	03-Jan	1	300	03-Jan	Francesco	PR03	1	300
5	5	04-Jan	10	1,000	04-Jan	Francesco	PR01	40	4,000
6	5	31-Jan	30	3,000	04-Jan	Francesco	PR01	40	4,000
			45	**4,610**				**85**	**8,610**

Figure 11.7: Sales and Shipments form a fan trap. When they get joined together, they produce duplicates

The join between Sales and Shipments produces a duplicate of measures: 40 and 4000 are repeated. As a consequence, the totals appear to be 85 and 8610, which are incorrect. This is a big problem.

The problem of duplicates of measures, today, is solved in various ways.

One possible solution is to let the duplication happen, and then try to artificially "de-duplicate" the measures with the help of some complex formula. In Tableau, this can be achieved by building a calculated measure that uses the LOD (Level of Detail) syntax. But the resulting formula will look quite complex and difficult to maintain. Moreover, there is always the risk that an end-user will accidentally create a sum of the original measure, producing an incorrect total in the reports. We definitely do not recommend this path. It does not make any sense for us to create a duplicate and then de-duplicate it. This is why Tableau has recently introduced a completely different way of handling the problem, as we will see later in this chapter.

Another possible solution is to avoid the duplication by creating an aggregated query, ad-hoc. If the requirement is the comparison of the sales quantity vs. the shipment quantity, the developer will aggregate Shipments and Sales to the same level of granularity. By doing so, Shipments and Sales will line up perfectly when joined, and the totals will be correct. However, some detail (such as the shipment date) will no longer be available. If there is a new requirement to see the shipment date, then a new query will be needed. But that new query, in turn, must not include the measures from Sales, for the reason that we have seen before. This leads to a multitude of queries, created ad-hoc for each requirement.

The ad-hoc approach today works fine, but it has a problem: every business requirement becomes a self-standing project. And this has a high cost.

The solution that we present in this book goes beyond ad-hoc. We want a solution that does not have any problem if the granularity is not identical. We want a solution where the measures are always correct. We want a solution that is easy to create, to use, and to maintain.

Visualizing the one-to-many relationship

Before proceeding, we would like to spend some words about the graphical notation for the cardinality between two tables. In particular, we are interested in the one-to-many relationship because that is the foundation of the USS approach. Until this point, to show a connection between two tables, we have used the "arrow" notation. Figure 11.8 contains an alternative notation, very popular and very intuitive.

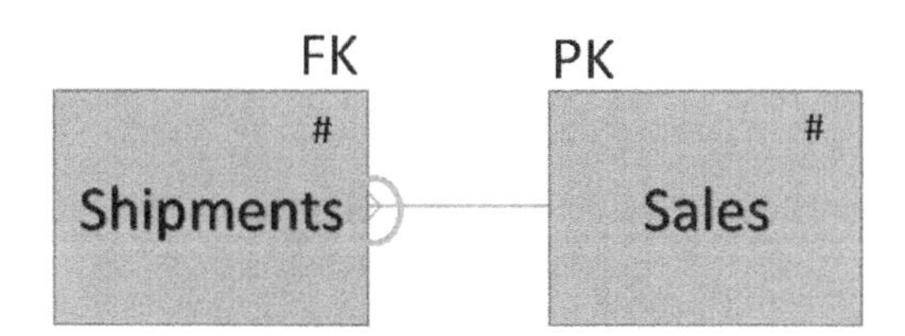

Figure 11.8: Crow's foot is an alternative notation for the one-to-many relationship

This is known as "crow's foot notation" because the connector (the symbol in the little circle in Figure 11.8) recalls the shape of the foot of a crow.

This notation shows the relationship between these two tables in a very intuitive way: a row of Sales may match multiple rows of Shipments, but each row of Shipments always matches at most one single row of Sales. With this notation, it appears very obvious that the "one" side is on the right, and the "many" side is on the left. Some people would refer to this figure as "many-to-one", to put in evidence that the "many" side is the one on the left. But the symbol of the connector also suggests the image of a "fan": not the classic electric fan that you may have at home, but rather a traditional manual fan, like the one of a Flamenco dancer, shown in Figure 11.9.

Figure 11.9: A Flamenco dancer holding a fan

A fan suggests the idea of "spreading". A fan trap takes a measure and spreads it into multiple copies, as you can see in Figure 11.10.

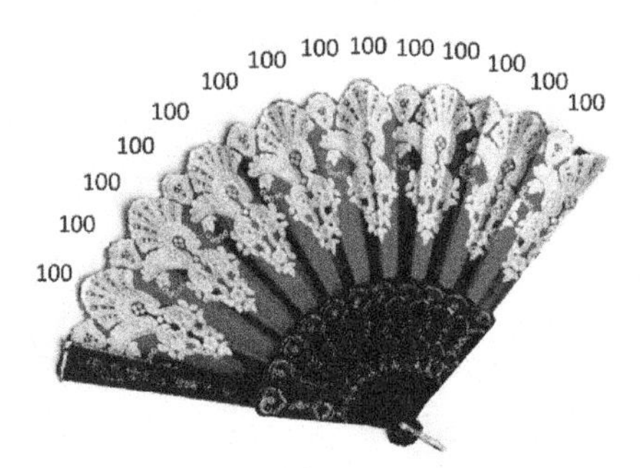

Figure 11.10: In a fan trap, a measure is spreading into multiple copies

Although we like the crow's foot notation and its analogy with the fan, we still prefer the notation with the arrow. The arrow suggests the concept of an "oriented connection", which is the foundation of the USS approach.

How the USS solves the fan trap

Fan traps are everywhere. They are probably the biggest risk existing today in business intelligence. And because the definition of fan trap in literature has always been too complex and too specific, this danger has never been properly recognized. Instead, if you look for fan traps in your data, based on our definition, you will probably find many of them.

It happens very frequently to get incorrect totals deriving from fan traps, because this danger is not very well known. Technologies do not seem to recognize duplicates of measures as errors. For example, the SQL language does not give any warning when a join is created between two tables that form a fan trap.

Fan traps are actually not a problem of a particular software, technology, or programming language. They are not a problem of spreadsheets, SQL, or BI tools. They are not even a problem of a database or an operating system. Fan traps are simply a logical problem: some particular combinations of tables cannot be joined together.

Some particular combinations of tables cannot be joined together.

You can verify this even with a pen and paper. Try to take the example of this chapter, based on Sales and Shipments. Look at the two tables, and try to draw a table where they both fit together. You will discover that you have no choice but duplicating the measures.

If we want to solve the problem of the fan traps, we must try to change our mindset completely. We must challenge the most consolidated and universally accepted "best practice" existing in business intelligence today: denormalization. Denormalization means that "two or more tables are joined together". The common perception in the data community is that denormalization is the right thing to do because merging tables improves the performance of our BI solution. This may probably be true. But in the presence of a fan trap, denormalization "kills the numbers".

So, can we imagine a world without denormalization? Can we imagine a world without the join? Yes, we can. Instead of the join, we can use the "in-memory association".

The problem of the fan trap can be solved by following the USS approach in combination with a BI tool that is capable of "in-memory association" (or simply association). The association is a way of merging two tables that look similar to a join, but it is created in memory, in the moment when the end-user creates a data visualization. Figure 11.11 shows the USS data model.

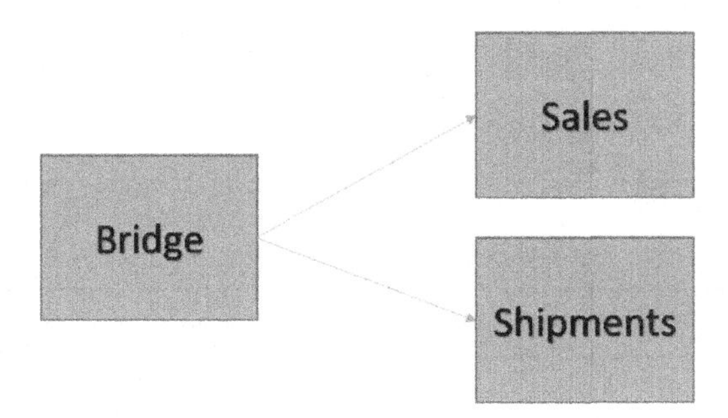

Figure 11.11: The USS data model. These lines this time represent an association

This model shows the tables connected by lines. These lines are identical to the ones that we have seen in all the figures until now. However, depending on the

BI tool that is being used, these lines may represent either a join or an association. In the case of a join, the tables are merged before being loaded in memory. In the case of an association, the tables are merged after. The next paragraph will clarify this concept with a practical implementation.

Most people think that "in-memory" is simply a synonym of "fast". But it's much more than that. When you work with a BI tool that is capable of association, the tables are loaded in memory separately, at their original granularity, and only later they get merged, in the moment of a data visualization. This means that the BI tool is always "aware of the original granularity of each table". Because of this, "in memory" is also a synonym of "no duplicates", which ultimately is a synonym of "correct numbers".

A traditional SQL query environment is usually not capable of association. If you create a standard join between Sales and Shipments, the result of the query will be a single merged table, and it will be loaded in memory as a single merged table. If the query retrieves a measure from Sales, that measures will be duplicated, and the resulting total will be incorrect.

But if you use a tool that is capable of association, the two tables will be loaded in memory at their original granularity. And then, if the end-user will create a visualization with all the data into one single table, the BI tool will still display the measures as repeated, but it will count them as non-repeated.

In the next paragraph, you will be able to see this amazing behavior with your own eyes. This is the real "magic" of the in-memory association.

Implementation with Microsoft Power BI

Let's see how a fan trap can be solved with the Unified Star Schema in combination with a BI tool capable of association: Microsoft Power BI.

Firstly, we need to look at the Bridge. In this example, the Bridge has two stages, one for Sales and one for Shipments. See Figure 11.12.

Stage	_KEY_Shipments	_KEY_Sales
Sales		1
Sales		2
Sales		3
Sales		4
Sales		5
Shipments	1	1
Shipments	2	2
Shipments	3	3
Shipments	4	4
Shipments	5	5
Shipments	6	5

Figure 11.12: The Bridge for Sales and Shipments

As we can see, the ID "5" of _KEY_Sales matches the IDs "5" and "6" of _KEY_Shipments. This is because, as we have seen before, the order of 40 Hard Disks was split into two shipments.

Now we can load into Power BI the three tables: Bridge, Sales, and Shipments. Figure 11.13 shows the Model section of Power BI.

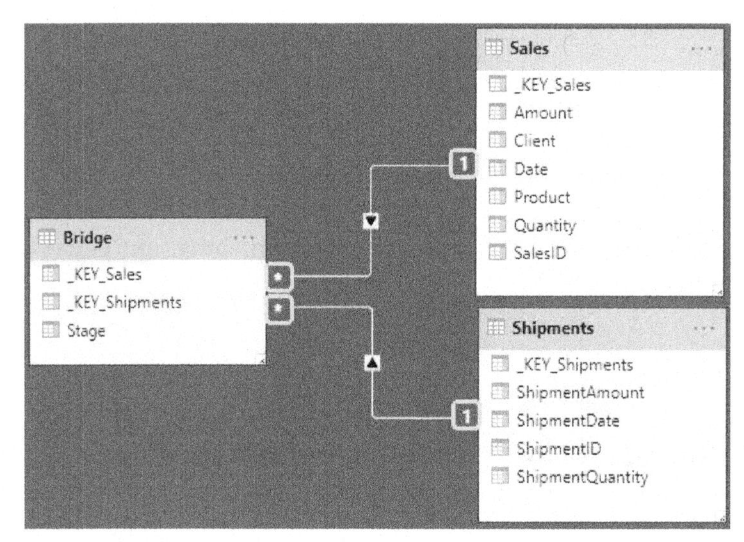

Figure 11.13: The lines look like joins in PowerBI, but in reality, they are associations

The model shows the tables connected by lines. These lines are very similar to the ones that we see in other BI tools. However, it is very important to understand that these lines are not joins: they are associations. They are, we can say, an indication of the way how the tables "will be merged in the future". By "future", we mean the moment when a particular visualization will be created in the report section.

Please note that Power BI, in the Model section, gives us the freedom to move the tables on the canvas as we want: this allows us to apply the ODM convention that we have defined in this chapter. The Bridge contains the FK pointing to Sales, and for this reason, it must stay on the left of Sales. The Bridge also contains the FK pointing to Shipments, and for this reason, it must stay on the left of Shipments too. In Power BI, it is very easy to apply the ODM convention because the tool automatically marks the PK with a "1" and the FK with a "*". So, in Power BI, the ODM convention can be achieved by applying a simple rule: the tables with the "*" must always stay on the left. Please note that a "*" should never be on both sides of a line. If this is the case, you should review your design. Chapter 13 will show you how to deal with many-to-many relationships.

The magic of the association can be seen by looking at the result in the Report section, shown in Figure 11.14.

ShipmentID	SalesID	ShipmentDate	ShipmentQuantity	ShipmentAmount	Date	Client	Product	Amount	Quantity
1	1	01 January 2019	1	100	01 January 2019	Bill	PR01	100	1
2	2	02 January 2019	1	70	02 January 2019	Bill	PR02	70	1
3	3	02 January 2019	2	140	02 January 2019	Francesco	PR02	140	2
4	4	03 January 2019	1	300	03 January 2019	Francesco	PR03	300	1
5	5	04 January 2019	10	1000	04 January 2019	Francesco	PR01	4000	40
6	5	31 January 2019	30	3000	04 January 2019	Francesco	PR01	4000	40
Total			**45**	**4610**				**4610**	**45**

Figure 11.14: Despite the fan trap, Power BI shows the correct totals

Although we can see the amount 4000 and the quantity 40 repeated, the displayed totals are correct: 4610 and 45. Power BI is capable of displaying the correct totals because they are calculated based on the original table, at the original granularity, which is available in memory. In other words, the tool "remembers how Sales was, before being displayed as merged with Shipments".

Is your BI tool capable of association?

Technology is in continuous evolution. A list of tools capable of association would risk becoming incorrect over time. For this reason, instead of a list of tools, this chapter provides you with a method to find out this information on your own. You need to create two tables. You can create them in two separate sheets of an Excel workbook, in two separate CSV files, or in any database. Figure 11.15 contains the first table, Films.

Film	Duration
Film1	100
Film2	100
Film3	100

Figure 11.15: The Films table contains a measure

The Films table has three rows and two columns. The column "Duration" is a measure. The total duration of the films is 300 minutes. So, the grand total that we expect to see in a report is 300. Figure 11.16 contains the second table, Genres.

Film	Genre
Film1	Comedy
Film2	Drama
Film3	Comedy
Film3	Drama

Figure 11.16: The Genres table contains a FK pointing to Films

The Genres table has four rows and two columns. In this table, the column "Film" is a FK, pointing to the PK of the Films table. You can see that "Film3" is both a Comedy and a Drama: this is the case where we will see different BI tools behaving in different ways.

Please note that the correct way of modeling this problem would be with three tables: Films, Genres, and FilmsGenres. Films would be as it is now, while Genres would be a list of all the existing genres, with no repetitions: in this case, two rows. Then FilmsGenres would be the classic "m-m table" that contains just two FK columns, pointing to the two tables. Anyway, even modeling it as three tables, the result would be the same: measures would be duplicated.

We have chosen to model this problem with just two tables for two reasons. First, the genres do not have any additional attributes. A comedy is a comedy, and we do not need any further columns that enrich this information. Second, and more importantly, we want to highlight that two tables are sufficient to form a fan trap.

In Figure 11.17, we can see how the two tables are connected. We can immediately notice that Films and Genres form a fan trap: Films contains a measure, and it gets exploded by Genres, which is on the left.

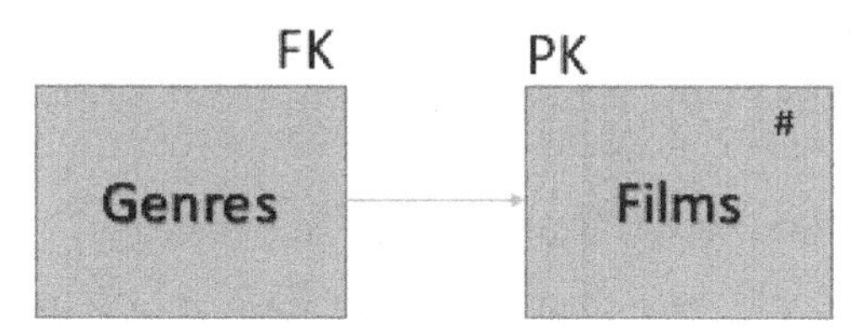

Figure 11.17: Films and Genres form a fan trap

Now the next step of the test is to load the two tables into your BI tool and display the three columns Genre, Film, and Duration.

If the displayed total is 400, it means that the BI tool creates a join.

If the displayed total is 300, it means that the BI tool creates an association.

Now that we have prepared the data set, we can perform our test on various BI tools.

Figure 11.18 shows the implementation with **Tibco Spotfire**. Spotfire shows a grand total of 400, which means that it creates a standard join. The two tables were merged before being loaded in memory, which is why Spotfire is not "aware of the original granularity of each table". It calculates the sum of the displayed measures as 400.

Duration per Genre, Film

(None)

Genre	Film	Sum(Duration)
Comedy	Film1	100
	Film3	100
Drama	Film2	100
	Film3	100
Grand total		400

Figure 11.18: Spotfire shows a total of 400, which means that the tool creates a join

Most BI tools behave like this because most BI tools are based on the SQL language. When numbers are duplicated, it is necessary to create an additional step of de-duplication. This can be achieved by using a particular syntax in the formulas. Most BI tools, in the end, can display the total as 300. What really matters is the awareness of the danger deriving from a fan trap.

Figure 11.19 shows the implementation with **Microsoft Power BI**. Power BI shows a grand total of 300, which means that the tool creates an association. The two tables were loaded in memory as separate tables and then merged only in the moment of the visualization.

Genre	Film	Duration
Comedy	Film1	100
Comedy	Film3	100
Drama	Film2	100
Drama	Film3	100
Total		**300**

Figure 11.19: Power BI shows a total of 300, which means that the tool creates an association

The tool is "aware of the original granularity of each table". It does not matter if the visualization shows the measure 100 repeated four times. The value 100 in memory appears only three times, and for this reason, the tool calculates the sum of those three measures and displays 300, which is the correct total.

Figure 11.20 shows the implementation with **QlikView**. QlikView shows a grand total of 300, which means that the tool creates an association. In this case, we are also displaying the subtotals. It appears that there are 200 minutes of comedy and 200 minutes of drama. However, the grand total is still 300.

Film Duration XL

Genre	Film	Duration
	Film1	100
Comedy	Film3	100
	Total	**200**
	Film2	100
Drama	Film3	100
	Total	**200**
Total		**300**

Figure 11.20: QlikView shows a total of 300, which means that the tool creates an association

Someone may object to this visualization as not being logical because it suggests that 200 + 200 = 300. And this would be a good objection. However, many managers ask for reports where the grand total is shown even when it would make more sense to omit it. Anyway, right or wrong, it is interesting to observe that different BI tools provide different totals starting from the same data source.

The most particular case is the one of **Tableau**. Until version 2020.1, Tableau was creating a standard join: multiple tables were merged into one denormalized table. Then, starting with version 2020.2, the tool has introduced a new feature called "new data model capabilities", which in fact has replaced the join with the association.

Please note that different vendors may give different names to the same feature: this new capability in Tableau has been named "relationship". But because there is not an industry standard, and because multiple names for the same thing risk to become confusing, we have chosen to call it consistently "association".

Figure 11.21 shows the implementation with Tableau, with all the versions until 2020.1. Please note that the test of this paragraph is based on the default behavior of a BI tool. Every BI tool has additional features that behave potentially in different ways. In Tableau, for example, it has always been possible to create multiple queries and merge them with a feature called "data blending". However, what we consider relevant is the default behavior.

Duration by Genre

Genre	Film	
Comedy	Film1	100
	Film3	100
	Total	200
Drama	Film2	100
	Film3	100
	Total	200
Grand Total		400

Figure 11.21: Tableau until version 2020.1 was showing a total of 400, which means that the tool was creating a join

Figure 11.22 shows the implementation with Tableau, with the version 2020.2.

Duration by Genre

Genre	Film	
Comedy	Film1	100
	Film3	100
	Total	200
Drama	Film2	100
	Film3	100
	Total	200
Grand Total		300

Figure 11.22: Tableau 2020.2 shows a total of 300, which means that the tool now creates an association

The difference between join and association, today, does not seem to be known at all. And even in the literature about data modeling, today, this differentiation seems to be a completely missing topic. And it's a pity because somebody would probably find it very interesting that a data set of seven rows produces different results on different BI tools.

Today everyone seems to be focused on performance, speed, and size. But how can we engineer a good BI solution with very large data sets if we are not even aware of these core principles that can also be observed on small data sets?

One more remark about the association. When you create a join, you need to decide if it's going to be an inner, left, right, or full outer join. When you create an association, instead, you do not need to make any decision on this matter. The decision has to do with "what non-matching elements should be kept in the resulting merged table", and it becomes irrelevant with the association because there is no merged table.

Figure 11.23 shows the data source editor of Tableau until version 2020.1.

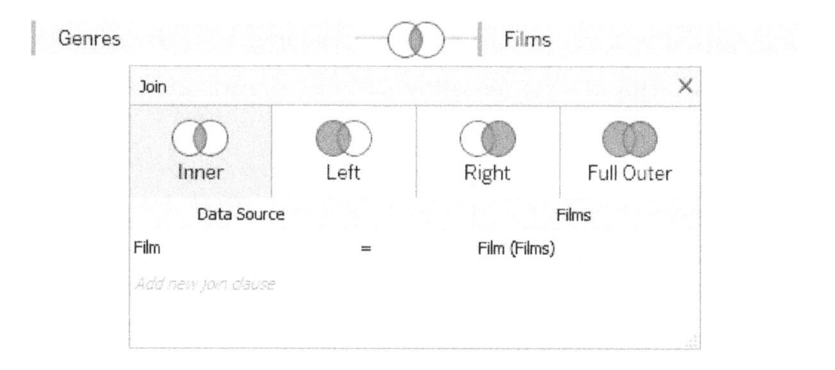

Figure 11.23: When a BI tool creates a join, like Tableau 2020.1, it prompts the end-user to choose the type of join

As you can see in the figure, the default option was the inner join, but the end-user could change it to left, right, or full outer.

Figure 11.24 shows the data source editor of Tableau 2020.2. In this version of Tableau, the end-user does not need to make any decision of inner, left, right, or full outer join. With the association, these concepts do not make any sense.

Figure 11.24: When a BI tool creates an association, like Tableau 2020.2, there is no longer a need to choose the type of join

Some developers say that the association is similar to a full outer join because it retrieves all the "non-matching elements". But the association is actually much better than a full outer join because it merges the tables at the very last moment.

We can summarize the benefit of the association with one simple phrase:

The in-memory association is immune to the fan trap.

Splitting the measures

When a fan trap occurs, using a BI tool that is capable of association is the best solution. But this is not always possible. If your organization has a BI tool that only creates the join, a different solution is needed.

A fair solution consists of "splitting the measures". Each table that is at risk of getting exploded in a fan trap needs to be split into two tables: one without measures, and one with measures.

Sales and Shipments form a fan trap, as we have seen earlier in Figure 11.4. Shipments is not at risk of getting exploded because the database does not have any table that "points" to Shipments. Consequently, for this table, no action is needed.

Sales, instead, is at risk of getting exploded by Shipments, and therefore action is needed.

According to this technique, Sales needs to be split into two tables. We keep the original name "Sales" for the main table, and create a second table we call "Sales_M", where the suffix "_M" stands for "Measure(s)". See Figure 11.25.

_KEY_Sales	SalesID	Date	Client	Product
1	1	01-Jan	Bill	PR01
2	2	02-Jan	Bill	PR02
3	3	02-Jan	Francesco	PR02
4	4	03-Jan	Francesco	PR03
5	5	04-Jan	Francesco	PR01

_KEY_Sales_M	Quantity	Amount
1	1	100
2	1	70
3	2	140
4	1	300
5	40	4,000

Figure 11.25: When your BI tool cannot create the association, split the measures

Now, here is the trick. The two tables that we have created must be connected in two different ways. And this is handled, of course, by the Bridge, as shown in Figure 11.26.

Stage	_KEY_Shipments	_KEY_Sales	_KEY_Sales_M	_KEY_Products
Sales		1	1	PR01
Sales		2	2	PR02
Sales		3	3	PR02
Sales		4	4	PR03
Sales		5	5	PR01
Shipments	1	1	EMPTY	PR01
Shipments	2	2		PR02
Shipments	3	3		PR02
Shipments	4	4		PR03
Shipments	5	5		PR01
Shipments	6	5		PR01

Figure 11.26: The Bridge in the case of split measures

The Sales stage is pointing to both Sales and Sales_M. This ensures that all the visualizations that are based uniquely on Sales will appear as if the table was not split. There is no risk of explosion here, because this stage has the same number of rows as the Sales table.

The Shipments stage is the interesting one. With the Bridge built this way, Shipments is pointing to Sales (see the highlighted rectangle in the figure), but it is not pointing to Sales_M. This is eliminating the fan trap because now the measures of Sales_M will no longer get exploded by Shipments. The main Sales table will still get exploded by Shipments, but there is no danger because Sales is now left with no measures.

This technique avoids the risk of fan trap, and it still keeps alive the functionality of "reducing Shipments based on attributes of Sales". For example, you can apply the filter SalesID = "5". This column is an attribute of Sales. By applying this filter, you will reduce the Bridge to only two rows (the last two rows in Figure 11.26, where _KEY_Sales = 5), resulting in a reduction of _KEY_Shipments to the IDs 5 and 6. Consequently, you will see the corresponding two rows of the Shipments table. The reference from Shipments to Sales is intact, and there are no duplicates of measures. The solution works!

Please note that with traditional dimensional modeling, it is usually considered "forbidden" to filter and group a fact table based on attributes from another fact table. But with the USS approach, instead, this operation is allowed.

To summarize, there are several actions that we can do now. We can use Sales to reduce Shipments, and vice versa (use Shipments to reduce Sales). We can use Shipments to reduce Products, and vice versa. We can use Sales to reduce Products and vice versa. We can also use Sales_M to reduce Products, and vice versa. But there is one action that we cannot do: use Sales_M to reduce Shipments and vice versa. This is not allowed because this connection has been intentionally broken. This is where we see a block marked as "EMPTY" in the Bridge. Sales_M and Shipments are now complete strangers to each other. A filter on one will discard all the rows of the other, and vice versa. This is the effect that we have intentionally built.

Please note that this solution solves the problem of the fan trap, but it breaks one of the connections. For this reason, we recommend this solution only as a "plan B". The recommended solution is always to use a BI tool capable of association because it does not have any limitation.

Moving all the measures to the Bridge

There is another possible solution to the fan trap when in-memory association is not available: moving all the measures to the Bridge.

In general, the measures originally belong to multiple tables. However, during the phase of the creation of the USS, they can be all be moved to the Bridge. Each measure must be placed in the stage corresponding to the table where it originates from: the sales quantity and the sales amount will be moved to the Sales stage, while the shipment quantity and the shipment amount will be moved to the Shipments stage. By doing so, no duplicates will happen, because the number of rows of a stage is always identical to the number of rows of its originating table. The Bridge will now be the only table containing measures, as shown in Figure 11.27.

Stage	_KEY_Shipments	_KEY_Sales	_KEY_Products	Sales Quantity	Sales Amount	Shipment Quantity	Shipment Amount
Sales		1	PR01	1	100		
Sales		2	PR02	1	70		
Sales		3	PR02	2	140		
Sales		4	PR03	1	300		
Sales		5	PR01	40	4000		
Shipments	1	1	PR01			1	100
Shipments	2	2	PR02			1	70
Shipments	3	3	PR02			2	140
Shipments	4	4	PR03			1	300
Shipments	5	5	PR01			30	3,000
Shipments	6	5	PR01			10	1,000

Figure 11.27: The Bridge now incorporates all the measures coming from multiple tables

This solution works very well, and it also makes the USS compatible with a special family of BI tools: the OLAP cubes. It is quite easy to imagine an OLAP cube where the Bridge acts as "the one and only fact table", while all the other tables (including the original facts) are treated as dimensions.

This solution is also ideal for the USS implementations with Looker. When a Looker model is created with the Bridge as the first table, and all the measures are in the Bridge, then Looker will no longer need to apply the complex "fanout formula". When this technique is applied, the implementation with Looker will be much simpler.

But let's remind it once more: the ideal solution to the fan trap is always the in-memory association.

The JSON fan trap

When we create a business intelligence solution, our data source sometimes may be in JSON format. Very often, we hear developers saying that this is not a problem because "the JSON files can be flattened". But flattening JSON files, unfortunately, is very similar to denormalizing tables: sometimes it can cause problems. One of these problems is the "JSON fan trap".

We define a "JSON fan trap" as a JSON structure that contains at least one measure and one nested array. For example, see Figure 11.28.

Duration is a measure, and Genre is a nested array. At the moment when we flatten this JSON file, the duration of Film3 will appear twice because this film is both a comedy and a drama.

FilmsGenres JSON.JSON

```
1  {
2  "results": [
3      {
4          "Film": "Film1",
5          "Duration": 100,
6          "Genre": [
7              "Comedy"
8          ]
9      },
10         {
11         "Film": "Film2",
12         "Duration": 100,
13         "Genre": [
14             "Drama"
15         ]
16     },
17     {
18         "Film": "Film3",
19         "Duration": 100,
20         "Genre": [
21             "Comedy",
22             "Drama"
23         ]
24     }
25 ]
26 }
```

Figure 11.28: An example of JSON fan trap

Figure 11.29 shows how Tableau interprets the schema.

Select Schema Levels

The schema levels you select determine which dimensions and measures are available for analysis in the worksheet.

Collapse Fields

	Schema	Example Value
☑	FilmsGenres JSON.JSON	
☑	results	
	Duration	*100*
	Film	*Film1*
☑	Genre	*["Comedy", ...]*

3 schema levels selected

Cancel OK

Figure 11.29: The Tableau "Select Schema Levels" window

Tableau recognizes that "Genre" is a nested array, and it gives the end-user a choice to keep it or discard it. We decide, of course, to keep it. Figure 11.30 shows how data is loaded.

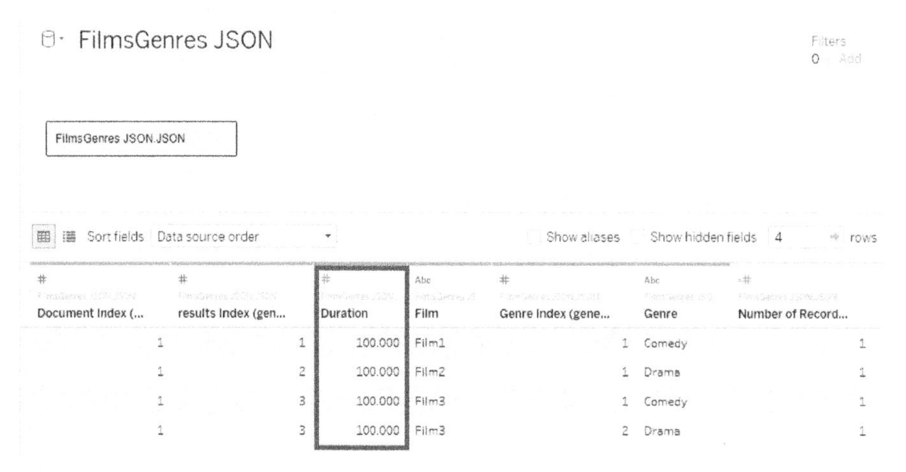

Document Index (...	results Index (gen...	Duration	Film	Genre Index (gene...	Genre	Number of Record...
1	1	100.000	Film1	1	Comedy	1
1	2	100.000	Film2	1	Drama	1
1	3	100.000	Film3	1	Comedy	1
1	3	100.000	Film3	2	Drama	1

Figure 11.30: The Tableau "Data Source" page shows the number 100 repeated four times

As you can see, the number 100 is repeated four times. This would lead us to think that Tableau will show a grand total of 400.

However, fortunately, Tableau handles this duplicate with a special automatic formula based on the LOD syntax. This formula adjusts the total, as you can see in Figure 11.31.

Despite loading the duplicated numbers, Tableau keeps account of how the structure was before being flattened. As a result, it displays a grand total of 300, which is the total that we would expect.

Things are very different when you are not using a BI tool that handles the JSON fan trap. For example, if the flattening operation is performed by a programming language and saved into a CSV file, then every BI tool (including Tableau) will show by default a grand total of 400.

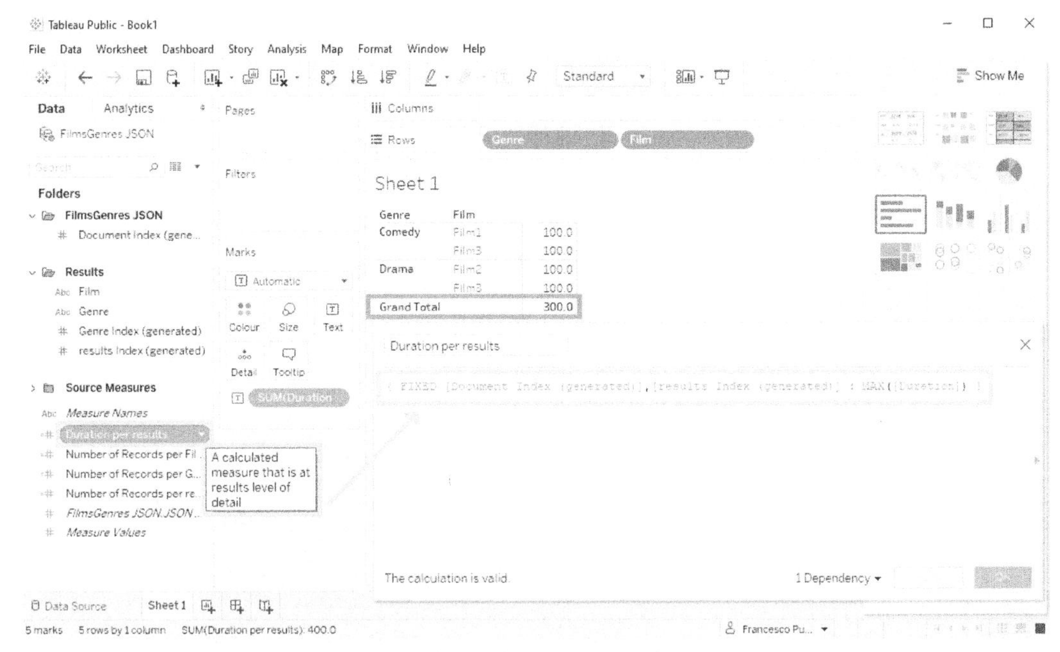

Figure 11.31: The Tableau worksheet shows the correct total

Our recommendation, in this case, is to avoid the flattening operation. Instead, each nested array needs to be converted into a separate relational table. By doing so, you will find yourself back in the classic relational scenario that is described by this book. Starting from this, by following our instructions, you will obtain the correct results.

CHAPTER 12

The Chasm Trap

In this chapter, become familiar with the Cartesian product, and then follow along with an example of a chasm trap based on LinkedIn, which illustrates that a chasm trap produces unwanted duplicates. Learn about how the chasm trap grows between linear and quadratic. Understand the method for the chasm trap row count, which helps to calculate the exact number of rows of the resulting table. See that the Bridge is based on a union, which does not create any duplicates. Finally, see an example of the JSON chasm trap and how it can be fixed.

The chasm trap, like the fan trap, is a problem that occurs in the vast majority of business intelligence projects today. The chasm trap and fan trap have one principle in common: some particular combinations of tables, when joined together, create unwanted duplications.

When you join together a combination of tables that form a chasm trap, the inevitable consequence will be an increased number of rows. This means that you will most likely experience poor performance because the data volume has become bigger than the size of the originating tables, although there isn't any increase of information. But there is also a second consequence, much more dangerous: when measures are involved, these measures will also be duplicated. Consequently, the totals will be incorrect, the same way as it happens in the fan trap. And this is something that we must avoid.

To have a full understanding of the chasm trap, we need to keep in mind the ODM convention introduced in the previous chapter, and we need to be familiar with the Cartesian product.

The Cartesian product

The Cartesian product is an operation that produces a table containing all the possible combinations of rows coming from two or more source tables. In a few rare cases, the Cartesian product can be an intentional operation that produces a sensible result. In all the other cases, it is unintentional, and it is giving an unwanted "explosion" of rows.

For an example of an intentional Cartesian product that produces a sensible result, imagine that we are running a summer event that lasts eight weeks, and we want to create a daily activity program. We can certainly list the days manually. But we can also create a Cartesian product between the Weeks table and the WeekDays table. Figure 12.1 shows the two tables.

Weeks:

Week
Week1
Week2
Week3
Week4
Week5
Week6
Week7
Week8

WeekDays:

WeekDay
Monday
Tuesday
Wednesday
Thursday
Friday
Saturday
Sunday

Figure 12.1: Weeks and WeekDays

The Weeks table has one column (Week) and eight rows, while the WeekDays table has one column (WeekDay) and seven rows.

They cannot be merged with a standard join because there is no common key. But it's possible to create a CROSS JOIN, which will produce a Cartesian product. The SQL syntax for the cross join is very simple: SELECT * FROM Weeks CROSS JOIN WeekDays

The resulting table will have 56 rows (8 x 7), partially shown in Figure 12.2.

Week	WeekDay
Week1	Monday
Week1	Tuesday
Week1	Wednesday
Week1	Thursday
Week1	Friday
Week1	Saturday
Week1	Sunday
Week2	Monday
Week2	Tuesday
Week2	Wednesday
...	...
...	...

Figure 12.2: This Cartesian product makes sense, as it creates all the combinations of Week and WeekDay

The Cartesian product has created all the 56 possible combinations between the two source tables. Each row represents one day of the event. Each combination makes sense because it represents something that exists.

In most cases, unfortunately, the Cartesian product is an unintentional operation. It produces a result that makes no sense at all. It's a mix of things that are not correlated with each other, like apples and pears.

Talking about apples and pears, let's use them as an example!

Figure 12.3 contains two tables representing the most common varieties of apples and pears. Both tables have just one column and four rows.

Apples:

Apple
Cortland
Fuji
Honey crisp
McIntosh

Pears:

Pear
Anjou
Bartlett
Comice
Forelle

Figure 12.3: Apples and Pears

We can apply the same SQL syntax as before: SELECT * FROM Apples CROSS JOIN Pears

The resulting table will have 16 rows (4 x 4), as partially shown in Figure 12.4.

Apple	Pear
Cortland	Anjou
Fuji	Anjou
Honey crisp	Anjou
McIntosh	Anjou
Cortland	Bartlett
Fuji	Bartlett
...	...
...	...

Figure 12.4: The Cartesian product creates 16 rows, but the combinations don't make any sense

This Cartesian product has created all the 16possible combinations between the two source tables. But these combinations do not represent anything that exists. Even if you want to mix apples and pears together, you should expect to see a total of 4 + 4 different varieties of fruits. Instead, the Cartesian product has created 4 x 4 combinations. These combinations do not make any sense.

If two tables have (n) and (m) rows, the Cartesian product always contains the number of rows equal to (n x m). We can say that the Cartesian product between two tables, in general, has a "quadratic growth". This is, of course, not good because it creates an explosion of redundant data. Let's see how this explosion can affect the scalability of a project of business intelligence.

Imagine that you have a start-up company. The first year your database is small, and you decide to build a BI solution that includes, by accident, a Cartesian product. Things look fine because your data initially is not too big. But then, if your data on the second year has tripled, your BI solution will be nine times bigger. If your data on the next year has become ten times bigger, your BI solution will be 100 times bigger. This is the meaning of quadratic growth. This is clearly not good, because the increase in the size of the BI solution does not reflect the increase in the actual information.

You can spend a lot of money trying to increase your hosting and computing capabilities, but this is not a good idea. The recommended action is to create a better design for your BI solution. The best is to have a BI solution with a linear growth. With a linear growth, when your data has become ten times bigger, your BI solution will also become ten times bigger and not 100.

The good news is that nobody would ever create a BI solution that has a quadratic growth: we have chosen this example just to show you the most extreme case. However, it's very common to find BI solutions that become much bigger than their original data source. A possible reason for this phenomenon is the "chasm trap".

Definition of the chasm trap

A "chasm trap" is a particular combination of tables where a table "X" gets exploded by two or more tables. See Figure 12.5. A chasm trap always has a minimum of three tables. We give the name "X" to the table "on the right", based on the ODM convention. This name helps to facilitate spoken communication. It indicates "the table that is pointed by multiple tables".

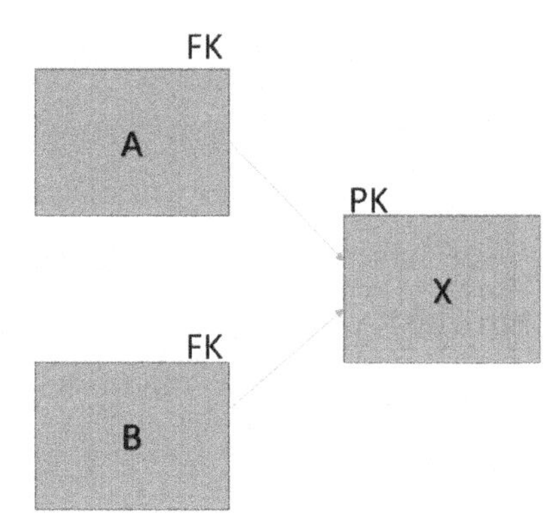

Figure 12.5: Schema of a chasm trap

Any table of a database can potentially be the table "X" of a chasm trap. Even table A (or table B) of this example can be, in turn, the table "X" of another chasm trap. This would form a chain of chasm traps or even a tree of chasm traps. This, of course, would create a much bigger explosion.

Moreover, this basic definition has only two tables, A and B, on the left of X, but in general, we can have on the left more tables A, B, C, D, E, and so on. But let's focus on the simplest configuration now: a chasm trap formed by three tables: A, B, and X. Looking at the schema, we can see that one row of X can match multiple rows of A, and simultaneously it can also match multiple rows of B. We can say that "X gets exploded by A and by B, simultaneously".

The core principle of the chasm trap is that the two explosions are "in conflict" with each other. The table "X" is not the only one that gets exploded: we can say that "A gets exploded by B, and B gets exploded by A". This conflict creates multiple combinations that are very similar to the "unintentional Cartesian product" that we have seen in the previous paragraph.

Please note that, in this definition, measures are not mentioned. A chasm trap is already a problem when measures are not involved. But of course, if measures are involved, the problem becomes exacerbated, as we will see later in this chapter.

Example based on LinkedIn

Let's understand the chasm trap through an example based on LinkedIn. This example does not contain measures. In LinkedIn, as we all know, each registered user can create a list of their skills and their spoken languages. Figure 12.6 contains the UserSkills and UserLanguages tables.

User	Skill
User1	SQL
User1	JavaScript
User1	Python
User2	SQL
User3	SQL
User3	Python
User3	PHP

User	Language
User1	English
User2	English
User2	French
User2	Spanish
User2	Chinese
User3	English
User3	German

Figure 12.6: The UserSkills and UserLanguages tables

Please spend a moment watching the two tables. User1 knows SQL, JavaScript and Python, and speaks only English. User2 knows only SQL and speaks four spoken languages. User3 has multiple skills and multiple spoken languages. As you can imagine, User3 will be the most interesting case.

Both tables, UserSkills and UserLanguages, contain a column Users that acts as a FK pointing to the PK of Users. Figure 12.7 shows this schema.

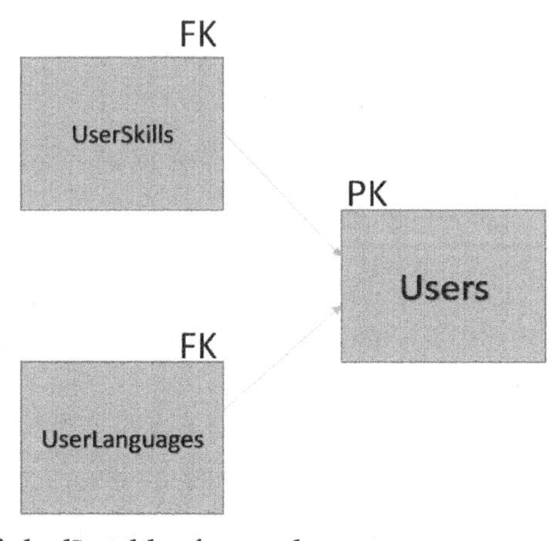

Figure 12.7: These three LinkedIn tables form a chasm trap

Please note that the correct way of modeling this problem would be with five tables: Users, Skills, Languages, UserSkills, and UserLanguages. The Users table would be as it is now. The Skills table would be a list of all the existing skills, with no repetitions, and the Languages table would be a list of all the existing spoken languages, with no repetitions. Then UserSkills would be the classic "m-m table" that contains just two FK columns, and UserLanguages likewise.

We have chosen to model this problem with just three tables for two reasons. First, Skills and Languages do not have any additional attribute—we all know what JavaScript means, as well as French, and there are no additional attributes in LinkedIn for them. Second, and more importantly, we want to highlight that three tables are sufficient to form a chasm trap.

So, let's move forward with our example based on three tables. What happens if we create a join that involves Users, UserSkills, and UserLanguages? See Figure 12.8 for the result.

User	Skill	Language
User1	SQL	English
User1	JavaScript	English
User1	Python	English
User2	SQL	English
User2	SQL	French
User2	SQL	Spanish
User2	SQL	Chinese
User3	SQL	English
User3	Python	English
User3	PHP	English
User3	SQL	German
User3	Python	German
User3	PHP	German

Figure 12.8: The join of the tables forming a chasm trap produces redundancy

This join produces redundancy, especially in the cases where a LinkedIn user has multiple skills and multiple spoken languages.

Let's look at the result with attention. Looking at User1, we can see that English got exploded by three skills. Looking at User2, we can see that SQL got exploded by four spoken languages. And looking at User3, we can see that skills and spoken languages have "exploded each other". For User3, we observe an "unintentional Cartesian product", similar to the one of apples and pears that we have seen earlier in this chapter. There are three skills combined with two spoken languages, which have produced six combinations (3 x 2 = 6). And these six combinations do not make any sense at all, like apples and pears.

Fortunately, the growth of this query is smaller than quadratic. The two source tables have seven rows each. The resulting table does not have 49 rows, but just 13. Where does this number of rows come from? Why 13?

The method for the chasm trap row count

There is a simple method that helps us predict the exact number of rows that a chasm trap will generate. We can call it the "method for the chasm trap row count".

Why do we need this? We need it because we want to know in advance whether our solution will work or not. If we produce a chasm trap without predicting how many rows it will generate, we are similar to an engineer who builds a tower without making any calculation of stability. A poor performance in a BI project is less tragic than a collapsing tower, that's clear. However, if we make this prediction in advance, and it turns out that the solution will have one trillion rows, we will probably have to stop and rethink our project differently. Calculating in advance the number of rows can save time and money.

For each ID of the table "X", we must count the number of rows of the tables A and B. Translated to our LinkedIn example, for each registered user, we must count the skills and the spoken languages, as shown in Figure 12.9.

User	CountSkills	CountLang	Multipl
User1	3	1	3
User2	1	4	4
User3	3	2	6
			13

Figure 12.9: The "method for the chasm trap row count"

After preparing the two columns (we have called them CountSkills and CountLang), we must make the multiplication, row by row. As you can see, for User3 we have 3 x 2 = 6. The total at the bottom is the number that we are looking for: in this case, the total is 13.

There is just one small additional trick. If a LinkedIn user has no skills or no spoken languages, the count will be 0. This 0 must be replaced with a 1, because a row will be generated anyhow, with a NULL value. We will see an example of this scenario in the next chapter.

The number of rows of a chasm trap depends on the data. Let's see the worst-case scenario and the best-case scenario. For a better understanding, let's make sure that table A and table B, consistent with the previous example, always have seven rows.

The worst-case scenario is when both A and B have only one row in the X table. In the case of LinkedIn, the worst-case scenario is when there is only one registered user that has seven skills and seven spoken languages, as shown in Figure 12.10.

User	CountSkills	CountLang	Multipl
User1	7	7	49
			49

Figure 12.10: Calculation of the number of rows of a chasm trap in a worst-case scenario

The result of the join will produce 49 rows. This is equivalent to a full Cartesian product, which is quadratic. This is the scenario that produces the greatest number of rows.

The best-case scenario, on the other hand, is when the rows of A and B are distributed across many IDs of X. In the case of LinkedIn, the best-case scenario is when there are seven registered users that have at most one skill and speak at most one language, as shown in Figure 12.11.

User	CountSkills	CountLang	Multipl
User1	1	1	1
User2	1	1	1
User3	1	1	1
User4	1	1	1
User5	1	1	1
User6	1	1	1
User7	1	1	1
			7

Figure 12.11: Calculation of the number of rows of a chasm trap in a best-case scenario

The result of the join will be seven rows, which is identical to the number of rows in the source tables. So, in the best-case scenario, we have a "linear growth".

We can also visualize this result of the best-case scenario, based on a random data set of seven LinkedIn users who are mono-skill and mono-language. The result of the query will have only seven rows, as shown in Figure 12.12.

User	Skill	Language
User1	SQL	English
User2	JavaScript	French
User3	Python	Spanish
User4	SQL	Chinese
User5	SQL	German
User6	SQL	English
User7	PHP	English

Figure 12.12: The best-case scenario is a small table

Of course, both cases, best and worst, are very unlikely. It is just an abstraction to find the upper and lower limit of the resulting table, depending on the values in the data source. The most likely scenario, clearly, is somewhere between these two extreme cases.

Let's now generalize and keep the simplification of the tables A and B having the same number of rows, and let's call "x" that number (the value of "x" in our LinkedIn example was 7). Let's call "y" the number of rows of the resulting query (the value of "y" in our LinkedIn example was 13, and in general, it could have been any number in the range between 7 and 49, depending on the values in the data source). We can now plot x and y and see the growth.

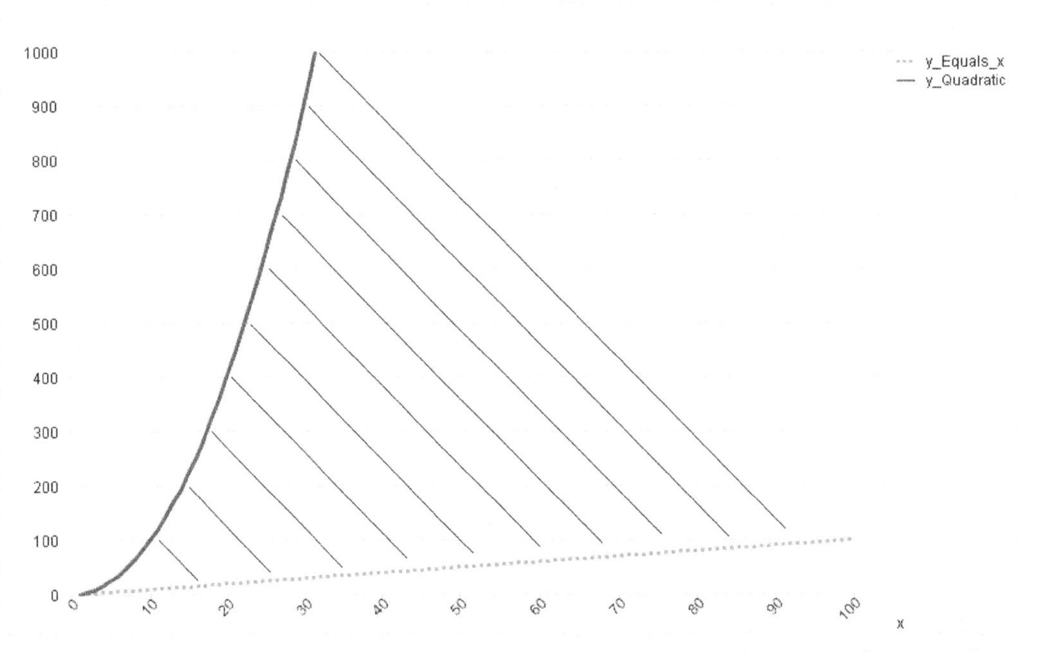

Figure 12.13: The Celtic harp. The "semi-quadratic" growth of a chasm trap is somewhere between linear and quadratic, depending on the values in the data source

The chasm trap has a number of rows between linear and quadratic. We can say, in general, that the chasm trap has a "semi-quadratic" growth. It is represented by Figure 12.13, which looks similar to a Celtic harp.

The chasm trap has a "semi-quadratic" growth.

Figure 12.13 shows the two extreme cases of linear growth vs. quadratic growth. The two axes are on a different scale, to allow for better visualization. The "semi-quadratic" growth is somewhere between these two extreme cases, depending on the values in the data source. The semi-quadratic growth is for sure better than quadratic, but it still not ideal. The ideal growth, if possible, is linear.

We will see later in this chapter that the USS approach always has a linear growth.

The chasm trap with measures

We now know that the chasm trap is when multiple one-to-many relationships create a large duplication of rows that do not add any useful information.

In the previous chapter, we introduced the fan trap, showing that a normal one-to-many relationship can explode a measure, producing incorrect totals. In this section, we will see a combination of these two problems, and we will call it the "chasm trap with measures". A "chasm trap with measures" is a chasm trap where at least one of the tables "on the left" contains a measure, as shown in Figure 12.14.

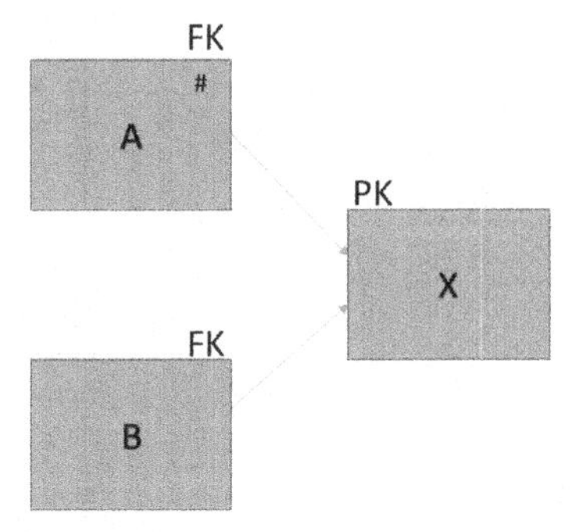

Figure 12.14: A chasm trap with measures means at least one of the tables "on the left" contains a measure

Table A now has a small symbol "#", indicating that it contains at least one measure. That measure is indeed correct within the granularity of the table A on its own. And it is also correct when A is joined with X, because X will not explode any row of A. But unfortunately, when B is added to the query, some of the rows of A will get exploded by B, and consequently, the measure will be duplicated, producing incorrect totals. Lets' take the example based on LinkedIn, and let's add to the UserSkills table a column containing the rating of the skills (from 1 to 5) that the registered users assign to themselves, as shown in Figure 12.15.

User	Skill	Rating
User1	SQL	3
User2	JavaScript	4
User2	Python	5
User2	SQL	5
User3	SQL	4
User3	Python	5
User3	PHP	5

Figure 12.15: The UserSkills table now contains a measure

Looking at this table, we can see that the rating of the SQL skill of the three LinkedIn users is 3, 5, and 4. So, if these three individuals belong to a team, the team leader can say that "the average rating of SQL within the team is 4.00". Figure 12.16 shows the results after adding table B to the query.

User	Skill	Rating	Language
User1	SQL	3 ✓	English
User1	JavaScript	4	English
User1	Python	5	English
User2	SQL	5 ✓	English
User2	SQL	5 ✗	French
User2	SQL	5 ✗	Spanish
User2	SQL	5 ✗	Chinese
User3	SQL	4 ✓	English
User3	Python	5	English
User3	PHP	5	English
User3	SQL	4 ✗	German
User3	Python	5	German
User3	PHP	5	German

Figure 12.16: The measure "Rating" gets duplicated, and therefore the average will be incorrect

Now that table B has been added, we can immediately notice the presence of duplicates. For example, for User2, we can see that the rating "5" appears four times instead of once: there are three unwanted duplicates. This happens because that LinkedIn user speaks four languages, and this creates a conflict. Likewise, for User3 we can see that the rating "4" appears twice instead of once because that LinkedIn user speaks two languages. Obviously, the spoken languages are not supposed to affect the rating of the skills! But unfortunately, they do. If we try to calculate the average knowledge of SQL within the team, the value will now be 4.429, instead of 4.00. The new measure 4.429 is incorrect, and this is due to the chasm trap.

The problem, in this case, may be solved by using a different formula, much more complex than just a simple average. But there are some drawbacks with this. First, the new formula is actually not so easy to create and to maintain. Second, when the business requirement is a bit more complex than a simple average, the complexity of the formula may become very difficult to handle.

Please note that the phenomenon of incorrect measures with chasm trap occurs quite frequently, and in most cases, nobody even realizes it. This is due to a few reasons. First of all, there is not much literature today about chasm traps with measures. Second, it's about the process of properly testing a BI solution: very often, the testing is made "by sample". In other words, the tester is verifying just some sample measures: if the tested measures are OK, then the assumption is that all the other measures are also OK. And this is clearly not a reliable testing method.

Instead of testing "by sample", the recommended approach is to draw a schema based on the Oriented Data Model convention, and detect the chasm traps. Then, if there is a query that joins the tables of a chasm trap with measures, there is a high probability that the totals will be incorrect. You can easily search and detect those cases that present a duplicate of measures. In this example, every LinkedIn user with multiple spoken languages (like User2 and User3) will inevitably have a duplicate of the measures related to the skills.

You can detect the errors in advance, even without the need of going through a traditional testing process. It is sufficient to visualize the list of users and the "CountLang" column that we have seen earlier in Figure 12.9. You need to sort by CountLang, descending. All the cases with CountLang > 1 will inevitably have a duplicated value of rating. This approach is deterministic: the probability of detecting all of the incorrect measures is 100%.

The traditional testing by sample is quite similar to looking for a needle in a haystack. If the errors are just a few, they will not be detected very easily. The USS approach, instead, introduces a "magnet" in the testing process: the magnet will attract the needle. If there is one error in a million, you will detect it instantly.

Many people say that the numbers in business intelligence are not supposed to always be perfect. This is very strange to hear. This may be true in data science, in the cases when we are trying to predict the future with the help of sophisticated mathematical algorithms. But in traditional business intelligence, we typically do something much easier: we try to "predict the past" with the help of the four arithmetic operations that we have learned at primary school. Having errors here is unacceptable! Numbers in this discipline are deterministic, not estimated! We must be able to produce numbers that are 100% accurate until the last decimal digit.

Now, imagine that this data with measures, instead of being used in a corporate report, is being used as a training set for a predictive algorithm of machine learning. It may handle the flow of water in a dam, a simulation of climate change, or even a landing on Mars. We believe that the training set that we provide to this algorithm, based on numbers that are completely deterministic, must be 100% accurate. If we use an accurate training data set, the prediction of our model is likely to improve.

To achieve a 100% accurate data set, detect and prevent the duplication of measures by following the USS approach.

How the USS solves the chasm trap

With the Unified Star Schema, the problem of the chasm trap is very easy to solve. To be more precise, the problem does not even exist.

The USS is based on the Bridge, and the Bridge is based on the union. When the end-users create a join between the Bridge and the various other tables, the result of the join is always a union of stages. It is important to understand that the union is immune to duplicates.

The union is immune to duplicates.

Tables A and B of our chasm trap will be in two separate stages, merged with a union. The values from A will be listed underneath the values from B, and there will be no duplicates, as we will see later in Figure 12.22. But before getting there, let's build the solution step by step.

First of all, we need to visualize again all the tables in our LinkedIn example. This time they have the usual additional KEY column, as recommended by the USS naming convention.

Figure 12.17 contains the UserSkills table. There is a new column called _KEY_UserSkills. The table, natively, does not have any unique identifier. So, we must add a surrogate key. The surrogate key of this example is textual, with the purpose of making this example easier to read. Also, please note that the column of the rating has been renamed to "SkillRating".

_KEY_UserSkills	User	Skill	SkillRating
US1	User1	SQL	3
US2	User1	JavaScript	4
US3	User1	Python	5
US4	User2	SQL	5
US5	User3	SQL	4
US6	User3	Python	5
US7	User3	PHP	5

Figure 12.17: The UserSkills table with an additional KEY column

Figure 12.18 contains the UserLanguages table. There is a new column called _KEY_UserLanguages. And for completeness, we have added a rating also here. The two columns of ratings have non-ambiguous and understandable names.

_KEY_UserLanguages	User	Language	LangRating
UL1	User1	English	5
UL2	User2	English	4
UL3	User2	French	3
UL4	User2	Spanish	5
UL5	User2	Chinese	2
UL6	User3	English	5
UL7	User3	German	2

Figure 12.18: The UserLanguages table with an additional KEY column and an additional measure

Figure 12.19 contains the Users table. The Users table has a unique identifier called "User". So, _KEY_Users is just a copy of that column. Please note that in the table, there is also "User4", which is missing in the other two tables.

_KEY_Users	User	User Name
User1	User1	User Name 1
User2	User2	User Name 2
User3	User3	User Name 3
User4	User4	User Name 4

Figure 12.19: The Users table

And now, it's time to visualize the Bridge, shown in Figure 12.20.

Stage	_KEY_UserSkills	_KEY_UserLanguages	_KEY_Users
UserSkills	US1	EMPTY	User1
UserSkills	US2		User1
UserSkills	US3		User1
UserSkills	US4		User2
UserSkills	US5		User3
UserSkills	US6		User3
UserSkills	US7		User3
UserLanguages	EMPTY	UL1	User1
UserLanguages		UL2	User2
UserLanguages		UL3	User2
UserLanguages		UL4	User2
UserLanguages		UL5	User2
UserLanguages		UL6	User3
UserLanguages		UL7	User3
Users			User1
Users			User2
Users			User3
Users			User4

Figure 12.20: The Bridge. UserSkills and UserLanguages do not point to each other

The two blocks marked as "EMPTY" tell us that the UserSkills stage does not point to UserLanguages, and the UserLanguages stage does not point to UserSkills, exactly as we expected. However, they both point to Users.

Please note that the Users stage does not point to any other table than itself. As we have seen before, its function is to create the full outer join effect, which in this case guarantees that User4 is available in the final dashboard, no matter if there are no skills and no spoken languages associated with that user.

Figure 12.21 shows the USS data model. With no surprise, we can see that all the tables are connected through the Bridge. As we have seen before, with the USS approach, the connection between two tables is always oriented. We have also seen that the FK is always on the side of the Bridge, while the PK is always on the side of the other tables. Consequently, if we follow the ODM convention, the Bridge is always on the left, and all the other tables are always on the right.

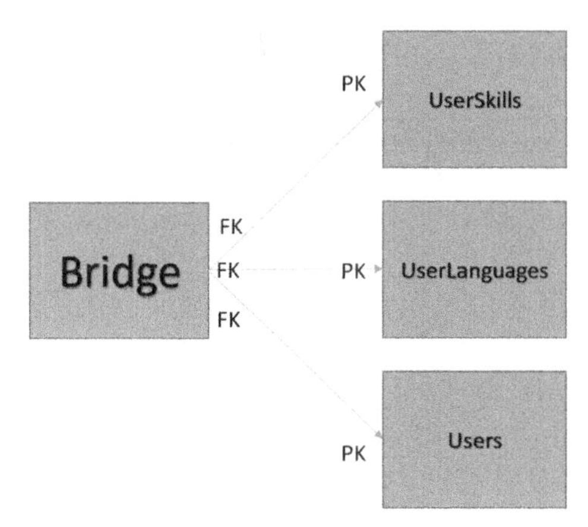

Figure 12.21: The USS solution to chasm traps

With the USS approach, the schema of the solution always looks the same: the Bridge points to all the other tables.

Figure 12.22 shows the result of the join.

Stage	_KEY_UserSkills	_KEY_UserLanguages	_KEY_Users	Skill	Skill Rating	Language	Lang Rating	User Name
UserSkills	US1		User1	SQL	3			User Name 1
UserSkills	US2		User1	JavaScript	4			User Name 1
UserSkills	US3		User1	Python	5			User Name 1
UserSkills	US4		User2	SQL	5			User Name 2
UserSkills	US5		User3	SQL	4			User Name 3
UserSkills	US6		User3	Python	5			User Name 3
UserSkills	US7		User3	PHP	5			User Name 3
UserLanguages		UL1	User1			English	5	User Name 1
UserLanguages		UL2	User2			English	4	User Name 2
UserLanguages		UL3	User2			French	3	User Name 2
UserLanguages		UL4	User2			Spanish	5	User Name 2
UserLanguages		UL5	User2			Chinese	2	User Name 2
UserLanguages		UL6	User3			English	5	User Name 3
UserLanguages		UL7	User3			German	2	User Name 3
Users			User1					User Name 1
Users			User2					User Name 2
Users			User3					User Name 3
Users			User4					User Name 4

No Duplicates!

Figure 12.22: The result of the join with the USS approach. No more duplicates of measures!

As you can see in the figure, the columns "Skill Rating" and "Lang Rating" do not interfere with each other anymore. When the end-user in a BI tool will drag and drop these columns, there will be no risk of creating any duplicates, and the totals of the measures will always be correct.

Implementation with Tableau

Let's make a practical implementation with Tableau. We will initially load the tables in their original format, following the traditional approach, and then we will load the tables based on the USS approach. As a reminder, Figure 12.23 shows the three tables in their original format.

User	User Name
User1	User Name 1
User2	User Name 2
User3	User Name 3
User4	User Name 4

User	Skill	SkillRating
User1	SQL	3
User1	JavaScript	4
User1	Python	5
User2	SQL	5
User3	SQL	4
User3	Python	5
User3	PHP	5

User	Language	LangRating
User1	English	5
User2	English	4
User2	French	3
User2	Spanish	5
User2	Chinese	2
User3	English	5
User3	German	2

Figure 12.23: The three tables in their original format

You can see that the SQL skill is rated 3, 4, and 5. Consequently, the correct average for the SQL skill is 4.00. This is the total that we will expect to see in Tableau. Figure 12.24 shows the resulting report in Tableau, based on the classic approach.

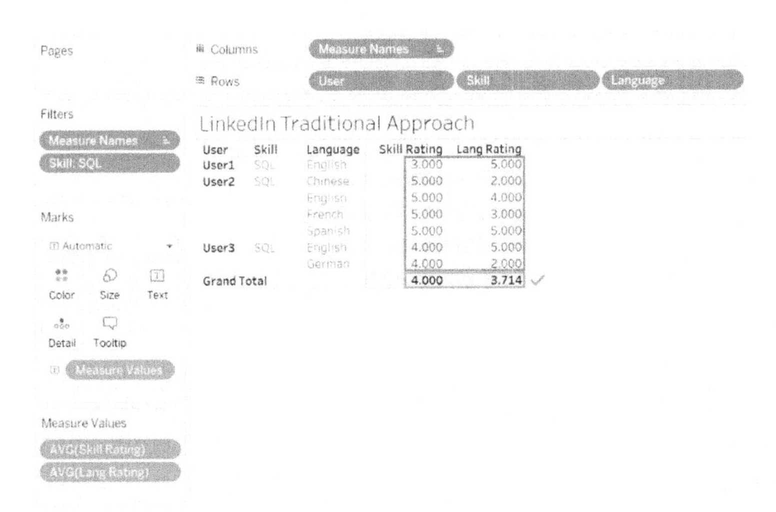

Figure 12.24: The result based on the traditional approach is correct, but it looks a bit incoherent

We have added a filter on the SQL skill. Tableau displays a total average of 4.00 for SQL, which is correct, despite the duplicates. This is possible because Tableau is capable of in-memory association. Other BI tools that don't have this capability would show a total average of 4.429, because this is the actual average of the numbers that you see in the figure, which are 3, 5, 5, 5, 5, 4, and 4.

Tableau is able to display the correct total, so it seems that there is no problem here. But in reality, there is still a problem: the visualization looks a bit incoherent.

If we remove the filter, it will be even harder to realize that the total average is incoherent with the displayed numbers, as shown in Figure 12.25.

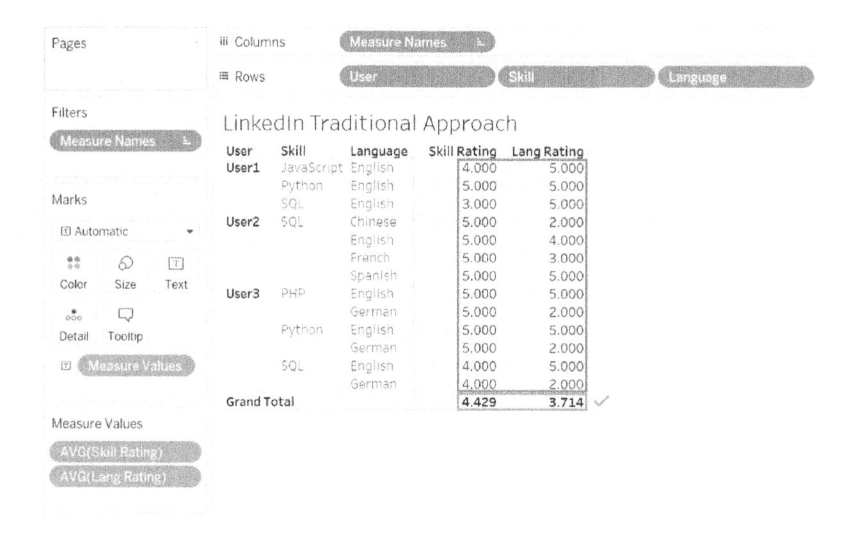

User	Skill	Language	Skill Rating	Lang Rating
User1	JavaScript	English	4.000	5.000
	Python	English	5.000	5.000
	SQL	English	3.000	5.000
User2	SQL	Chinese	5.000	2.000
		English	5.000	4.000
		French	5.000	3.000
		Spanish	5.000	5.000
User3	PHP	English	5.000	5.000
		German	5.000	2.000
	Python	English	5.000	5.000
		German	5.000	2.000
	SQL	English	4.000	5.000
		German	4.000	2.000
Grand Total			4.429	3.714

Figure 12.25: With a larger data set, not many people will realize that the totals are not coherent with the displayed numbers

What is the point of displaying duplicates if we actually have to disregard them? It would be much better to avoid the creation of these duplicates in the first place! This is where the Unified Star Schema makes a difference.

Figure 12.26 shows the data model in Tableau based on the USS approach.

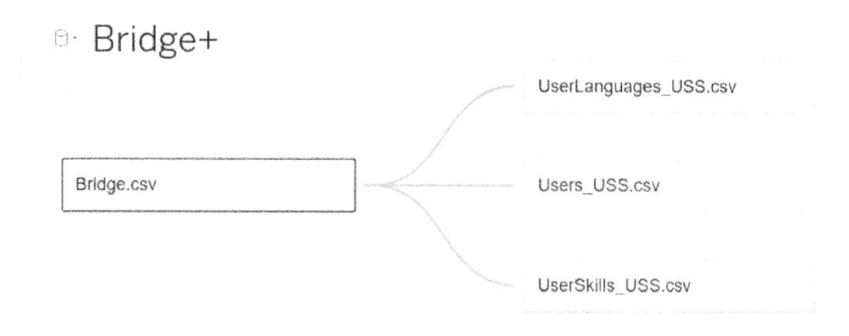

Figure 12.26: The data model of LinkedIn implemented in Tableau, based on the USS approach

The solution based on the USS approach always looks the same.

Thanks to the Unified Star Schema, we have now eliminated the duplicates. Figure 12.27 shows the same totals as before, but this time it's easy to verify that they are coherent with the displayed numbers.

LinkedIn USS Approach

Stage	User	Skill	Language	Skill Rating	Lang Rating
UserLanguages	User1	Null	English		5.000
	User2	Null	Chinese		2.000
			English		4.000
			French		3.000
			Spanish		5.000
	User3	Null	English		5.000
			German		2.000
UserSkills	User1	JavaScript	Null	4.000	
		Python	Null	5.000	
		SQL	Null	3.000	
	User2	SQL	Null	5.000	
	User3	PHP	Null	5.000	
		Python	Null	5.000	
		SQL	Null	4.000	
Grand Total				4.429	3.714

Figure 12.27: With the USS approach, the totals are coherent with the displayed numbers

It is easy to verify, with a pocket calculator, that the displayed numbers are coherent: 31/7=4.429 and 26/7=3.714. This was not the case before.

The Unified Star Schema creates no duplicates because it is based on the union, and the union is immune to duplicates. The resulting report looks fully coherent.

Chasm Trap with multiple tables

Until now, we have seen the chasm trap with just two tables on the left: A and B. To have a full understanding of the chasm trap and its growth, let's have a brief look at the case of three tables A, B, and C, shown in Figure 12.28.

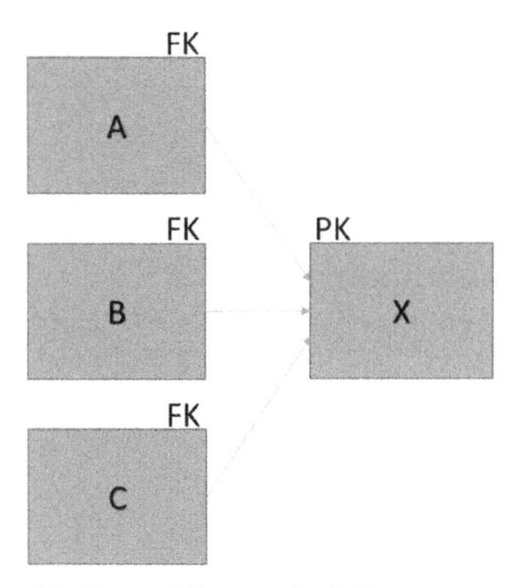

Figure 12.28: The chasm trap with three tables on the left

If the three tables (A, B, C) have (m, n, o) rows respectively, a Cartesian product will have (m x n x o) rows.

In the LinkedIn example, if we add a new table "UserProjects" that has seven rows, then the resulting worst case, equivalent to a Cartesian product, will have (7 x 7 x 7) = 343 rows. In other words, the worst-case with a chasm trap with (A, B, C) has a cubic growth. The best case is still linear.

If we look at the USS approach, instead, the growth is always linear. There is no best or worst case. If the three tables (A, B, C) have (m, n, o) rows, the Bridge will have (m + n + o) rows. The size of the Bridge has an order of magnitude proportional to the sum of the rows of the tables, and not to the multiplication.

In the LinkedIn example, the Bridge will have (7 + 7 + 7) = 21 rows. 21 rows are better than 343 rows, especially considering that they contain the same information.

The USS approach always has a linear growth.

Let's keep the simplification of A and B and C having the same number of rows, and call that number "x", as we have done before. Let's call "y" the number of rows of the resulting join. The chasm trap with (A, B, C) has a number of rows between linear and cubic. The USS approach, instead, always has a linear growth. In the case of three tables, the resulting query has a number of rows equal to (x + x + x) = 3x rows. Figure 12.29 contains this plot.

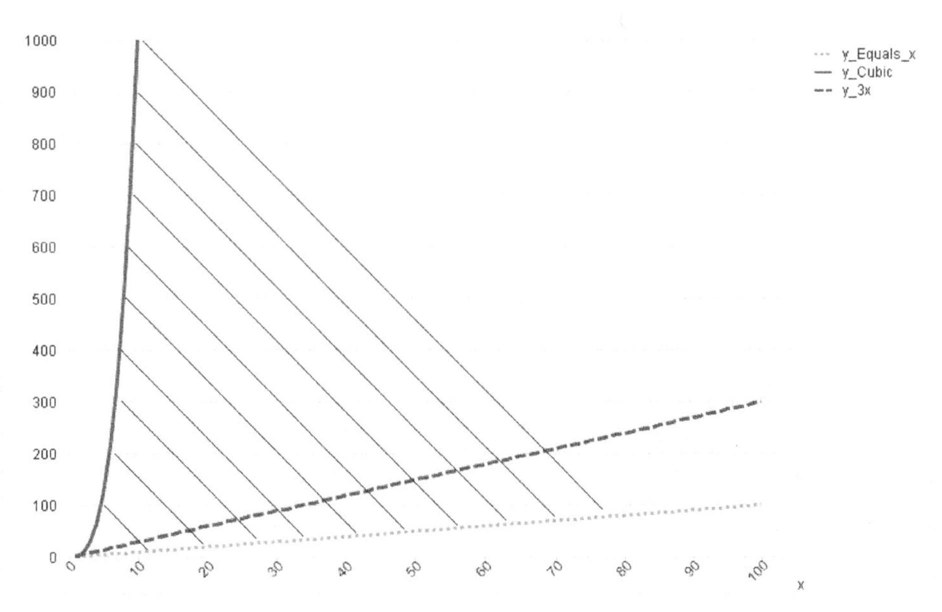

Figure 12.29: The "Celtic harp" in the cubic case, which shows that the USS approach always has a linear growth

The figure compares the growth of a standard join of a chasm trap with the growth of the USS approach. In this case, the tables "on the left" are three (A, B, and C). The traditional approach will fall somewhere into the zone between the two extreme lines (linear and cubic), while the USS approach always has a linear growth equal to 3x.

If we have ten tables "on the left" (A, B, C, D, E, F, G, H, I, and J), then the chasm trap will have a growth up to X^10, while the USS approach will have a linear growth equal to 10x.

When the size of the data source scales, the USS approach is the best solution because its growth is always linear.

The JSON chasm trap

When we create a business intelligence solution, our data source sometimes may be in JSON format. As we have seen in the previous chapter, very often we hear developers saying that this is not a problem because "the JSON files can be flattened". But flattening JSON files, unfortunately, is very similar to denormalizing tables: sometimes it can cause problems. One of these problems is the "JSON chasm trap".

We define the "JSON chasm trap" as a JSON structure that contains at least two nested arrays. If the arrays contain measures, the problem becomes exacerbated.

The JSON file in Figure 12.30 contains a list of LinkedIn users. For each user, there are two nested arrays: Skills and Languages. Both arrays contain the rating, which is a measure. At the moment when we flatten this JSON file, the two arrays will explode each other, exactly as a relational chasm trap does. Languages will explode Skills, and Skills will explode languages.

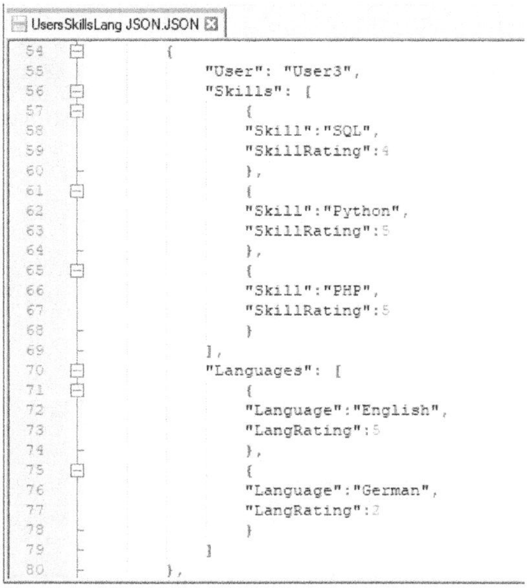

UsersSkillsLang JSON.JSON

```
{
    "User": "User3",
    "Skills": [
        {
        "Skill":"SQL",
        "SkillRating":4
        },
        {
        "Skill":"Python",
        "SkillRating":5
        },
        {
        "Skill":"PHP",
        "SkillRating":5
        }
    ],
    "Languages": [
        {
        "Language":"English",
        "LangRating":5
        },
        {
        "Language":"German",
        "LangRating":2
        }
    ]
},
```

Figure 12.30: An example of JSON chasm trap with measures

Figure 12.31 shows how Tableau interprets the schema.

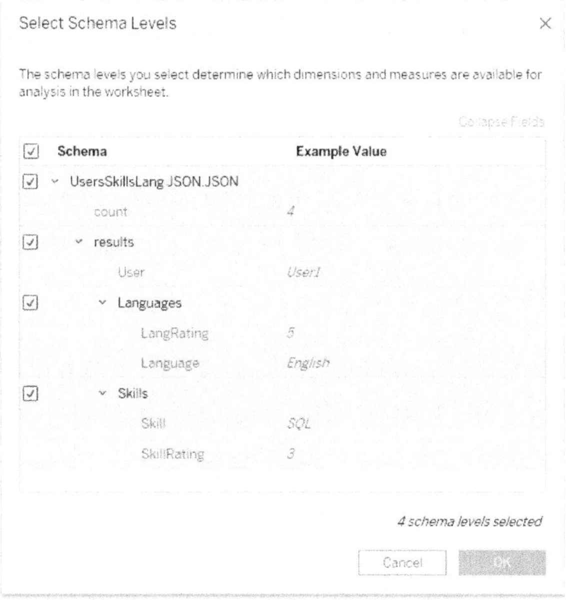

Select Schema Levels

The schema levels you select determine which dimensions and measures are available for analysis in the worksheet.

Collapse Fields

Schema	Example Value
UsersSkillsLang JSON.JSON	
count	4
results	
User	User1
Languages	
LangRating	5
Language	English
Skills	
Skill	SQL
SkillRating	3

4 schema levels selected

Cancel OK

Figure 12.31: The Tableau "Select Schema Levels" window

Tableau recognizes that "Languages" and "Skills" are nested arrays, and it gives the end-user the choice to keep them or discard them. We decide, of course, to keep them both. Figure 12.32 shows how this data is loaded.

UsersSkillsLang JSON

Filters 0 | Add

UsersSkillsLang JSON.JSON

Sort fields Data source order   Show aliases   Show hidden fields 14 rows

Doc...	Count	res...	Lan...	Lang Rating	Language	Skil...	Skill	Skill Rating	User	Nu...
1	4.00000	1	1	5.00000	English	1	SQL	3.00000	User1	1
1	4.00000	1	1	5.00000	English	2	JavaScript	4.00000	User1	1
1	4.00000	1	1	5.00000	English	3	Python	5.00000	User1	1
1	4.00000	2	1	4.00000	English	1	SQL	5.00000	User2	1
1	4.00000	2	2	3.00000	French	1	SQL	5.00000	User2	1
1	4.00000	2	3	5.00000	Spanish	1	SQL	5.00000	User2	1
1	4.00000	2	4	2.00000	Chinese	1	SQL	5.00000	User2	1
1	4.00000	3	1	5.00000	English	1	SQL	4.00000	User3	1

Figure 12.32: The Tableau "Data Source" page shows the ratings duplicated

In the first rectangle, you can see that the spoken language of User1, English, gets exploded by the three skills. In the second rectangle, you can see that the skill of User2, SQL, gets exploded by the four spoken languages. In both cases, the ratings are duplicated. This would lead us to think that Tableau will show an incorrect average.

However, fortunately, Tableau handles these duplicates with a special automatic formula based on the LOD syntax. This formula adjusts the totals, as you can see in Figure 12.33.

Despite loading the duplicated numbers, Tableau keeps account of how the structure was before being flattened. As a result, it displays a total average of 4.429 and 3.714, which are the correct totals.

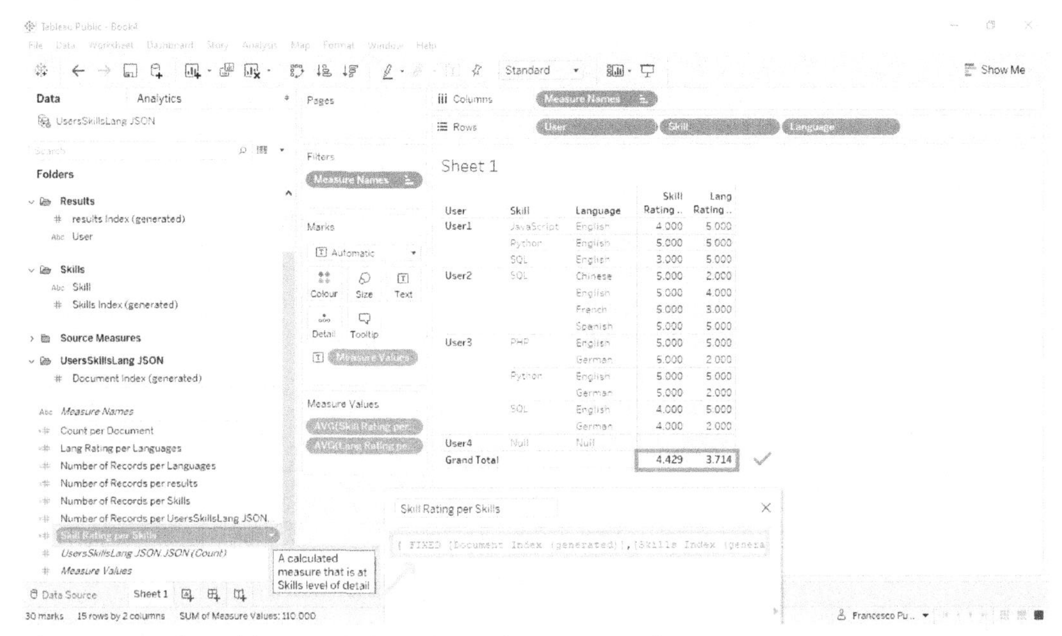

Figure 12.33: The Tableau worksheet shows the correct total

Things are very different when you are not using a BI tool that handles the JSON fan trap. For example, if the flattening operation is performed by a programming language and saved into a CSV file, then every BI tool (including Tableau) will show by default a total average of 4.615 and 3.846, which are the incorrect totals that are calculated in the presence of duplicates. You can obtain these numbers by typing into your calculator the values that you see in the figure and dividing by 13.

Our recommendation, in this case, is to avoid the flattening operation. Instead, each nested array needs to be converted into a separate relational table. By doing so, you will find yourself back in the classic relational scenario that is described by this book. Starting from this, by following our instructions, you will obtain the correct results.

CHAPTER 13

Multi-Fact Queries

In this chapter, distinguish between multiple facts "with direct connection" versus multiple facts "with no direct connection". See that a many-to-many relationship corresponds to a dangerous chasm trap with measures. Learn that although the best operation with a many-to-many relationship is the union, the union is difficult to create and can be confusing. Explore how BI tools are capable of building aggregated virtual rows, and how the USS approach is based on the Bridge, which naturally embeds the union. Follow along with an implementation in Spotfire to see how easy the end-users can build a valuable dashboard.

Traditional dimensional modeling puts the fact table at the center of a star/snowflake schema, and the dimensions all around. But what happens if we want to create a query that involves two or more fact tables at the same time?

First thing first: what is a fact table? According to the traditional definition, a fact table is a table where each row represents an event associated with a process, and it usually contains the numerical measurement associated with that event. A fact table tells us a story that puts together multiple business entities: it may tell us that a client bought a product on a certain date, or that a shipment of an order was fulfilled on a certain date, or that a warehouse at some point in time had a certain stock of products, and so on.

Recall that the USS approach does not classify the tables as facts or dimensions because we consider it to be a limitation. Also, sometimes we find a table that does not fit within the definition of a fact or dimension. With the USS approach, tables are just tables. The only relevant thing is whether or not a table contains measures, and this can occur to any table.

Fact tables may also reference other fact tables. We have seen it before, and in this chapter, we will go deeper into this topic.

Computing together multiple fact tables is usually not a problem for a developer who knows SQL. But this is a problem for end-users with no data expertise because multi-fact queries are often not available in the standard package of reports or in the self-service BI capabilities that are available to them. Or, when they are, they typically offer just aggregated measures, with no option of drilling down into the detail. In today's scenario of business intelligence, there is too much dependency on developers, and this is a problem that needs to be solved.

This chapter integrates that part of the theory that traditional dimensional modeling has left to the "creativity of the developer". We want to present a solution to multi-fact queries that is "fully integrated", with a "capability of drill down", and available as "self-service BI" for the users with no data expertise.

Let's explain a bit better what we mean by these three expressions:

- By "**fully integrated**", we mean that the end-users have one single integrated access point to the information. Any filter that the end-users will select, on any report, will propagate across all the other reports.

- By "**capability of drill down**", we mean that the information may appear initially aggregated, but then the end-users will have the possibility to drill into every single detail of information without being data experts.

- By "**self-service BI**", we mean a BI solution where a new question can be answered without the need of a developer. The infrastructure has been prepared in advance, and the end-users can perform their analysis by simply interacting with an intuitive graphical interface.

Multi-fact queries with direct connection (one-to-many)

In past chapters, we have seen the example based on Sales and Shipments shown in Figure 13.1.

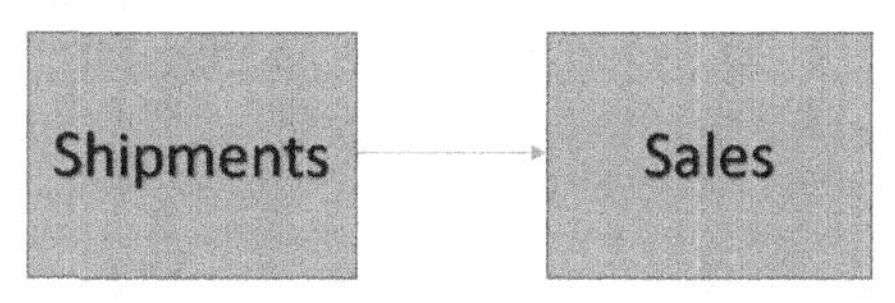

Figure 13.1: Sales and Shipments are an example of two fact tables with a direct connection (one-to-many)

In this example, the two fact tables are directly connected: Shipments contains the column SalesID: a FK that points to the PK of Sales. This is an example of a one-to-many relationship between fact tables.

Sales and Shipments are both good examples of transactional fact tables: each row represents a single event associated with a process, and it contains the numerical measurement associated with that event. They both capture the many-to-many relationship across dimensions such as Products, Clients, and Calendar. The dimensions are conformed. Or, to say it in a different way, the fact tables reference the dimensions using the same level of granularity.

This is the ideal scenario for traditional dimensional modeling. It is quite easy to create two separate star schemas and two separate queries that use the same dimensions. However, is it possible to create a query that involves Sales and Shipments together, as well as all of their related attributes, and provide full detail for drill down? Also, is this an easy query that any end-user could create? With the traditional approach, the answer is no.

With the USS approach, this problem was solved, as we have seen in chapter 11.

Figure 13.2 shows the Unified Star Schema containing two fact tables. This time we added Clients, Products, and Calendar because we want to show a more complete example of the Unified Star Schema.

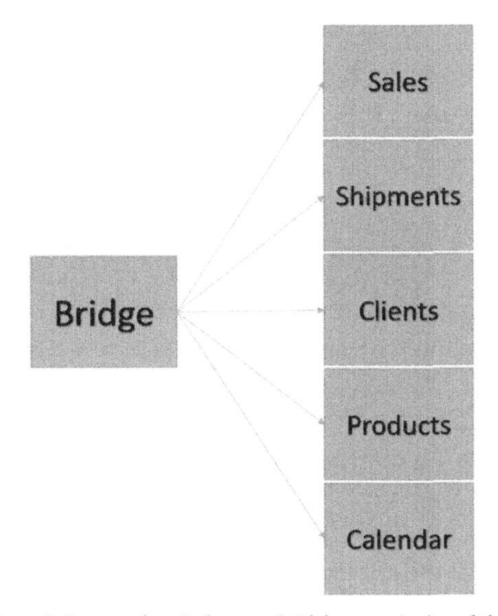

Figure 13.2: The Unified Star Schema for Sales and Shipments (multi-fact one-to-many)

Note that the Bridge always has the FKs pointing to the PKs of the other tables, no matter if they are facts, dimensions, or anything else. For this reason, if we apply the ODM convention, the Unified Star Schema is always represented with the Bridge on the left and all the other tables on the right.

The USS approach has solved the case of two fact tables that have a direct connection. The next step, more generally, is the case of two fact tables that are not directly connected. This means that there isn't any key that is unique in one table and available in the other. This is the case of the many-to-many relationship, and it is the most interesting case.

Multi-fact queries with no direct connection (many-to-many)

The two tables in Figure 13.3 have no direct connection. There isn't any FK pointing to a PK. According to the ODM convention, they cannot be connected with any direct line, as we have seen in chapter 11.

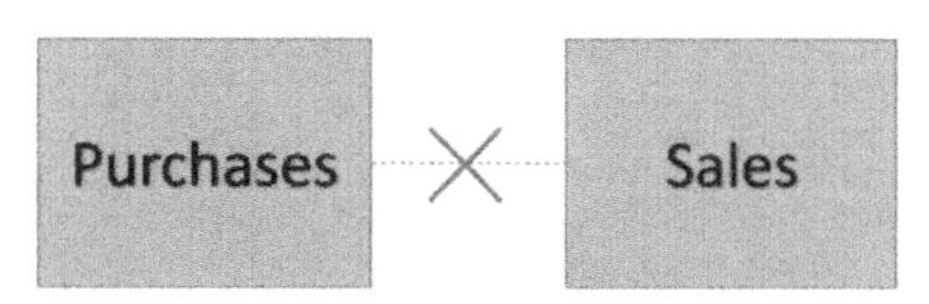

Figure 13.3: Sales and Purchases are facts with no direct connection (many-to-many)

So now you may wonder: why should we create a query involving these two tables if they are not directly connected? Are they like apples and pears? Is it a Cartesian product?

The answer is no. They are not like apples and pears, because they have something in common: the dimensions. The two tables have no direct connection, but they are indirectly connected through the common dimensions.

Example based on sales and purchases

Let's see an example. Let's imagine that our business consists of buying products from a supplier and selling them to our clients. The table "Purchases" describes the process of buying products from the supplier, and the table "Sales" describes the process of selling them to the client. So, the two tables have at least one common dimension: Products. The date is also a common dimension: we can call it "Calendar".

Now the question is, should we connect Sales and Purchases through the product? Or through the date? Or maybe through a combination of product and date? Or, rather than product and date, should we connect them through their aggregates, such as "product category" and "month"? Let's begin by connecting Sales and Purchases through Products, at the granularity of the ProductID. See Figure 13.4.

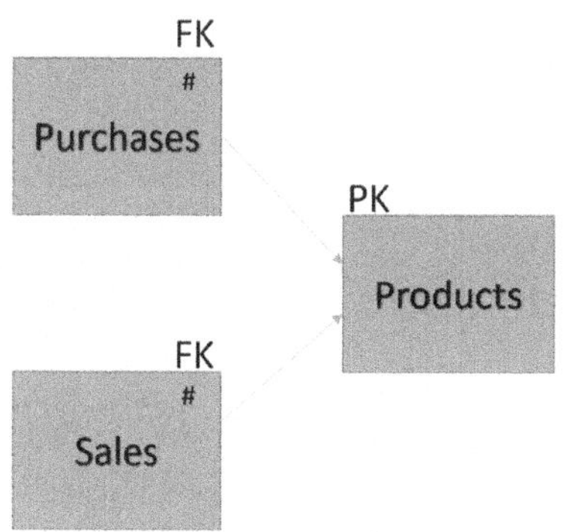

Figure 13.4: Sales and Purchases, connected through Products, form a chasm trap with measures

If we connect Sales and Purchases through Products, we notice that the three tables form a chasm trap with measures. A chasm trap, as a reminder, is a combination of tables where a table "X" gets exploded by two or more tables. The table "X" in this case is Products because it has two tables on the left. Both tables on the left, in this case, contain measures. A join on a chasm trap with measures gives incorrect totals, and it must be avoided. What if we connect Sales and Purchases through the Calendar table? See Figure 13.5.

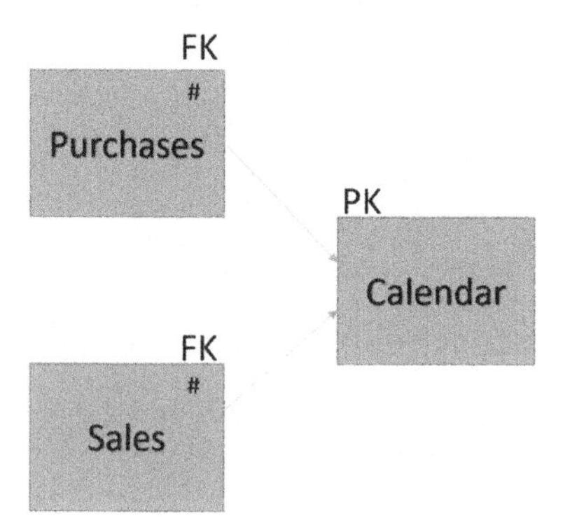

Figure 13.5: Sales and Purchases, connected through Calendar, form a chasm trap with measures

If we connect Sales and Purchases through Calendar, the three tables form again a chasm trap with measures. The table "X" this time is Calendar because it has two tables on the left. Same as above: a join of these three tables must be avoided.

And what happens if we connect Sales and Purchases directly?

Let's have a look at the two tables. Sales is the same as the previous examples, as shown in Figure 13.6.

SalesID	Date	Client	Product	Quantity	Amount
1	01-Jan	Bill	PR01	1	100
2	02-Jan	Bill	PR02	1	70
3	02-Jan	Francesco	PR02	2	140
4	03-Jan	Francesco	PR03	1	300
5	04-Jan	Francesco	PR01	40	4000

Figure 13.6: The Sales table

The last row of Sales is highlighted because it is a bigger transaction than the others.

Purchases is shown in Figure 13.7.

PurchID	Purch Date	Prod ID	Prod Name	Purch Quantity	Purch Price	Purch Amount
1	01-Dec	PR01	Hard Disk Drive	10	80	800
2	01-Dec	PR02	Keyboard	10	40	400
3	01-Dec	PR03	Tablet	10	220	2200
4	01-Dec	PR04	Laptop	10	350	3500
5	04-Jan	PR01	Hard Disk Drive	60	80	4800

Figure 13.7: The Purchases table

The highlighted row of Purchases is a refill of stock of hard disk drives. Let's imagine that in December, each product was purchased from a supplier in the quantity of ten units each. Then in January, when a client made an order of 40 units of PR01 (Hard Disk Drive), a new purchase of 60 units was immediately made.

As we can see, these two tables don't point directly to each other: they don't have each other's key. Sales does not have the purchase ID, and Purchases does not have sales ID. But they have two things in common: the product and date.

Please note that the columns may have, at times, different names in the two tables, but they represent the same thing. In this case, "Product" and "Prod ID" represent the same thing: they are the FK to Products. Likewise, "Date" and "Purch Date" are the identifier of the date when the event has happened: they are the FK to Calendar. Let's join the two tables through the product. The SQL query for this join is shown in Figure 13.8.

```
SELECT
[Sales].[SalesID],
[Sales].[Date],
[Sales].[Client],
[Sales].[Product],
[Sales].[Quantity],
[Sales].[Amount],
[Purchases].[PurchID],
[Purchases].[Purch Date],
[Purchases].[Prod ID],
[Purchases].[Prod Name],
[Purchases].[Purch Quantity],
[Purchases].[Purch Price],
[Purchases].[Purch Amount]
From [Sales]
FULL OUTER JOIN [Purchases]
ON [Sales].[Product] = [Purchases].[Prod ID]
```

Figure 13.8: An example of SQL code creating a direct join between Sales and Purchases

The result of the SQL query is shown in Figure 13.9.

SalesID	Date	Client	Product	Quantity	Amount	PurchID	Purch Date	Prod ID	Prod Name	Purch Quantity	Purch Price	Purch Amount
1	01-Jan	Bill	PRO1	1	100	1	01-Dec	PRO1	Hard Disk Drive	10	80	800
1	01-Jan	Bill	PRO1	1	100	5	04-Jan	PRO1	Hard Disk Drive	60	80	4800
2	02-Jan	Bill	PRO2	1	70	2	01-Dec	PRO2	Keyboard	10	40	400
3	02-Jan	Francesco	PRO2	2	140	2	01-Dec	PRO2	Keyboard	10	40	400
4	03-Jan	Francesco	PRO3	1	300	3	01-Dec	PRO3	Tablet	10	220	2200
5	04-Jan	Francesco	PRO1	40	4000	1	01-Dec	PRO1	Hard Disk Drive	10	80	800
5	04-Jan	Francesco	PRO1	40	4000	5	04-Jan	PRO1	Hard Disk Drive	60	80	4800
						4	01-Dec	PRO4	Laptop	10	350	3500
					8710							17700

Figure 13.9: The join of Sales and Purchases is not good because it produces duplicates of measures

The result of the query does not look good. We can see duplicates, and consequently, the totals are incorrect. In general, it is hard to imagine a use case when a many-to-many join is a sensible choice, especially when measures are involved.

Many-to-many joins rarely make sense, especially when measures are involved.

Note that this many-to-many join produces the same result as a join on a chasm trap with measures. In general, we can say that "many-to-many" and "chasm trap" are the same thing. A many-to-many relationship is equivalent to a chasm trap where the table "X" is omitted. Figure 13.10 shows that "many-to-many" and "chasm trap" are the same thing.

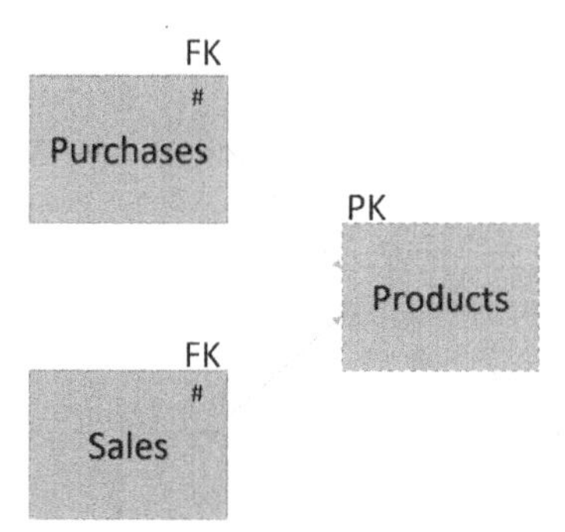

Figure 13.10: The direct join Sales-Purchases is equivalent to a chasm trap with measures, where the Products table is omitted

The direct join Sales-Purchases is equivalent to a chasm trap with measures where the Products table is omitted. Why Products? Because our SQL query creates the join based on the Product ID. If the SQL join was based on the Date, this would be equivalent to a chasm trap with measures where the omitted table "X" is the Calendar table.

A many-to-many relationship is equivalent to a chasm trap where the table "X" is omitted.

Let's focus now on the number of rows. The result of the query, as seen earlier in Figure 13.9, has eight rows. Where do these eight rows come from? Why exactly eight?

The answer can be found by applying the "method for the chasm trap row count" that we have shown in the previous chapter: we group both tables by the IDs of table "X" (in this case, the product ID), and we count the rows. If we have a 0, we must replace it with a 1. The multiplication will give us the number of rows for each product. The grand total at the bottom is the number that we are searching for.

Now we need to look at the tables, and we need to answer two questions. How many rows do we have in Sales per each Product? If you look at the Sales table, earlier in this chapter, you can see that we have (2,2,1,0) rows. This means that we have two rows with PR01, two rows with PR02, one row with PR03, and no rows with PR04. And how many rows do we have in Purchases, per each Product? We have (2,1,1,1) rows. Let's put these numbers in a spreadsheet, replace the 0 with 1, and make the multiplication. See Figure 13.11.

Product	CountSales	CountPurch	Multiplication
PR01	2	2	4
PR02	2	1	2
PR03	1	1	1
PR04	0 (->1)	1	1
			8

Figure 13.11: The method for the chasm trap row count, replacing a 0 with a 1

PR01 appears twice in both tables. So, a Cartesian product generates four rows. PR02 appears twice in Sales and only once in Purchases, so it remains two rows. PR03 appears once in both tables, so it remains one row. PR04 is the most interesting. It does not appear in Sales, but it appears in Purchases. So, it creates one row, where the Sales part remains NULL. The grand total is 8. So, the method works.

A join between two tables that are in a many-to-many relationship is, in general, a dangerous operation: it is likely to explode the rows, generate duplicates of measures, and produce incorrect totals. In most cases, it gives only problems and no added value. When the relationship between two tables is many-to-many, we recommend to never create a join.

Instead of creating a many-to-many join, it is recommended to create a union.

The union

The union puts the values of a table underneath the values of the other table, and the columns with the same business meaning need to be "piled up" in a shared column. See Figure 13.12.

Source	SalesID	Date	Client	Product	Quantity	Amount	PurchID	Prod Name	Purch Quantity	Purch Price	Purch Amount
Sales	1	01-Jan	Bill	PR01	1	100					
Sales	2	02-Jan	Bill	PR02	1	70					
Sales	3	02-Jan	Francesco	PR02	2	140					
Sales	4	03-Jan	Francesco	PR03	1	300					
Sales	5	04-Jan	Francesco	PR01	40	4000					
Purch		01-Dec		PR01			1	Hard Disk Drive	10	80	800
Purch		01-Dec		PR02			2	Keyboard	10	40	400
Purch		01-Dec		PR03			3	Tablet	10	220	2200
Purch		01-Dec		PR04			4	Laptop	10	350	3500
Purch		04-Jan		PR01			5	Hard Disk Drive	60	80	4800

Figure 13.12: Union between Sales and Purchases. The columns with the same business meaning are "piled up"

When you create a union, it is always recommended to add a column "Source", to track where each row originates from, as you can see in the figure.

In this figure, we can also see that the Date column has values coming both from Sales and from Purchases. The values are piled up into one single column because they have the same business meaning. The same occurs with the Product column.

Some developers tend to also pile up Quantity and Amount, but we recommend avoiding this. They have similar names, but they have different business meanings. When creating formulas, you may need to split them up again. It makes no sense to merge two things if later you will need to unmerge them again.

The union is always the best way to merge two fact tables that are in a many-to-many relationship. Unfortunately, however, the union is usually a bit difficult to create.

Many BI tools support the union only when the tables are identical, but they do not support it when "only some columns need to be piled up", which is our case right now. Consequently, an end-user typically cannot obtain a union like the one shown in Figure 13.12 by simply dragging and dropping columns in a BI tool.

With some other BI tools, like Spotfire, the union between "non-identical" tables is actually possible. However, this requires the end-users to make some difficult technical decisions, and this is not ideal for business users.

Even the SQL language, with the union, is a bit tedious. If we want to create a union between two tables, they must have an identical structure. The name and the position of the columns of the two tables must be perfectly matching. This constraint is forcing the SQL developers to create "empty columns" and "renamed columns". Figure 13.13 contains an example of SQL syntax for the union with empty columns and renamed columns.

As you can see in the second part of the SQL query, the developer is forced to create four empty columns named "Sales ID", "Client", "Quantity", and "Amount". These four columns need to be placed in the opportune position, matching the positions of the first half of the query. Furthermore, the column "Purch Date" must be renamed as "Date" and the column "Prod ID" must be renamed as "Product". Not only the second part must adapt to the first, but also the first needs to adapt to the second: as you can see, five empty columns have been created in the first half. If the two tables of the union do not have an identical structure, the SQL language will produce a syntax error.

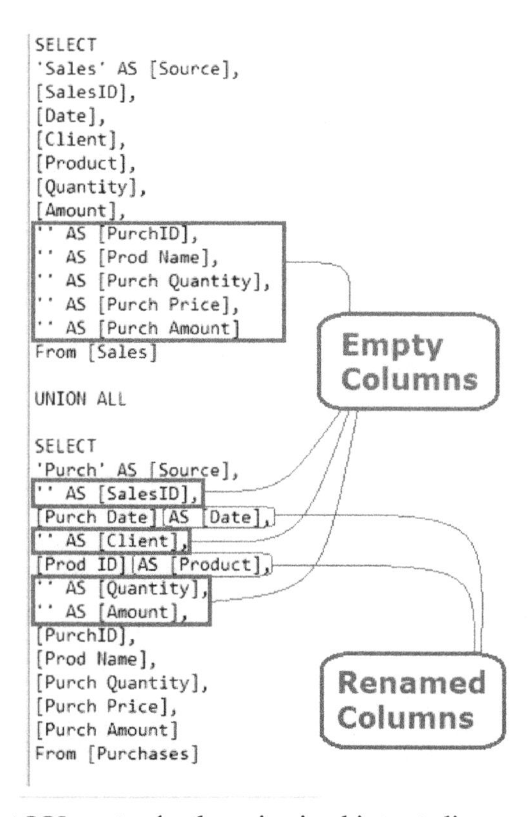

Figure 13.13: The correct SQL syntax for the union is a bit too tedious

---

The SQL syntax for the union requires a lot of attention, and the maintenance is a bit time-consuming. But this is, unfortunately, a price to pay, because the union is the only good way to merge the tables that are in a many-to-many relationship.

Please note that other programming languages have a much easier syntax to create an operation equivalent to the SQL union. In Python and in R, for example, there is no need to have an identical structure: the operation can be easily created based on the column names, regardless of the position, and the empty columns will be created automatically, with no need to mention them in the code. This is the reason why many programming languages are better than SQL in handling complex queries and data transformations. These languages are particularly recommended also for the implementation of the Unified Star Schema.

The spring effect of aggregation in BI tools

The union is just the first step. After the union, the aggregation is needed.

When creating the union between two tables with (n, m) rows, the resulting number of rows will be the sum (n + m). If there is a risk of identical rows, we recommend using the SQL command "UNION ALL", to avoid the risk of loss of data. You can think of the union of two tables as two decks of playing cards piled up, and eventually shuffled. See Figure 13.14.

Figure 13.14: The union of two tables is like two decks of playing cards piled up and eventually shuffled

When you pile up and shuffle the cards, they are "merged" but not "aggregated". Let's explain what we mean by "aggregated".

When you pile up two decks of 52 cards, you will have 104 cards. No matter how much you shuffle them, they will still be 104. Each card will be either red or blue. They are merged, but they are not aggregated. By "aggregated," we mean that two or more cards "melt together" into one single card, which has a bit of red and a bit of blue. With the cards, of course, this will not happen. But it will happen with data.

So, back to data: imagine that you have two tables, and these tables are called "RedTable" and "BlueTable". They both have 52 rows. If you create a union, the resulting table will have 104 rows. No matter if you change the order of the resulting query, the rows will still be 104. Each row will be coming either from RedTable or from BlueTable, exactly as it happens with the cards.

If we want to compute together the measures from two different tables, after the union, we need to create an aggregation. Within a BI tool, this is very easy to achieve because it is somehow "automatic". We need to display in our visualization the measures and only a subset of the attributes, such as the product category, the product supplier, the year, etc. Displaying a subset of the attributes will automatically aggregate the rows.

To better understand the automatic aggregation inside a BI tool, you can think of a metal spring like the one in Figure 13.15.

Figure 13.15: The BI tools always try to aggregate data, similarly to a spring that tries to shrink to its resting position

A metal spring always tries to shrink to its resting position. The spring can be stretched manually, but when you release it, it will shrink again.

BI tools behave in a similar way. An attribute with a fine granularity is equivalent to a strong stretch. An attribute with a less fine granularity is equivalent to a weaker stretch. When there is no attribute, there is no stretch.

Figure 13.16 shows how a BI tool (in this case, Spotfire) operates the aggregation.

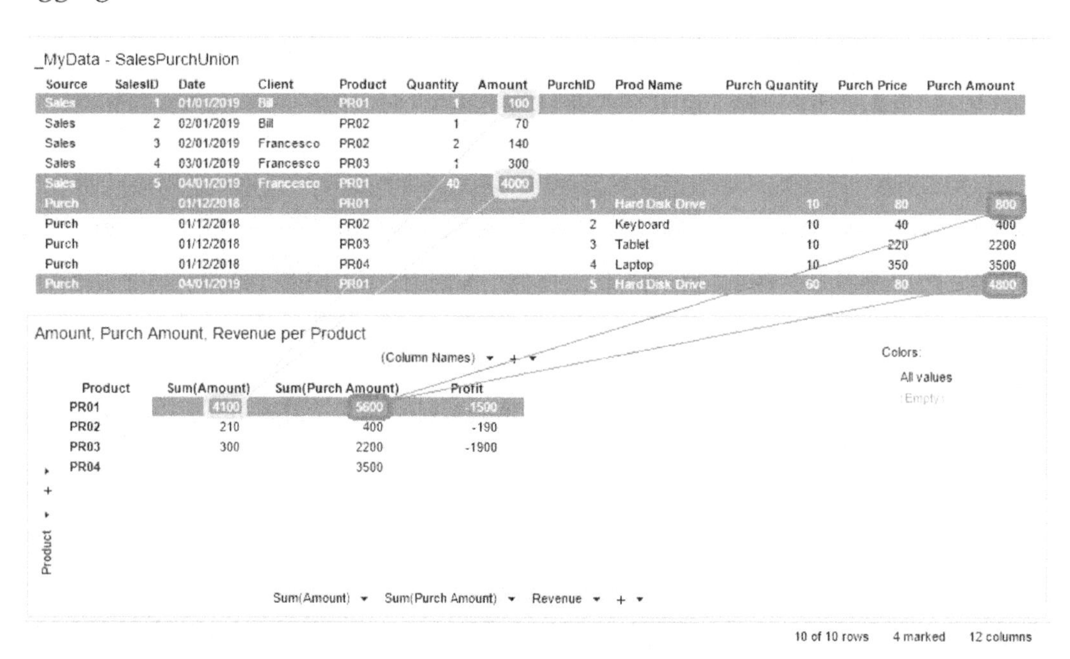

_MyData - SalesPurchUnion

Source	SalesID	Date	Client	Product	Quantity	Amount	PurchID	Prod Name	Purch Quantity	Purch Price	Purch Amount
Sales	1	01/01/2019	Bill	PR01	1	100					
Sales	2	02/01/2019	Bill	PR02	1	70					
Sales	3	02/01/2019	Francesco	PR02	2	140					
Sales	4	03/01/2019	Francesco	PR03	1	300					
Sales	5	04/01/2019	Francesco	PR01	40	4000					
Purch		01/12/2018		PR01			1	Hard Disk Drive	10	80	800
Purch		01/12/2018		PR02			2	Keyboard	10	40	400
Purch		01/12/2018		PR03			3	Tablet	10	220	2200
Purch		01/12/2018		PR04			4	Laptop	10	350	3500
Purch		04/01/2019		PR01			5	Hard Disk Drive	60	80	4800

Amount, Purch Amount, Revenue per Product

Product	Sum(Amount)	Sum(Purch Amount)	Profit
PR01	4100	5600	-1500
PR02	210	400	-190
PR03	300	2200	-1900
PR04		3500	

Figure 13.16: Every measure inside a BI tool gets automatically aggregated

The upper half of the figure contains a table of ten rows: it is the union of Sales and Purchases. This is equivalent to the two decks of cards piled up. If you look at the first column (Source), you will notice that the first five rows come from Sales, and the second five rows come from Purchases. Even if you change their order (for example, you sort by date), you will still have ten rows, and each row will come either from Sales or from Purchases. Either red or blue. By simply changing the order, you will never have the sales amount and the purchase amount on the same row. The columns SalesID and PurchID are producing the effect of a full stretch of the spring because they are at the finest possible granularity.

The lower half of the figure, instead, shows a table with only four rows: it is a different visualization, aggregated. Because the most detailed columns have been removed, the table has been automatically aggregated, like a spring that gets partially released. There is only one column now: Product. It has only four distinct values, and for this reason, the table is now aggregated into four rows. This is equivalent to a weaker stretch of the spring.

Let's focus now on "Amount" (coming from Sales) and "Purch Amount" (coming from Purchases). In the upper half of the figure, there are ten rows, and you will not find a row where they are both populated, because each row comes either from Sales or from Purchases. But if you look at the lower part of the figure, then yes, you now have rows with both measures populated.

We call "aggregated virtual rows" those rows that we see in a BI tool after the automatic aggregation. They are virtual because they do not exist in the detailed data that is loaded in memory. However, they are visible in reports and dashboards. The aggregated virtual rows are "multi-color": they have information coming from multiple tables at the same time. Now we can say that the rows are "aggregated". Now you can see, at last, the sales amount and the purchase amount on the same row. Thanks to the aggregated virtual rows, we are now able to calculate for each product the profit: the sales amount minus purchase amount.

BI tools are capable of building aggregated virtual rows, where the measures coming from multiple fact tables can be compared and computed together.

It is very important to understand the incredible flexibility of the "union combined with the aggregation".

Most developers think that they must choose how to join two fact tables based on business requirements. If they are asked to calculate the profit by product, they will create a join based on product. They cannot join at the original granularity because this would produce duplicates of measures. For this reason, they are forced to aggregate the two tables to the granularity of the product, with the obvious drawback that some detail is no longer available. Later, if they are asked to calculate the profit by month, they will have to create a new join, based on the two tables aggregated to the month granularity. Later, if they are asked to calculate the profit by product category and year, they will have to create a new join based on product category and year. Later, if they are asked to display the detail of the sales, they will have to create a new query that contains the detail of the sales.

With multi-fact data, using the traditional approach based on the join, each business requirement needs a different query.

Instead, when using the union combined with the automatic aggregation of a BI tool, everything is much easier: one single query can create all the possible combinations. When you prepare the union, you just need to "pile up" all the common business elements: only later you will decide if you want to display the measures by product, by date, by a combination of product and date, by month, and so on. Figure 13.17 shows a visualization of the profit by month.

The figure shows a visualization of the profit by month. This visualization is not coming from a new query: it is just a different aggregation of the same query as before. The "union combined with the aggregation" offers all the possible visualizations, with just one query.

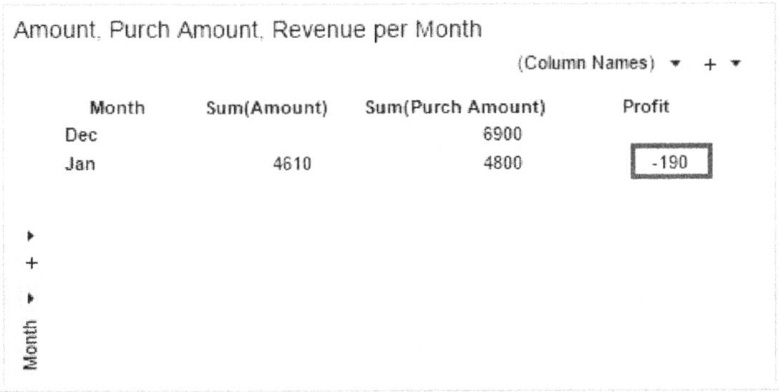

Amount, Purch Amount, Revenue per Month

(Column Names)

Month	Sum(Amount)	Sum(Purch Amount)	Profit
Dec		6900	
Jan	4610	4800	-190

Month

Figure 13.17: When using the union, the same multi-fact query can satisfy multiple business requirements

Figure 13.18 shows one more visualization: purchase amount by product and month.

Purch Amount per Product and Month

Month

Product	Dec	Jan
PR01	800.00	4800.00
PR02	400.00	
PR03	2200.00	
PR04	3500.00	

Product

Sum(Purch Amount)

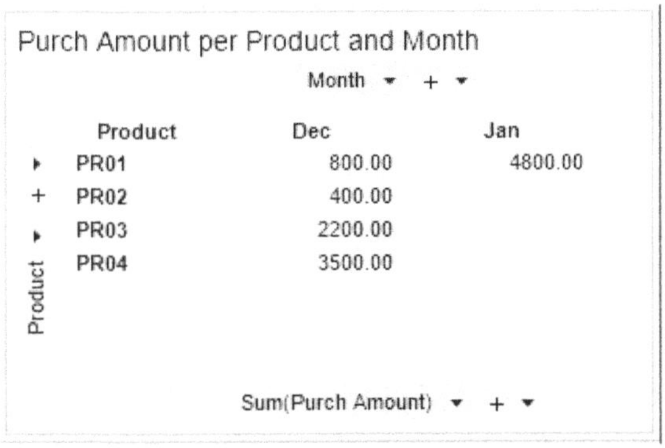

Figure 13.18: The same multi-fact query can show an aggregation of purchase amount by product and month

This flexibility is the same as what we normally experience in Excel when using the Pivot tables. But the added value here is that we are working on multiple fact tables that are in a many-to-many relationship.

The union combined with the automatic aggregation of a BI tool is a very powerful and flexible solution. The end-users will have the freedom to pivot their data in all possible ways, with no risk of duplicates, with full integration, with drill-down always available, and with a very intuitive graphical interface.

The combination of union and aggregation allows us to compare and compute together multiple fact tables. One single query can offer incredible flexibility of visualizations.

But the union, as we know, has some drawbacks. The main drawback is that it's not user-friendly to create. BI tools don't always allow to create the union of non-identical tables, and the SQL language with the union is particularly tedious. Another drawback is that the resulting table is a mix that does not represent a specific business entity: it contains columns that come from different sources. For example, in the SQL query of Figure 13.13, we have created an artificial column called "Sales ID" within the Purchases table, which obviously makes no sense and sounds very confusing.

We would like to find a better solution.

How the USS solves multi-fact queries

The Unified Star Schema is based on the union. But it is better than the union, because it is easier to use, and it does not mix the tables. The end-users will create a join. In reality, what happens behind the scene is a combination of join and union. You may wonder: how is it possible that a join produces a union? It is possible because the Bridge, by itself, is already a union. It is a union of stages.

Please note that a data expert must create the Bridge. It cannot be created by a business user. But there is good news: this effort is only needed once, at the beginning of the project. New business requirements typically do not need any amendment to the Bridge. An amendment is only needed when a data structure change occurs, or when the project is expanded to new data sources.

The schema of the USS solution looks like in Figure 13.19.

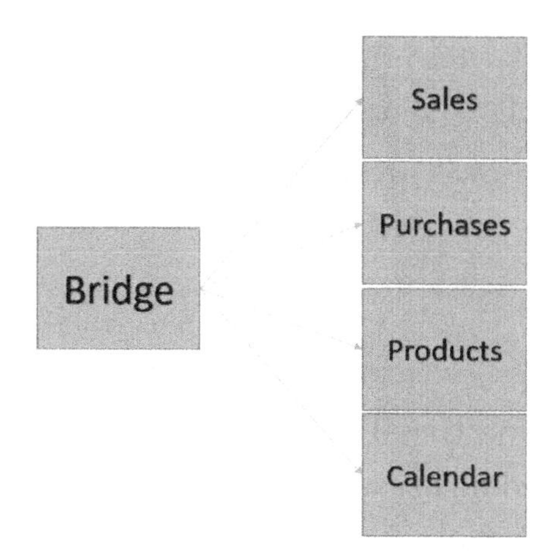

Figure 13.19: The Unified Star Schema for Sales and Purchases (multi-fact many-to-many)

Not surprisingly, the schema already looks familiar. Every USS data model will look like this!

Now let's have a look at the Bridge. Because we have four tables, we already know that the Bridge will have four stages and five columns, as shown in Figure 13.20.

Stage	_KEY_Sales	_KEY_Purchases	_KEY_Products	_KEY_Calendar
Sales	1		PR01	01-Jan
Sales	2		PR02	02-Jan
Sales	3	EMPTY	PR02	02-Jan
Sales	4		PR03	03-Jan
Sales	5		PR01	04-Jan
Purch		1	PR01	01-Dec
Purch		2	PR02	01-Dec
Purch	EMPTY	3	PR03	01-Dec
Purch		4	PR04	01-Dec
Purch		5	PR01	04-Jan
Products			PR01	
Products			PR02	
Products			PR03	
Products			PR04	
Calendar				01-Jan
Calendar				02-Jan
Calendar				03-Jan
Calendar				04-Jan
Calendar				05-Jan
Calendar				06-Jan
...	...	...	...	...

Figure 13.20: The Bridge always looks the same

The Bridge always looks the same. One stage per each table and the FKs populated when available. The two blocks marked as "EMPTY" tell us that the Sales stage does not point to Purchases, and the Purchases stage does not point to Sales, exactly as we expected. However, they both point to the common dimensions, and this is what brings value.

In the Bridge, we can also see that both Products and Calendar do not point to anything other than themselves. These stages are useful because they guarantee that every value of the dimension is visible even when no facts are associated with it. For example, on 05-Jan and 06-Jan, nothing happened: no sales and no purchases. Despite this, 05-Jan and 06-Jan will appear in the end-user reports, thanks to the Calendar stage. This is what we have called the full outer join effect.

Implementation with Tibco Spotfire

It is easy to create a dashboard using Tibco Spotfire when the data has been prepared with the USS approach. Any end-user with no data expertise can easily do it. The first step is always to load the Bridge, as shown in Figure 13.21.

After that, it is sufficient to add all the other tables that are needed. With Spotfire, this is achieved by giving the command "Insert Columns" and add all the tables one by one. We can start by loading Sales, as shown in Figure 13.22.

Worksheet:

Bridge — Refresh

☑ Ignore empty rows

Data preview:

Name	Stage	_KEY_Sales	_KEY_Purchases	_KEY_Products	_KEY_Calendar
Type	String	Integer	Integer	String	Date
Included	☑	☑	☑	☑	☑
Data row	Sales	1		PR01	01/01/2019
Data row	Sales	2		PR02	02/01/2019
Data row	Sales	3		PR02	02/01/2019
Data row	Sales	4		PR03	03/01/2019
Data row	Sales	5		PR01	04/01/2019
Data row	Purch		1	PR01	01/12/2018
Data row	Purch		2	PR02	01/12/2018
Data row	Purch		3	PR03	01/12/2018
Data row	Purch		4	PR04	01/12/2018
Data row	Purch		5	PR01	04/01/2019
Data row	Products			PR01	
Data row	Products			PR02	
Data row	Products			PR03	
Data row	Products			PR04	
Data row	Calendar				01/01/2019
Data row	Calendar				02/01/2019
Data row	Calendar				03/01/2019
Data row	Calendar				04/01/2019
Data row	Calendar				05/01/2019
Data row	Calendar				06/01/2019
Data row	...			...	

Help — OK — Cancel

Figure 13.21: In the BI tool, the first step is always to load the Bridge

Worksheet:

Sales — Refresh

☑ Ignore empty rows

Data preview:

Name	_KEY_Sales	SalesID	Date	Client	Product	Quantity	Amount
Type	Integer	Integer	Date	String	String	Integer	Integer
Included	☑	☑	☑	☑	☑	☑	☑
Data row	1	1	01/01/2019	Bill	PR01	1	100
Data row	2	2	02/01/2019	Bill	PR02	1	70
Data row	3	3	02/01/2019	Francesco	PR02	2	140
Data row	4	4	03/01/2019	Francesco	PR03	1	300
Data row	5	5	04/01/2019	Francesco	PR01	40	4000

Help — OK — Cancel

Figure 13.22: The Sales table is being imported into Spotfire

As you can see, Sales now has the additional column "_KEY_Sales", following the USS naming convention.

The Sales table is being imported into Spotfire. Thanks to the USS naming convention, Spotfire automatically recognizes how to create the join. The end-user does not need to be a data expert. The only thing to remember is to turn the default join into a "left join". The first result is immediately visible, as can be seen in Figure 13.23.

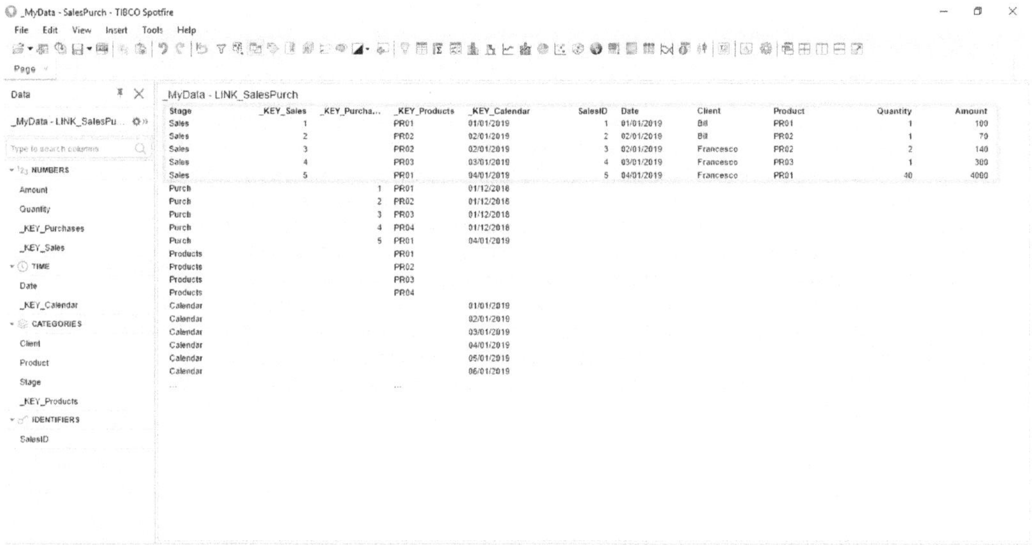
_MyData - SalesPurch - TIBCO Spotfire
File Edit View Insert Tools Help
Page
Data
_MyData - LINK_SalesPu...
Type to search columns
NUMBERS
Amount
Quantity
_KEY_Purchases
_KEY_Sales
TIME
Date
_KEY_Calendar
CATEGORIES
Client
Product
Stage
_KEY_Products
IDENTIFIERS
SalesID
_MyData - LINK_SalesPurch
Stage _KEY_Sales _KEY_Purcha... _KEY_Products _KEY_Calendar SalesID Date Client Product Quantity Amount
Sales 1 PR01 01/01/2019 1 01/01/2019 Bill PR01 1 100
Sales 2 PR02 02/01/2019 2 02/01/2019 Bill PR02 1 70
Sales 3 PR02 02/01/2019 3 02/01/2019 Francesco PR02 2 140
Sales 4 PR03 03/01/2019 4 03/01/2019 Francesco PR03 1 300
Sales 5 PR01 04/01/2019 5 04/01/2019 Francesco PR01 40 4000
Purch 1 PR01 01/12/2018
Purch 2 PR02 01/12/2018
Purch 3 PR03 01/12/2018
Purch 4 PR04 01/12/2018
Purch 5 PR01 04/01/2019
Products PR01
Products PR02
Products PR03
Products PR04
Calendar 01/01/2019
Calendar 02/01/2019
Calendar 03/01/2019
Calendar 04/01/2019
Calendar 05/01/2019
Calendar 06/01/2019
... ...

Figure 13.23: The first table (Sales) has been correctly imported

Then it is sufficient to repeat the process for each table that needs to be loaded. See Purchases in Figure 13.24. Same process: "Insert Columns", select the table, left join, and press OK. The second stage is now integrated.

When adding Products, data begins to become really interesting because Products is pointed by three stages, as you can see in Figure 13.25.

Client	Product	Quantity	Amount	PurchID	Purch Date	Prod ID	Prod Name	Purch Quantity	Purch Price	Purch Amount
Bill	PR01	1	100							
Bill	PR02	1	70							
Francesco	PR02	2	140							
Francesco	PR03	1	300							
Francesco	PR01	40	4000							
				1	01/12/2018	PR01	Hard Disk Drive	10	80	800
				2	01/12/2018	PR02	Keyboard	10	40	400
				3	01/12/2018	PR03	Tablet	10	220	2200
				4	01/12/2018	PR04	Laptop	10	350	3500
				5	04/01/2019	PR01	Hard Disk Drive	60	80	4800

Figure 13.24: The second table (Purchases) has been correctly imported

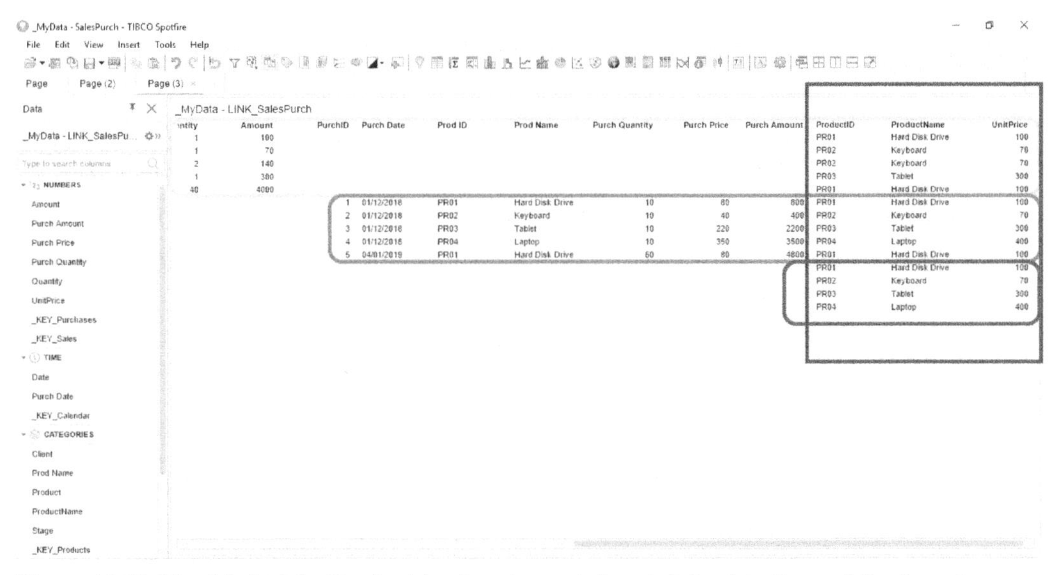

ntity	Amount	PurchID	Purch Date	Prod ID	Prod Name	Purch Quantity	Purch Price	Purch Amount	ProductID	ProductName	UnitPrice
1	100								PR01	Hard Disk Drive	100
1	70								PR02	Keyboard	70
2	140								PR02	Keyboard	70
1	300								PR03	Tablet	300
40	4000								PR01	Hard Disk Drive	100
		1	01/12/2018	PR01	Hard Disk Drive	10	80	800	PR01	Hard Disk Drive	100
		2	01/12/2018	PR02	Keyboard	10	40	400	PR02	Keyboard	70
		3	01/12/2018	PR03	Tablet	10	220	2200	PR03	Tablet	300
		4	01/12/2018	PR04	Laptop	10	350	3500	PR04	Laptop	400
		5	04/01/2019	PR01	Hard Disk Drive	60	80	4800	PR01	Hard Disk Drive	100
									PR01	Hard Disk Drive	100
									PR02	Keyboard	70
									PR03	Tablet	300
									PR04	Laptop	400

Figure 13.25: The third table (Products), when imported, gets joined to three of the four stages

The rectangle on the right, in the figure, shows that Products is populated in all the three stages. In other words, one single left join has created the union of three denormalized tables. The end-user has created a join, but the result is a combination of a join and a union.

When adding Calendar, all data is finally loaded and ready to be analyzed. The fourth table (Calendar), when imported, gets populated in all the stages except Products, as expected. See Figure 13.26.

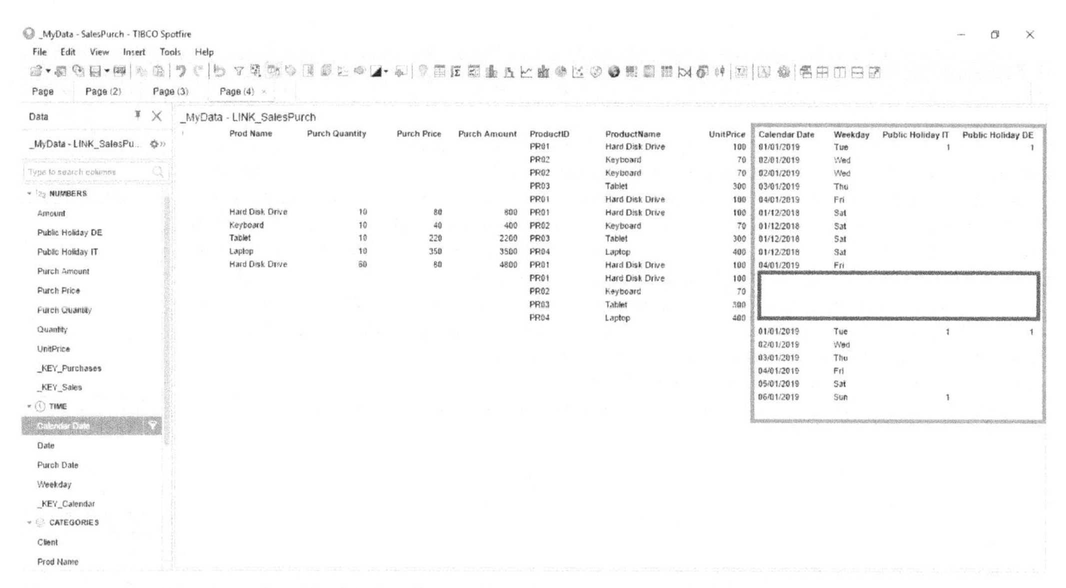

Prod Name	Purch Quantity	Purch Price	Purch Amount	ProductID	ProductName	UnitPrice	Calendar Date	Weekday	Public Holiday IT	Public Holiday DE
				PR01	Hard Disk Drive	100	01/01/2019	Tue	1	1
				PR02	Keyboard	70	02/01/2019	Wed		
				PR02	Keyboard	70	02/01/2019	Wed		
				PR03	Tablet	300	03/01/2019	Thu		
				PR01	Hard Disk Drive	100	04/01/2019	Fri		
Hard Disk Drive	10	80	800	PR01	Hard Disk Drive	100	01/12/2018	Sat		
Keyboard	10	40	400	PR02	Keyboard	70	01/12/2018	Sat		
Tablet	10	220	2200	PR03	Tablet	300	01/12/2018	Sat		
Laptop	10	350	3500	PR04	Laptop	400	01/12/2018	Sat		
Hard Disk Drive	60	80	4800	PR01	Hard Disk Drive	100	04/01/2019	Fri		
				PR01	Hard Disk Drive	100				
				PR02	Keyboard	70				
				PR03	Tablet	300				
				PR04	Laptop	400				
							01/01/2019	Tue	1	1
							02/01/2019	Wed		
							03/01/2019	Thu		
							04/01/2019	Fri		
							05/01/2019	Sat		
							06/01/2019	Sun	1	

Figure 13.26: The fourth table (Calendar), when imported, gets joined to three of the four stages

Loading these tables is extremely easy because the end-user does not need to know how to connect the tables. This exercise has already been done by the data expert who has created the Bridge. Now that all tables have been loaded, the end-user can proceed with the analysis.

Even if the data set contains multiple fact tables in a many-to-many relationship, there is no risk of duplicates or incorrect totals. The solution is fully integrated, the drill-down is available, and the self-service analysis can be performed with maximum flexibility.

This example shows that the USS approach makes self-service BI possible also in the complex scenario of multiple fact tables with no direct connection.

CHAPTER 14

Loops

In this chapter, learn more about loops and five traditional techniques to solve them. See that the USS approach is based on the Bridge, which naturally embeds the union. Consequently, the USS approach is a very good solution to the loops. Follow along with an implementation in SAP Business Objects, which will illustrate that with the USS approach, the end-users can have a real "self-service experience".

A loop is a topology of entities (A, B, C, etc.) where we have multiple possible paths to go from one entity to another. See Figure 14.1.

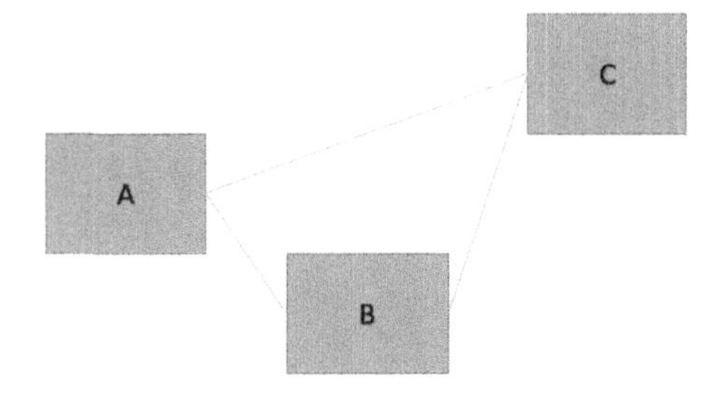

Figure 14.1: A loop

From A to B, you can go either directly or via C. This is a loop.

Loops are one of the most common challenges in data modeling. The solutions that have been proposed by various software vendors are only partially solving the problem. This chapter presents a different solution based on design, and compatible with all technologies.

Example based on CRM

A Customer Relationship Management (CRM) is a system that handles the relationships and interactions between an organization and its customers. Examples of interactions are emails, phone calls, deals, opportunities, and more.

Each interaction involves one employee of the organization and one customer. Each employee usually follows multiple customers, and each customer can be potentially followed by multiple employees. In other words, customers and employees are in a many-to-many relationship. This is how the CRM process usually works.

So, let's choose an example based on three fact tables: Emails, Phonecalls, and Deals. Each of these tables points to both Customers and Employees. So, we have three facts sharing two dimensions. See Figure 14.2.

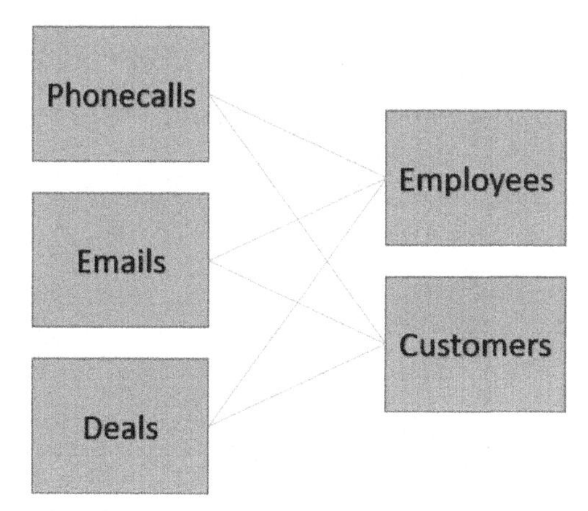

Figure 14.2: In a CRM, most tables are connected to Employees and Customers, which creates multiple loops

There are multiple loops in this model. For example, the path from Phonecalls to Employees can be either direct, or via Customers and Emails, or via Customers and Deals.

As we have seen in chapter 9, if we have five tables, we can build at most four connections. The fifth connection will inevitably create a loop. In this example, based on five tables, we have six connections: too many. Each of these six connections is a Foreign Key that contains some unique information. Disregarding this information is a loss of data, which of course, we want to avoid. So, this is a problem. How can we solve it?

Solving loops using traditional techniques

The solutions that have been proposed by the various BI vendors across the years are somehow working, but they usually create either some limitations, or a bit of confusion, or both. Solutions include:

- Solution 1: Aliases
- Solution 2: Contexts
- Solution 3: Query Plan
- Solution 4: Disregarding FKs
- Solution 5: Ad-hoc

Solution 1: Aliases

A very common solution, which can be adopted in every technology, is given by "aliases". An "alias" is a repetition of a table with a different name. In Figure 14.3, for example, Employees is replaced by three aliases: "Employees of Phonecalls", "Employees of Emails", and "Employees of Deals".

The solution with aliases removes the loops, and in many cases, it works fine. But in other cases, like this one, it creates some confusion. For example, the end-user of a dashboard will need to search for a particular employee in multiple places instead of just one. This is confusing. Not to mention the filters, which will create a conflict. A filter on one particular Employee of emails will potentially result in multiple Employees of deals. This is confusing too.

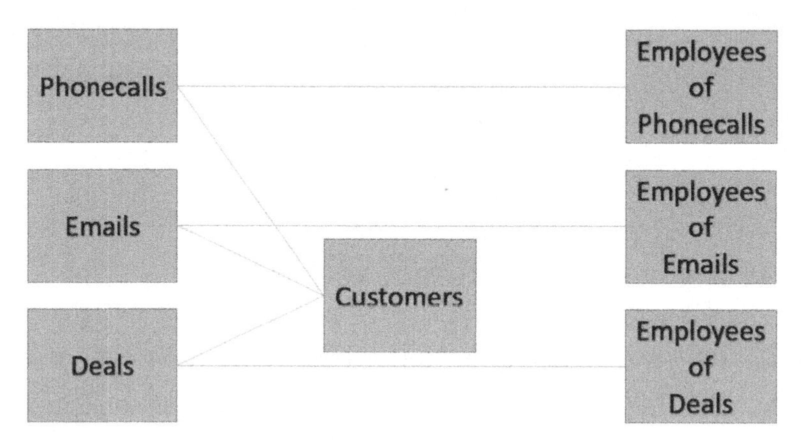

Figure 14.3: The loops, in any technology, can be solved with aliases

The solution based on aliases is easy to create, but the user experience in some cases is not very good.

Solution 2: Contexts

A brilliant solution called "contexts" was introduced a long time ago by SAP Business Objects. By applying this solution to our example, the six connections must be grouped into three contexts. As a rule of thumb, we can say that there is one context for each fact table. Thanks to this solution, invented by Business Objects, it is possible to create and maintain one single table for Employees and one single table for Customers. These tables can be utilized in multiple contexts, such as Phonecalls, Emails, or Deals. See Figure 14.4.

But there is a drawback in this solution: queries in Business Objects cannot use multiple contexts at the same time. If, for example, the end-user wants to create a query involving Phonecalls, Emails, Employees, and Customers, the tool will produce an error message of "incompatible objects" because it is using two contexts: the one of Phonecalls and the one of Emails. It is possible to change this setting, but then the problem will only be shifted. The multi-context query can be executed as a set of multiple queries that will be merged later. But in reality, they do not properly merge.

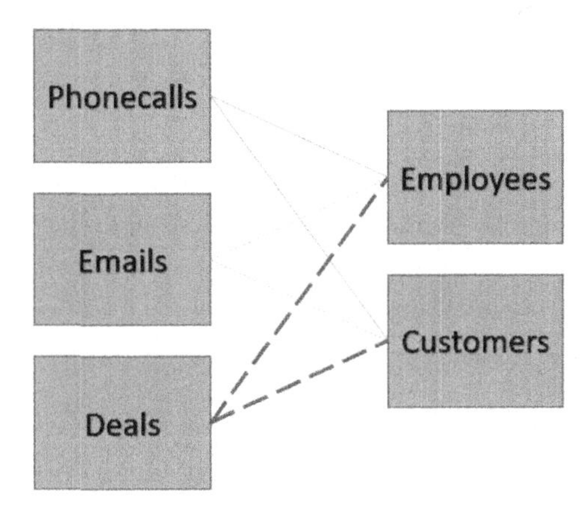

Figure 14.4: The loops in Business Objects can be solved with contexts

The solution based on contexts in some cases works well. But in some other cases, the end-users will have a hard time dealing with the issue of "incompatibility".

Solution 3: Query plan

Another solution, very much specific to the adopted technology, is the "query plan". Some BI tools, like Incorta, ingest all possible connections, regardless of whether or not they generate loops. Then some of the connections will get automatically disabled, based on the particular visualization created by the end-user.

Figure 14.5 shows an example of this solution.

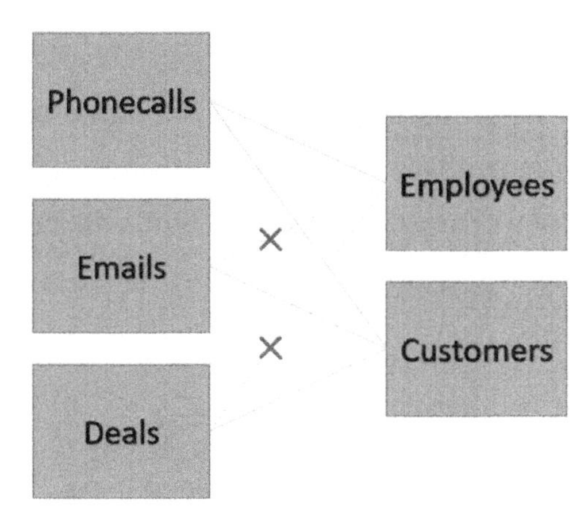

Figure 14.5: The loops, in some technologies, can be solved with the Query Plan

In the figure, you can see that the connections Emails-Employees and Deals-Employees have been automatically disabled, while Phonecalls-Employees remains active. This is probably happening because a particular visualization is focused on Phonecalls, Employees, and possibly Customers.

Figure 14.6 contains an example from Incorta based on AdventureWorks, a Microsoft demo database.

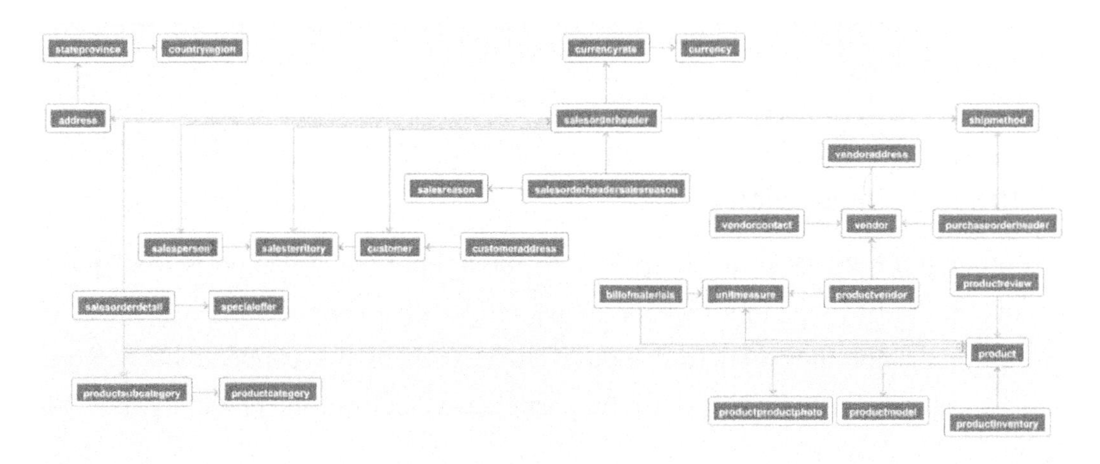

Figure 14.6: A Data Model in Incorta

This data model contains 29 tables and 32 connections. The maximum number of connections, to avoid loops, would be 28. So, the data model contains loops.

Incorta ingests all possible connections, ideally reading them from the Foreign Keys of the source system, but also allowing the operation of adding/editing them manually. Of course, too many connections would cause a loop. However, Incorta has a smart engine that decides, based on the particular visualization created by an end-user, what "subset" of the existing connections to use, and what to discard. Figure 14.7 contains an example of the Incorta "Query Plan".

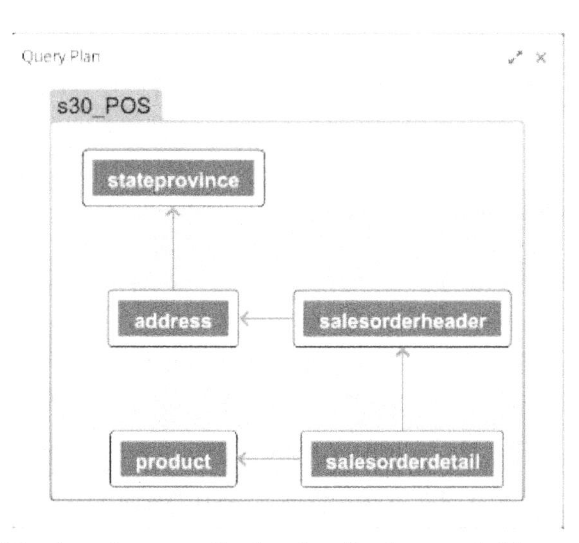

Figure 14.7: A Query Plan based on a particular visualization created by an end-user

The main data model has multiple loops, and it would be impossible to use all the tables and all the connections at the same time. However, a report from an end-user typically uses only a subset of the existing tables and connections, and this subset is likely to be free from loops. Each visualization has its own Query Plan. In this case, for example, the end-user has created a visualization that involves only five of the existing 29 tables, and only four of the 32 existing connections. These five tables and four connections do not form any loop. So, the problem is solved!

Figure 14.8 shows the 29 available tables, and it highlights the five that were used for this particular visualization.

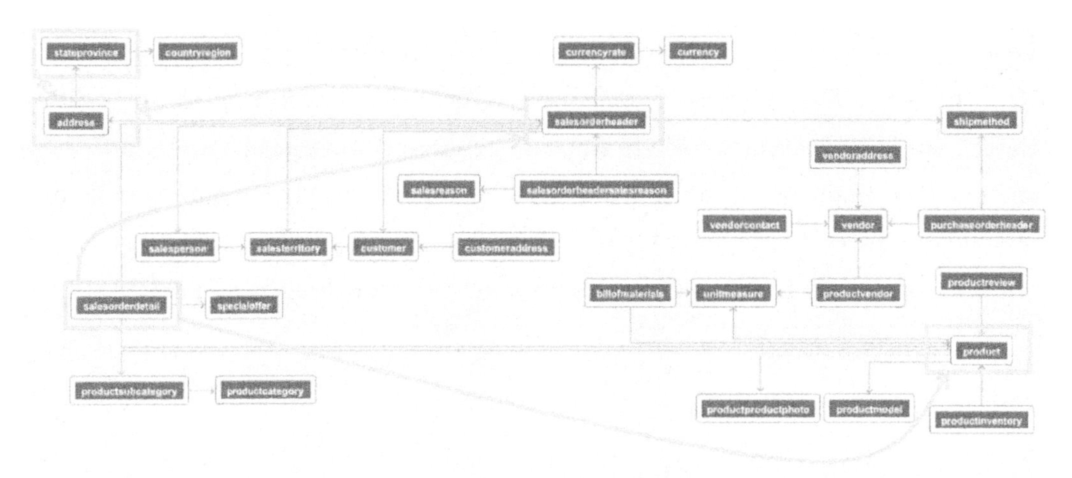

Figure 14.8: The subset chosen by the Query Plan

The solution based on the Query Plan, in this case, works well.

But one question remains: what happens if the end-user creates a particular visualization that forms a loop? Will it generate an error message of incompatibility? Will it automatically disregard some of the needed connections? And if this is the case, are the results going to be correct?

Solution 4: Disregarding FKs

A very common solution, unfortunately, is the one of disregarding some of the existing connections. It means that some of the Foreign Key columns will simply not be used. In some cases, this solution may work because Foreign Keys are sometimes redundant. In other cases, disregarding FKs is a loss of information.

Figure 14.9 shows the example of a loop that we have seen in chapter 9.

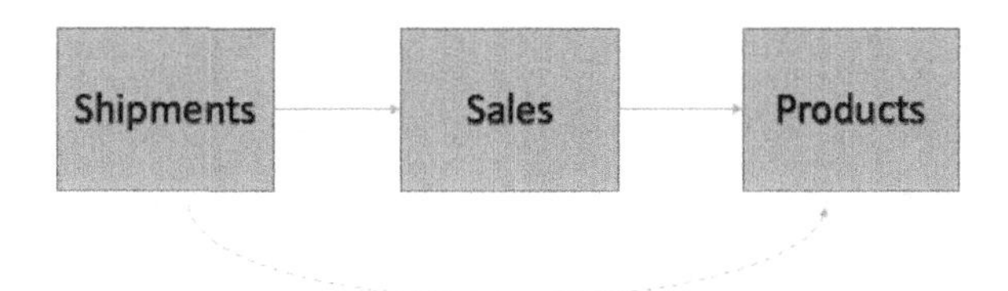

Figure 14.9: An example where disregarding FKs can actually be a good solution

Shipment points to Sales, and Sales points to Products. If also Shipments points to Products, it is reasonable to assume that the product ID in Shipments is identical to the one available in Sales. For this reason, we can say that the product ID in Shipments is "redundant", and it can be safely disregarded. We can say that "Shipments is connected to Products through Sales". The solution will work fine.

However, the solution will not work with our CRM example. Figure 14.10 shows four of our five tables.

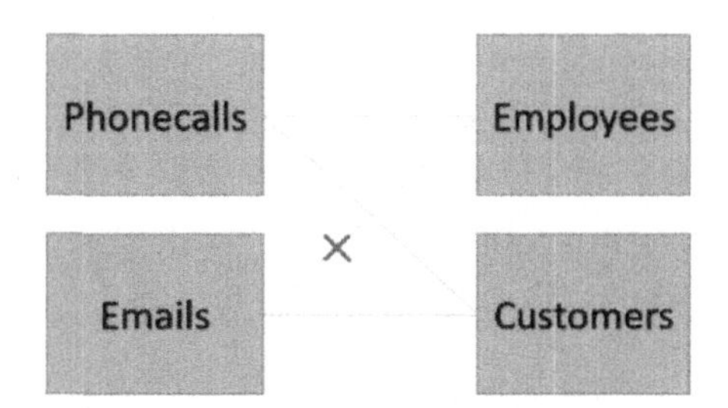

Figure 14.10: An example where disregarding FKs does not work

So, let's focus on these four tables. Each row of the Phonecalls table tells us a story: on a certain date, an employee was making a phone call to a customer. The Phonecalls table has two FKs: one points to Employees, and one points to Customers. Likewise, each row of the Emails table tells us a story: on a certain date, an employee was sending an email to a customer. The Emails table also has two FKs: one points to Employees, and one points to Customers.

Figure 14.10 shows an example of "disregarding FKs". The direct connection from Emails to Employees has been disregarded. In this case, unfortunately, the solution cannot work. Let's explain why.

The "Employee ID" column from Emails contains some information that is not available anywhere else: it tells us "who sent that email". We cannot say that "Emails is connected to Employees through Customers and Phonecalls". If we were applying this logic, we would make the assumption that a particular email to a customer was sent by the same employee who was also calling that customer. This assumption is not true. Moreover, Phonecalls is on the left of Customers: it means that a customer could have received multiple calls, potentially from multiple employees. So, this solution simply does not work.

Disregarding Foreign Keys is, in general, a synonym of "loss of data", and our recommendation is to avoid this solution.

Solution 5: Ad-hoc

The most common solution to the problem of the loops, unfortunately, is the ad-hoc. It means that, for each new business requirement, there is a developer who is writing a new query or building a new report with a BI tool. The choice of "what connections to use" in is made by the developer, case by case.

When receiving a new business requirement, the developer will probably search for a similar project that was done in the past, create a copy of that project, and adapt the copy to the new business requirement.

This is, of course, a solution that we do not recommend: each new business requirement becomes a new self-standing project which will need to be maintained. The ad-hoc approach is actually the reason why today every organization has hundreds of projects. They are all similar, but they are all slightly different, and no one in the organization really knows which one to use.

But this book is going in the opposite direction: we want to build a data structure that serves as a foundation to be used to satisfy all the possible business requirements.

Solving loops with the union

The best way to solve loops is the union.

Yes, the union is indeed the best solution to several problems!

We have three fact tables: Emails, Phonecalls, and Deals. If they are merged together with the union, then the schema becomes very simple, and it has no loops. See Figure 14.11.

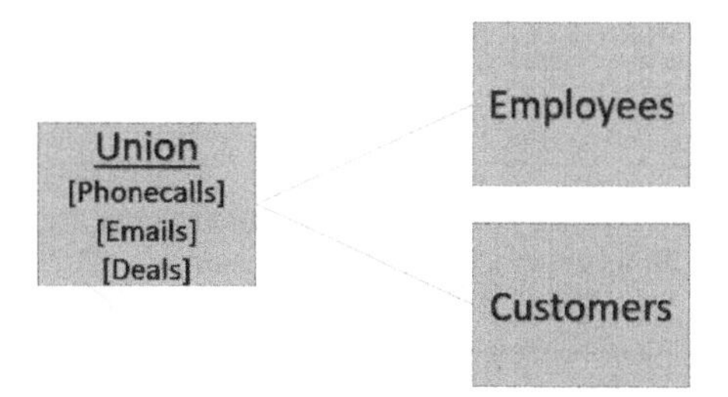

Figure 14.11: If the three tables are merged into one, the schema becomes very simple and it has no loops

Please note that the three fact tables cannot be merged with a join, because they are in a many-to-many relationship. Many-to-many joins must be avoided.

The three tables must be merged with a union.

So, let's visualize the solution. Let's start by looking at the three tables. Figure 14.12 shows data from Phonecalls, Figure 14.13 from Emails, and Figure 14.14 from Deals.

Call Date	Employee ID	Customer ID	Call Status	Topic	Long description
01-Jan	Emp1	A	Busy	Sell new insurance	Busy
02-Jan	Emp1	A	Answered	Sell new insurance	Was not interested
02-Jan	Emp2	B	No answer	Phone survey	No answer
03-Jan	Emp2	B	Answered	Phone survey	Survey completed
03-Jan	Emp2	C	Answered	Phone survey	She declined the survey
...	...	...	...	...	...

Figure 14.12: The Phonecalls table

Sent Date	Employee ID	Customer ID	Subject	Body
01-Jan	Emp1	C	Email survey	Dear Customer, ...
01-Jan	Emp1	D	Email survey	Dear Customer, ...
01-Jan	Emp1	E	Email survey	Dear Customer, ...
02-Jan	Emp3	A	Incident 1234 solved	We have solved...
...	...	...	...	...

Figure 14.13: The Emails table

Employee ID	Customer ID	Signed Date	Valid From Date	Link to Doc
Emp4	A	15-Jan	01-Jul	https://docs..
Emp4	F	15-Jan	01-Apr	https://docs..
Emp4	G	15-Jan	01-Jul	https://docs..
...	...	...	...	...

Figure 14.14: The Deals table

The union is shown in Figure 14.15.

Source	Date	Employee ID	Customer ID	Call Status	Topic	Long description	Subject	Body	Valid From	Link to Doc
Phonecalls	01-Jan	Emp1	A	Busy	Sell new insurance	Busy				
Phonecalls	02-Jan	Emp1	A	Answered	Sell new insurance	Was not interested				
Phonecalls	02-Jan	Emp2	B	No answer	Phone survey	No answer				
Phonecalls	03-Jan	Emp2	B	Answered	Phone survey	Survey completed				
Phonecalls	03-Jan	Emp2	C	Answered	Phone survey	She declined the survey				
Emails	01-Jan	Emp1	C				Email	Dear...		
Emails	01-Jan	Emp1	D				Email	Dear...		
Emails	01-Jan	Emp1	E				Email	Dear...		
Emails	02-Jan	Emp3	A				Incident	We have		
Deals	15-Jan	Emp4	A						01-Jul	https://docs..
Deals	15-Jan	Emp4	F						01-Apr	https://docs..
Deals	15-Jan	Emp4	G						01-Jul	https://docs..
...	...	...	...						...	...

Figure 14.15: The union of the three fact tables

Look at the two highlighted columns. Employee ID is one column, but it actually contains three columns piled up, coming from the three original tables.

So, three columns are now merged into one single column. The same can be said for Customer ID: one column contains three columns piled up.

The union solves the problem of the loops because it reduces the number of tables, and consequently, it reduces the number of connections needed. The connections are not lost—they are just piled up.

However, recall that the union also has two drawbacks. It is not user-friendly, and the resulting table is a mix that does not represent a specific business entity.

How the USS solves the loops

The Unified Star Schema is based on the union. But it is better than the union, because it is easier to use, and it does not mix the tables.

The end-users will create a left join. In reality, what happens behind the scene is a combination of a join and a union. And let's not forget that the BI tools also create an automatic aggregation. The schema of the CRM example, with the USS approach, is shown in Figure 14.16. In this model, there are no loops.

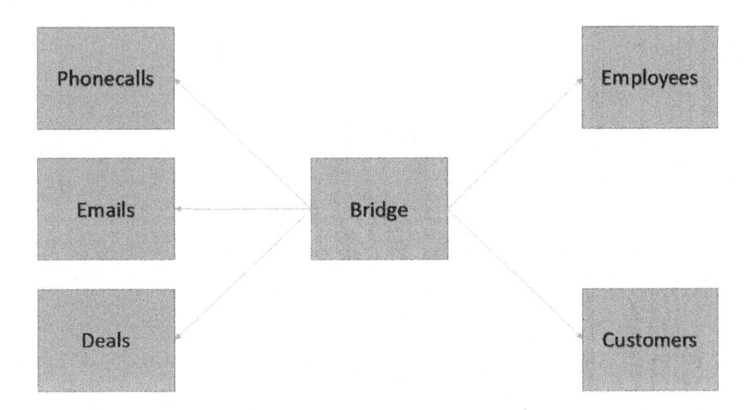

Figure 14.16: The USS solution to the loops

Initially, we had six connections, and now we have only five. Does it mean that we have lost one connection? Certainly not. The five lines that you see in Figure 14.16 are just the connections of the tables to the Bridge. We can call them the "trivial connections". But the real information about "who points to what" is embedded inside the Bridge.

Let's have a closer look at the Bridge now. When we have five tables, the Bridge will have five stages and six columns. See Figure 14.17.

Stage	_KEY_Phonecalls	_KEY_Emails	_KEY_Deals	_KEY_Employees	_KEY_Customers
Phonecalls	1			Emp1	A
Phonecalls	2	EMPTY	EMPTY	Emp1	A
Phonecalls	3			Emp2	B
Phonecalls	4			Emp2	B
Phonecalls	5			Emp2	C
Emails		1		Emp1	C
Emails	EMPTY	2	EMPTY	Emp1	D
Emails		3		Emp1	E
Emails		4		Emp3	A
Deals			1	Emp4	A
Deals	EMPTY	EMPTY	2	Emp4	F
Deals			3	Emp4	G
Employees				Emp1	
Employees				Emp2	
Employees				Emp3	
Employees				Emp4	
Employees				Emp5	
Employees				Emp6	
Customers					A
Customers					B
Customers					C
Customers					D
Customers					E
Customers					F
Customers					G
Customers					H

Figure 14.17: The Bridge embeds all the six connections that were forming a loop earlier. They can be seen in the top-right corner of the figure

The Bridge always looks the same. One stage per table and the FKs are populated only when available. The stages of Employees and Customers ensure the full outer join effect—everything as usual.

But let's have a closer look at all the "FKs inside the Bridge". This analysis will give you a full understanding of the mechanism of the Unified Star Schema.

Let's call "block" each rectangle in Figure 14.17. If we exclude the Stage column, we have 25 blocks in total, and only 11 of them are populated. Please spend a moment in visualizing and counting the 11 populated blocks.

The six blocks at the top right of the figure correspond to the six connections that you have seen at the beginning of this chapter, in Figure 14.2. These are the six "real connections" that actually say "who points to what".

The remaining five blocks, positioned in the diagonal, are the "trivial connections". These are the five connections that you have seen earlier in Figure 14.16, and these are the ones that the end-users will actually implement inside the BI tools.

With the USS approach, the end-users will only need to implement the "trivial connections". The "real connections" that actually say "who points to what" are already embedded inside the Bridge.

Let's see it with a practical implementation.

Implementation with SAP Business Objects

In Business Objects, the connections of the tables are defined in an environment called the "Universe". The end-users are not supposed to deal with this. So, in theory, the end-users should not need to care about connections at all.

But unfortunately, things are not as easy.

The main problem is that, with traditional dimensional modeling, there are multiple ways of connecting the tables, depending on the business requirements. This leads to the creation of multiple universes, and for the end-users it is very difficult to choose what universe they should use.

The second problem is that, with traditional dimensional modeling, the loops have never been really solved. The solution is up to the creativity of the developer, or in some cases it is up to the technology in use. As we have seen, Business Objects has created a solution called "contexts".

So, let's start by solving the loops with the traditional approach, using the technique of the contexts. Figure 14.18 shows that the context "Phonecalls" consists of the two highlighted joins: Phonecalls-Employees and Phonecalls-Customers.

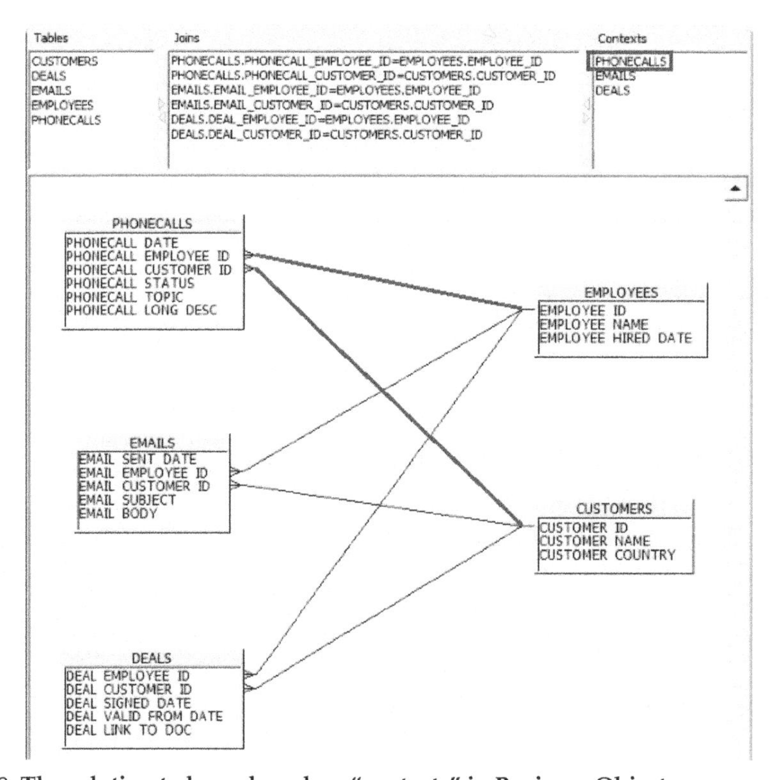

Figure 14.18: The solution to loops based on "contexts" in Business Objects

When the end-user creates a query that involves data coming from Phonecalls, Employees, and Customers, the tool will automatically resolve the query by using the "Phonecalls" context. So far, so good.

But if the end-user decides to add to the query an object that comes from Emails or from Deals, then the problem of "incompatibility" arises, as can be seen in Figure 14.19.

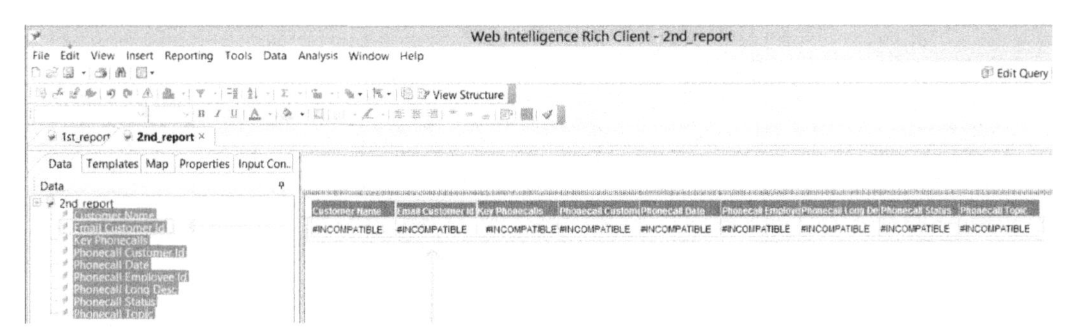

Figure 14.19: By adding any object not belonging to the context, the objects become "incompatible"

The column "Email Customer ID" comes from Emails. This table needs to use a join that does not belong to the "Phonecalls" context. For this reason, a separate query is created. But then, the objects of the two queries become "incompatible", and they will not fit into the same visualization.

The end-user has the freedom to drag and drop all the objects: the tool will create separate queries, and all the objects will be available for visualization. But then, based on the initial choice of visualization, some of the objects will be marked as "incompatible". See Figure 14.20.

In Business Objects, by using contexts, the end-users have limited freedom. This solution only works if the end-users have a technical understanding of the underlying schema, which of course, we cannot expect from the business users. As a consequence, the reports in the presence of loops are usually created by data experts, and the business users cannot have proper self-service BI experience.

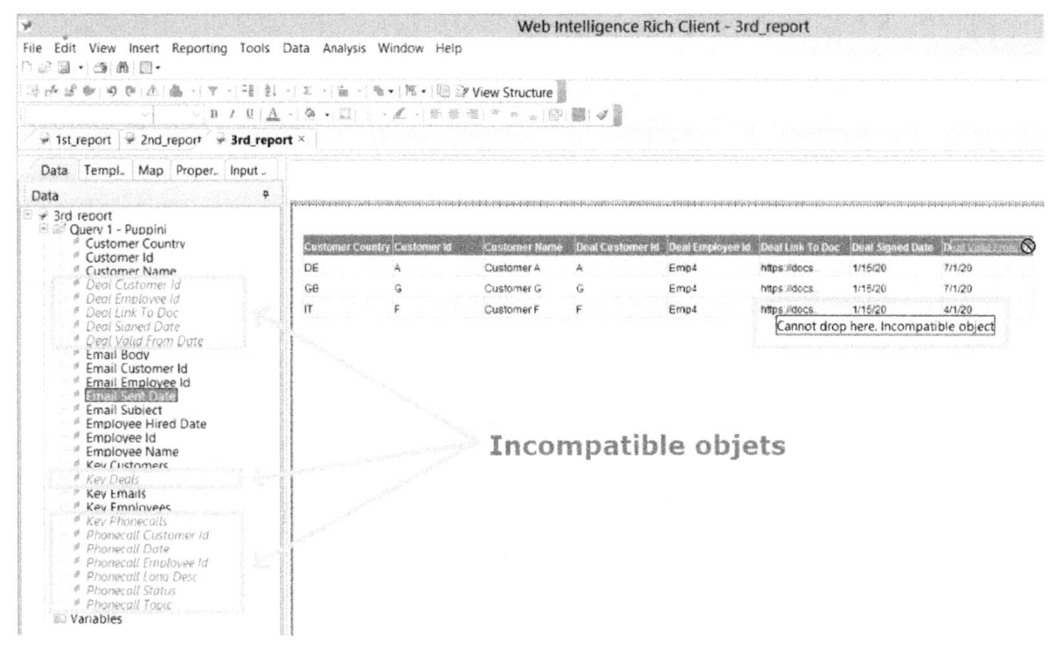

Figure 14.20: Some objects are incompatible with each other

Let's now implement the solution based on the Unified Star Schema.

With the Unified Star Schema, everything becomes easier. There are no incompatible combinations of objects. The end-users can drag and drop all the objects that they need, without any risk. Figure 14.21 shows the implementation of the USS with Business Objects.

The Unified Star Schema in Business Objects looks as always, with the Bridge in the middle and all the other tables around the Bridge.

Figure 14.22 shows a user report where all the available columns can be visualized and computed together.

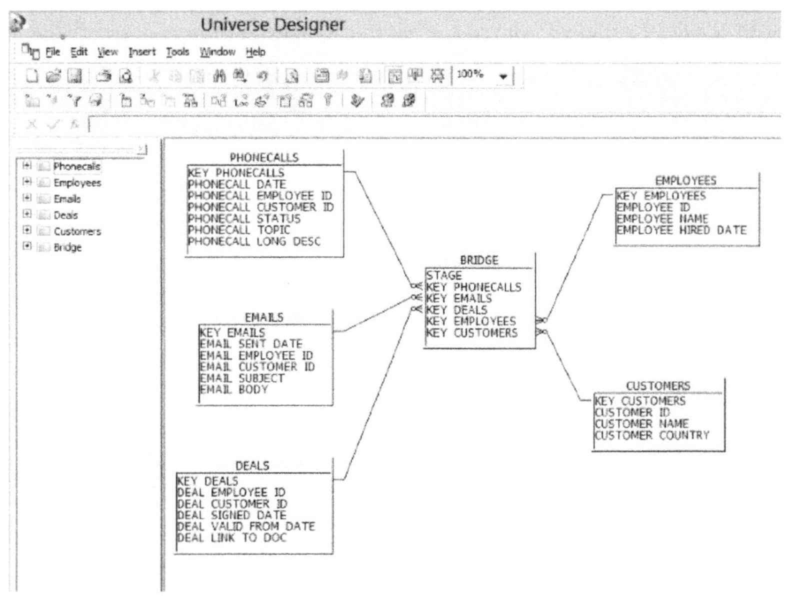

Figure 14.21: Implementation of the USS with Business Objects

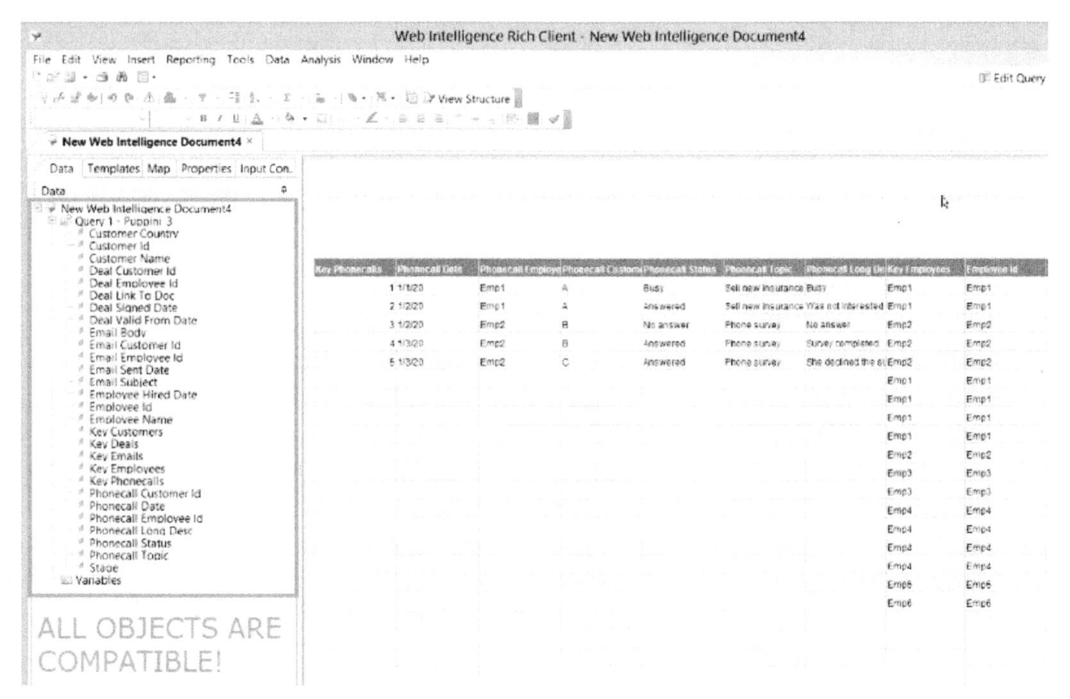

Figure 14.22: With the USS approach, everything is compatible with everything

---

With the USS approach, the end-users will be free to drag and drop whatever they need, with no limitation. Everything is compatible with everything, despite the presence of loops. The business users can have a proper "self-service experience".

CHAPTER 15

Non-Conformed Granularities

In this chapter, learn about non-conformed granularities through an example. See that creating a BI solution, when the dimensions are non-conformed, can present a number of challenges which have been traditionally solved by either creating ad-hoc queries or by building dashboards that are not integrated. Learn that the Unified Star Schema introduces a solution called "re-normalization". Witness the benefits, including that the developers are only needed for the setup phase of the USS, and that the USS does not depend on the business requirements, so the end-users will be free to implement their personalized reports and dashboards.

Up to this point, we have seen several examples where facts and dimensions had the same granularity. In the Multi-Fact example, both Sales and Purchases were referencing Products by using the Product ID. Likewise, in the CRM example, we have seen that three fact tables (Phonecalls, Emails, and Deals) were all referencing Employees and Customers by using Employee ID and Customer ID. These were all examples of "conformed granularities".

When it comes to multi-fact queries, the common perception in the data community is that the granularities must be conformed because this is the only way facts can be compared and computed together. But things are different with the USS approach.

With the USS approach, there is no need for conformed granularities.

Example based on sales and targets

Sales and Targets are non-conformed by nature.

Many organizations set a target for their sales, but the targets are never as detailed as sales. You typically do not set a target for each client, but rather for a group of clients, such as the country. And you typically do not set a target for each product, but rather for a group of products, such as the product line.

Sales and Targets are two fact tables, and they both reference Clients and Products, but at different granularities. The question is: how do we connect these four tables together? See Figure 15.1.

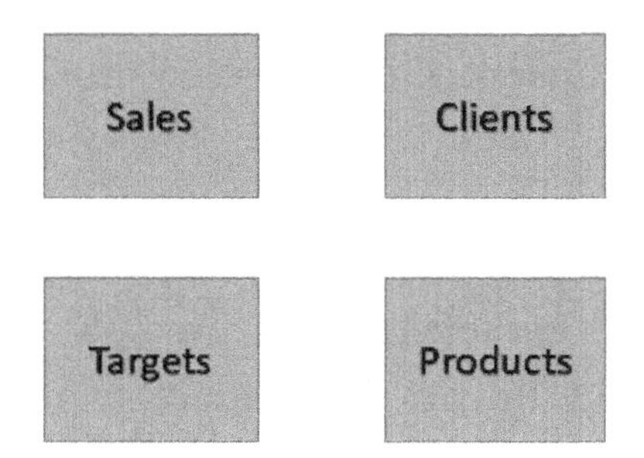

Figure 15.1: How do we connect Sales, Targets, Clients, and Products together?

Well, connecting Sales to Clients and Products is very easy, because Sales contains the client ID and the product ID. The problem is the Targets table. How can we integrate this table with the other three? See Figure 15.2.

The experienced developer would solve the problem by aggregating Sales to the granularity of Targets. This solution works, but it has a drawback: when we want to drill down into the detail of the Sales, we must create a new, separate query. The two queries will not be integrated. When the end-user creates a filter on the first one, that filter will not automatically propagate to the second one: it has to be created manually. In other words, the two queries "do not talk to each other". Furthermore, we want to avoid using a developer every time that an end-user has a new question—this is actually the ad-hoc approach that we want to eliminate.

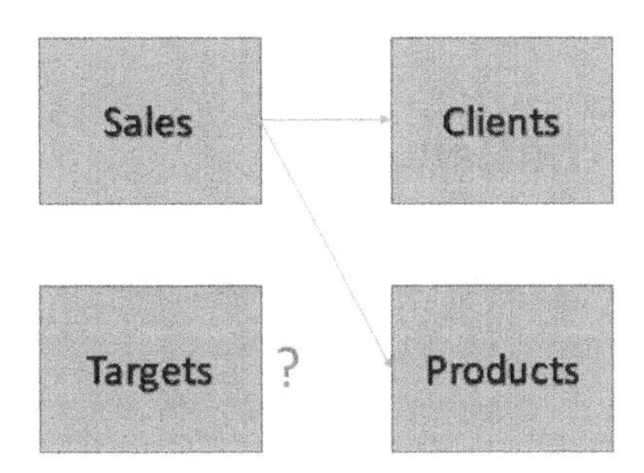

Figure 15.2: The challenge is how to connect Targets with the other three tables

The end-users may want to see the sales compared with the targets. Additionally, they may want to see the detail of the sales. Then they may want to see all the clients, regardless of whether or not they have bought anything. They may want to see all the products, regardless of whether or not they have been sold. They may want to see the percentage of sales versus targets on a double-entry table by product line and country, and so on.

These are all examples of reports that are very commonly requested. Typically, in organizations, a new business requirement needs to go through a process of finding budget, allocating resources, writing documentation, attending meetings, waiting, developing, testing, detecting bugs, waiting again, testing again, and more. Once the report has been delivered, it needs to be maintained. If there are many reports, the end-users will start getting confused. At some point, nobody will know if a particular report is in use at all—but just to be on the safe side, the obsolete reports will continue to be maintained, even if no one is using them. This is painful and expensive.

So, wouldn't it be great to integrate multiple fact tables at different levels of granularity without the need for ad-hoc solutions, and without being dependent on developers every time that a new question arises?

Yes! Read on!

Understanding the challenges

We have prepared a data set that looks very simple. But we will see that it is full of challenges.

See Figure 15.3 for data on Clients. Please note that the column "Country Name" is a denormalized column. Most likely, in the original transactional system, there was a separate reference table called "Countries", where each Country was appearing only once. In other words, we can say that the original transactional system was probably in third normal form, while this table is clearly not.

Client ID	Client Name	Client Segment	Country ID	Country Name
CL01	Client 01	Standard	US	United States
CL02	Client 02	Standard	US	United States
CL03	Client 03	Gold	MX	Mexico
CL04	Client 04	Gold	IT	Italy
CL05	Client 05	Standard	IT	Italy
CL06	Client 06	Gold	IT	Italy
CL07	Client 07	Standard	ES	Spain
CL08	Client 08	Gold	ES	Spain
CL09	Client 09	Standard	ES	Spain

Figure 15.3: The Clients table

Figure 15.4 contains the data for Products. Please note that the column "Product Line Name" is a denormalized column. Most likely, in the original transactional system, there was a separate reference table called "ProductLines", where each product line was appearing only once. In other words, we can say that the original transactional system was probably in third normal form, while this table is clearly not.

Product ID	Product Name	Product Line Code	Product Line Name
PR01	Prod1	C	Clothing
PR02	Prod2	C	Clothing
PR03	Prod3	C	Clothing
PR04	Prod4	A	Accessories
PR05	Prod5	A	Accessories
PR06	Prod6	A	Accessories

Figure 15.4: The Products table

Figure 15.5 contains the data for Sales. The Sales table, in our example, consists of the five white columns that appear in the figure. But none of these five columns contains a FK that points to Targets.

For this reason, the columns in grey need to be created during the data transformation process. The goal is to create inside Sales the additional column "Target Key" that points to Targets. This step is always recommended, even with the traditional approach. Sales and Targets are in a one-to-many relationship, and unfortunately, it is very common to see these two tables treated as if they were in a many-to-many relationship.

Sales ID	Sales Date	Client ID	Country ID	Product ID	Product Line	Target Key	Sales Amount
1	01-Jan	CL01	US	PR01	C	US-C	100
2	02-Jan	CL02	US	PR02	C	US-C	100
3	03-Jan	CL03	MX	PR03	C	MX-C	100
4	04-Jan	CL04	IT	PR04	A	IT-A	100
5	05-Jan	CL05	IT	PR05	A	IT-A	100
6	06-Jan	CL06	IT	PR01	C	IT-C	100
7	07-Jan	CL07	ES	PR02	C	ES-C	100
8	08-Jan	CL08	ES	PR03	C	ES-C	100
9	09-Jan	CL01	US	PR04	A	US-A	100
10	10-Jan	CL02	US	PR05	A	US-A	100
11	11-Jan	CL03	MX	PR01	C	MX-C	100
12	12-Jan	CL04	IT	PR02	C	IT-C	100
13	13-Jan	CL05	IT	PR03	C	IT-C	100
14	14-Jan	CL06	IT	PR04	A	IT-A	100
15	15-Jan	CL07	ES	PR05	A	ES-A	100
16	16-Jan	CL08	ES	PR01	C	ES-C	100
17	17-Jan	CL01	US	PR02	C	US-C	100
18	18-Jan	CL02	US	PR03	C	US-C	100
19	19-Jan	CL03	MX	PR04	A	MX-A	100
20	20-Jan	CL04	IT	PR05	A	IT-A	100

Figure 15.5: The Sales table

Figure 15.6 contains the data for Targets. Looking at the figure, we see that the organization has set a target for each combination of country and product line. Consequently, each row of the Targets table is uniquely identified by the combination of the two columns, "Country ID" and "Product Line". To avoid composite keys, it has been chosen to create inside Targets the additional column "Target Key". This is another example of a transformation that is always recommended, also in the traditional approach. Consolidating the PK into one single column is usually a good practice.

Country ID	Product Line	Target Key	Target Amount
US	C	US-C	40,000
US	A	US-A	20,000
MX	C	MX-C	30,000
MX	A	MX-A	15,000
IT	C	IT-C	20,000
IT	A	IT-A	10,000
ES	C	ES-C	14,000
ES	A	ES-A	5,000

Figure 15.6: The Targets table

Now the two fact tables are ready: Sales can easily point to Targets. Sales is the hunter, and Targets is the prey. The four tables appear in Figure 15.7.

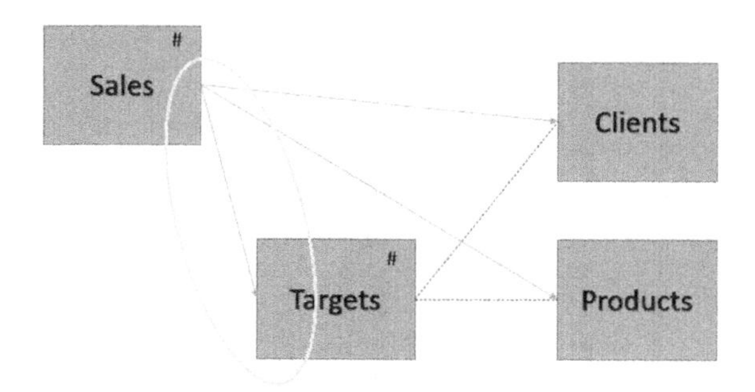

Figure 15.7: Although Sales and Targets are now connected, how do we connect Targets to Clients and Products?

We have made a step forward, but the process of data preparation is not finished yet. The Targets table is connected to the dimensions by a dotted line. This is because Targets "would like" to point to Clients and Products, but it cannot. It does not have the Client ID nor the Product ID. Targets is actually using these two dimensions, but on a different granularity, more aggregated.

If we connect Targets to Clients by the "Country ID" column, this will be a many-to-many relationship because the "Country ID" column is not unique in Clients. Likewise, if we connect Targets to Products by the "Product Line" column, this will be a many-to-many relationship because the "Product Line" column is not unique in Products. But as we know, many-to-many joins must be avoided.

Some developers solve this problem by using an interesting solution: adding a new column where they assign a "random but appropriate" Foreign Key. See Figure 15.8.

Country ID	Product Line	Target Key	Target Client ID	Target Product ID	Target Amount
US	C	US-C	CL02	PR02	40,000
US	A	US-A	CL02	PR05	20,000
MX	C	MX-C	CL03	PR02	30,000
MX	A	MX-A	CL03	PR05	15,000
IT	C	IT-C	CL05	PR02	20,000
IT	A	IT-A	CL05	PR05	10,000
ES	C	ES-C	CL08	PR02	14,000
ES	A	ES-A	CL08	PR05	5,000

Figure 15.8: The technique of "random but appropriate" Foreign Key

The Targets table now has two new columns called "Target Client ID" and "Target Product ID". This may sound strange because Targets does not have such detailed granularity. For Italy, the developer has chosen the client CL05. Why CL05? It is a random choice, but it is appropriate because CL05 is from Italy. Alternatively, it would have been OK to choose CL04 or CL06, but not the others. For the clothing product line, the developer has chosen the product PR02. Why PR02? It is a random choice, but it is appropriate because PR02 is a product of clothing. Alternatively, it would have been OK to choose PR01 or PR03, but not the others.

This solution works fine, but we do not recommend it because it is not a very "clean" solution. The user experience will not be perfect: when the end-user selects a filter on CL05, a target amount will appear associated with that particular client, which is not reflecting the truth.

The solution that we are proposing in this chapter is completely different, and it is much better.

Let's look again at our four tables in Figure 15.7. In this data model, we can also notice the risk of loops. As soon as we create a connection between Targets and the two dimensions, we will have four tables and five connections. As we have seen in chapter 9, with four tables, we can build at most three connections. The fourth and fifth connection will inevitably create loops.

Last but not least, Targets contains measures, and it gets exploded by Sales. So, Sales and Targets form a fan trap. With just four tables, we are detecting a lot of problems:

1. Fan traps
2. Many-to-many relationships
3. Loops
4. Non-conformed granularities

How do we solve all these problems? The Unified Star Schema, as we have seen in the previous chapters, can solve the first three of these problems. Non-conformed granularities are a new challenge, and we solve it with "re-normalization".

The Re-normalization

Data is given to us. The word "data" comes from Latin, and it means "given".

In many cases, the data that we receive is already denormalized. This means that we receive "joined tables". Very often, they have been joined as a courtesy to us because the common perception in the data community is that business intelligence should use denormalized tables.

But denormalized tables can lead to problems and limitations. We can explain this concept by using an analogy with Lego.

Imagine that you buy a box of Legos. Imagine that, when you open it, you find out that some of the pieces are glued together. Are you going to be happy?

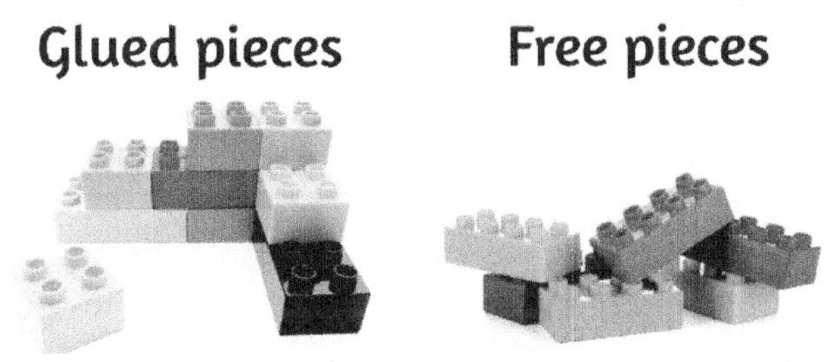

Figure 15.9: Is it better to have glued Lego pieces, or free Lego pieces?

If the pieces are glued together, you will have limited freedom in your Lego constructions.

With data, something very similar happens: if we receive denormalized tables, it is a bit like receiving glued Lego pieces! Please keep in mind the terminology: "denormalized" is equivalent to "glued", while "normalized" is equivalent to "free".

The solution is simple: unglue the bricks!

We call "re-normalization" a special process of turning a denormalized table into the original normalized tables. Re-normalization means "unglue the bricks". See Figure 15.10.

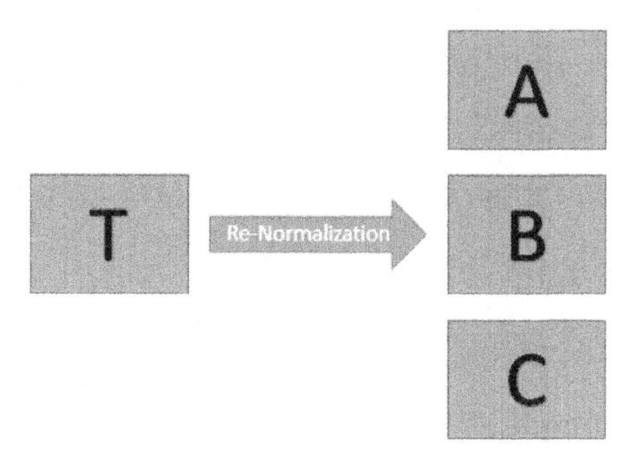

Figure 15.10: Re-normalization of T into the original tables A, B, and C

The letter "T" stands for "Transformed". T is a denormalized table, while A, B, and C are the original tables.

Re-normalization is quite an unusual process in business intelligence, but it is presented here because it has a very important role in dealing with non-conformed granularities.

As we have seen in chapter 10, the transformation of the original tables (A, B, and C) into a table T is unfortunately irreversible, because T has probably lost some data. Now that we actually want to roll it back, we have a real challenge: how can we restore the data that was lost?

There are two options to deal with this challenge. Either you communicate to your data providers that you want to receive the original normalized tables, or you just re-normalize them yourself, with the awareness that some information may be impossible to restore.

The first option is the best, but it usually needs to go through a slow process of decision making. Most likely, your data provider will tell you that it's not possible, although it actually is. If this is the case, you can go for the second option: undo the work that someone has done. Unglue the bricks.

Let's be clear: denormalized tables can be OK sometimes. If the pieces are glued in the shape of a castle, and you wanted to build exactly a castle, then it's all OK!

But in general, re-normalizing is just a small effort, and it gives you back your full freedom. You can still build a castle, but you can do it your own way.

You may think that the re-normalization of dimensions will lead to a snowflake schema, but this is not the case. The Unified Star Schema is always a star schema, and never a snowflake. The connection of Targets to Countries will happen through the Bridge, as well as the connection of Targets to ProductLines. With the USS approach, each relationship needs to be one-to-many, and it will be handled by the Bridge.

It's time to the see solution. So… let's get started and "unglue the bricks"!

The Clients table breaks into two tables: Clients and Countries. See Figure 15.11.

Clients:

Client ID	Client Name	Client Segment	Country ID
CL01	Client 01	Standard	US
CL02	Client 02	Standard	US
CL03	Client 03	Gold	MX
CL04	Client 04	Gold	IT
CL05	Client 05	Standard	IT
CL06	Client 06	Gold	IT
CL07	Client 07	Standard	ES
CL08	Client 08	Gold	ES
CL09	Client 09	Standard	ES

Countries:

Country ID	Country Name
US	United States
MX	Mexico
IT	Italy
ES	Spain
AF	Afghanistan
AL	Albania
DZ	Algeria
...	...

Figure 15.11: Re-normalization of Countries

The Countries table has been detached from the Clients table. We say that "Countries has been re-normalized".

Please note that if you manage to receive the original normalized tables from your data providers, you will be able to see also all those countries that were lost during the process of denormalization, such as Afghanistan, Albania, and Algeria. Instead, if you create the re-normalization on your own, you will be able to obtain only the countries until the dotted line in Figure 15.11, because the others are impossible to restore.

The Products table also breaks into two tables: Products and ProductLines. See Figure 15.12.

Products:

Product ID	Product Name	Product Line Code
PR01	Prod1	C
PR02	Prod2	C
PR03	Prod3	C
PR04	Prod4	A
PR05	Prod5	A
PR06	Prod6	A

ProductLines:

Product Line Code	Product Line Name
C	Clothing
A	Accessories
X	Special

Figure 15.12: Re-normalization of ProductLines

In this case, we say that "ProductLines has been re-normalized". And probably, if you receive the original normalized tables from your data providers, you will find a product line "X" that otherwise would have been lost. This is even more critical because the list of countries can always be found on the Internet, while the same cannot be said for the list of product lines of your organization.

Now that the bricks are unglued, let's build our castle!

In Figure 15.13 you can see the "re-engineered" data source after the process of re-normalization.

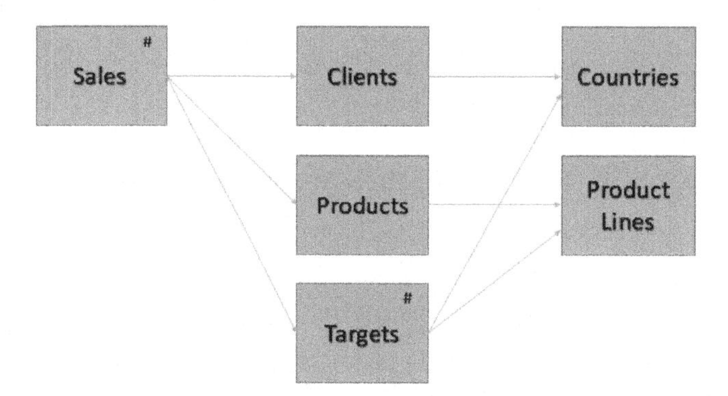

Figure 15.13: The schema of the re-normalized data source

Thanks to re-normalization, we have completely eliminated the evil "many-to-many" connection of Targets to the dimensions, and we have avoided the technique of "random but appropriate" Foreign Keys. Targets now points to Countries and to ProductLines. These connections are correct because they are one-to-many. Each row of Targets is associated with one and only one row of Countries. Each row of Targets is associated with one and only one row of ProductLines. Target is the hunter, and the two dimensions are the prey. Targets is on the left, and the two dimensions are on the right. All correct.

Note that the structure contains some loops, as we expected. We have six tables and seven connections. But this is not a problem because in chapter 14 we have shown how the USS approach solves the loops.

Now that we have re-normalized our data source, we are ready to build the USS.

How the USS solves non-conformed granularities

The structure of the USS is always the same: the Bridge points to all the other tables, as shown in Figure 15.14.

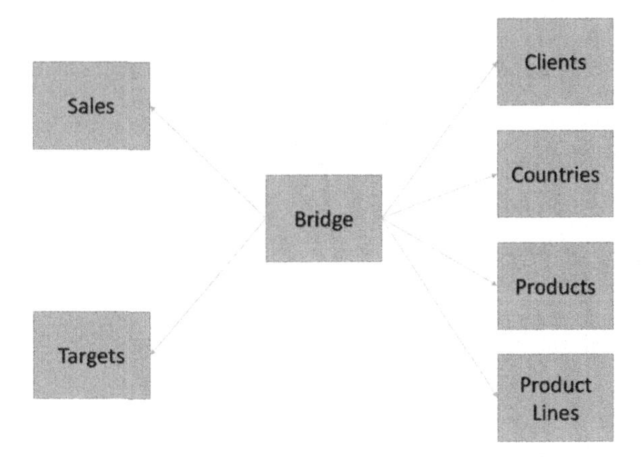

Figure 15.14: The USS solution to non-conformed granularities

With the USS approach, there is no need for conformed granularities. Thanks to the process of re-normalization, it is possible to build a Unified Star Schema that handles different granularities, with extreme simplicity.

Please note that the schema in the figure this time is not following the ODM convention. The ODM convention is useful when we need to interpret a complex data source. Now that the job is done, we are free to arrange our data model as we prefer, because in any case, we know that the Bridge is always hunter, and all the other tables are prey.

Figure 15.15 takes a closer look at the Bridge.

Stage	_KEY_Sales	_KEY_Targets	_KEY_Clients	_KEY_Countries	_KEY_Products	_KEY_ProductLines
Sales	1	US-C	CL01	US	PR01	C
Sales	2	US-C	CL02	US	PR02	C
Sales	3	MX-C	CL03	MX	PR03	C
Sales	...	...	...	...	...	...
Sales	19	MX-A	CL03	MX	PR04	A
Sales	20	IT-A	CL04	IT	PR05	A
Targets		US-C		US		C
Targets		US-A		US		A
Targets		MX-C		MX		C
Targets		MX-A		MX		A
Targets		IT-C		IT		C
Targets		IT-A		IT		A
Targets		ES-C		ES		C
Targets		ES-A		ES		A
Clients			CL01	US		
Clients			CL02	US		
Clients			CL03	MX		
Clients			CL04	IT		
Clients			CL05	IT		
Clients			CL06	IT		
Clients			CL07	ES		
Clients			CL08	ES		
Clients			CL09	ES		
Countries				AD		
Countries				AF		
Countries				...		
Countries				ES		
Countries				IT		
Countries				MX		
Countries				US		
Products					PR01	C
Products					PR02	C
Products					PR03	C
Products					PR04	A
Products					PR05	A
Products					PR06	A
ProductLines						A
ProductLines						C
ProductLines						X

Figure 15.15: The Bridge in the example based on non-conformed granularities

The Sales stage has the key to the original dimensions (Clients and Products) and also the key to the new re-normalized dimensions (Countries and ProductLines).

We call "derived keys" those keys that need to be added after a process of re-normalization. The columns _KEY_Countries and _KEY_ProductLines, in the Sales stage, represent derived keys.

They are called "derived" because they are usually not available in an explicit way, and for this reason, we must "derive" them. For each _KEY_Clients, there is a unique _KEY_Countries. For each _KEY_Products, there is a unique _KEY_ProductLines. This operation of "deriving" can be achieved by applying a simple lookup, similar to the VLOOKUP in Excel. This is an additional effort, but it has a huge payback: the possibility to work with non-conformed granularities in an extremely easy and powerful way.

Please note that _KEY_Countries is a derived key only in the Sales stage. In the other stages, _KEY_Countries is a normal key because it was already available in an explicit way, and there was no need to derive it with a lookup. The same is true for _KEY_ProductLines—it is a derived key only in the Sales stage.

Implementation with QlikView

Now that we have illustrated the theory and the concepts, let's move to a practical example, based on QlikView. Figure 15.16 contains the Unified Star Schema implemented in QlikView.

This figure looks like a traditional star schema. But it's not. Sales and Targets are two fact tables. With traditional dimensional modeling, they would be at the center of two distinct star schemas. Products and ProductLines are two levels of the same dimension. With traditional dimensional modeling, they would probably form a snowflake schema. Likewise, Clients and Countries are also two levels of the same dimension. So, graphically it appears like a star schema. But in reality, not even one of the rules of traditional dimensional modeling is applied to this solution.

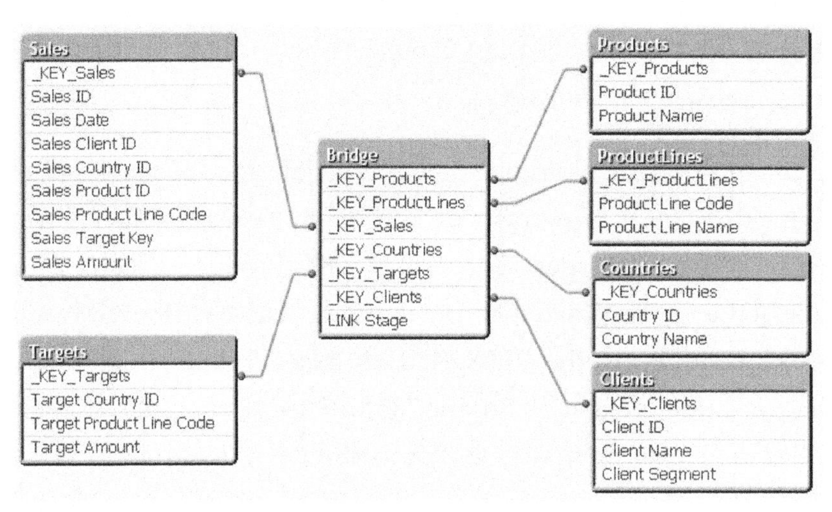

Figure 15.16: The Unified Star Schema implemented in QlikView

With this solution, we do not need to aggregate Sales to the granularity of Targets. Thanks to this, the drill-down of Sales is fully available in the query. There is also no dependency on developers because the end-users can easily build this dashboard on their own. All the connections will be automatically handled by the Bridge and by the USS naming convention.

The advantage of this solution for the end-users is huge. Not only will they find multiple answers in one single dashboard, but they will also benefit from "full integration". In other words, if a filter is applied, this will propagate simultaneously to all the other dashboards and reports, no matter if the tables are at different levels of granularity. This is all made possible by the process of re-normalization.

Let's better explain this functionality by looking at the next two figures.

Figure 15.17 shows several reports integrated into one single page.

Sales vs Target

Country Name	Product Line Name	Sales Amount	Target Amount	Sales vs Target	Sales vs Target %
		2,000	**154,000**	**-152,000**	**-98.70%**
United States	Accessories	200	20,000	-19,800	-99.00%
United States	Clothing	400	40,000	-39,600	-99.00%
Mexico	Accessories	100	15,000	-14,900	-99.33%
Mexico	Clothing	200	30,000	-29,800	-99.33%
Italy	Clothing	300	20,000	-19,700	-98.50%
Italy	Accessories	400	10,000	-9,600	-96.00%
Spain	Accessories	100	5,000	-4,900	-98.00%
Spain	Clothing	300	14,000	-13,700	-97.86%

Sales per Client (including Clients with no Sales)

Client Name	Country Name	Sales Amount
		2,000
Client 01	United States	300
Client 02	United States	300
Client 03	Mexico	300
Client 04	Italy	300
Client 05	Italy	200
Client 06	Italy	200
Client 07	Spain	200
Client 08	Spain	200
Client 09	Spain	0

Sales Detail

Sales ID	Sales Date	Client Name	Country Name	Product Name	Product Line Name	Sales Amount
						2,000
1	01/01/2019	Client 01	United States	Prod1	Clothing	100
2	02/01/2019	Client 02	United States	Prod2	Clothing	100
3	03/01/2019	Client 03	Mexico	Prod3	Clothing	100
4	04/01/2019	Client 04	Italy	Prod4	Accessories	100
5	05/01/2019	Client 05	Italy	Prod5	Accessories	100
6	06/01/2019	Client 06	Italy	Prod1	Clothing	100
7	07/01/2019	Client 07	Spain	Prod2	Clothing	100
8	08/01/2019	Client 08	Spain	Prod3	Clothing	100

Products Sold
Prod1
Prod2
Prod3
Prod4
Prod5

Products Unsold
Prod6

Figure 15.17: With the USS approach, one single dashboard can deliver multiple answers with just one query

The dashboard shows Sales vs. Target, as well as the sales detail, the clients with no sales, the products sold, and the products unsold. These reports can also be created with traditional dimensional modeling, but with multiple queries. The problem of using multiple queries is that "they do not talk to each other". They can be displayed on the same page, but they do not have "full integration". With the USS approach, instead, there is full integration.

What does it mean "full integration"? We can see it in Figure 15.18.

If the end-user selects, for example, Spain, the entire dashboard will reflect that selection. It is sufficient to apply the filter only in one place, and the filter will propagate simultaneously to all the other dashboards and reports, no matter if the tables are at different levels of granularity.

Sales vs Target

Country Name	Product Line Name	Sales Amount	Target Amount	Sales vs Target	Sales vs Target %
		400	**19,000**	**-18,600**	**-97.89%**
Spain	Accessories	100	5,000	-4,900	-98.00%
Spain	Clothing	300	14,000	-13,700	-97.86%

Sales per Client (including Clients with no Sales)

Client Name	Country Name	Sales Amount
		400
Client 07	Spain	200
Client 08	Spain	200
Client 09	Spain	0

Sales Detail

Sales ID	Sales Date	Client Name	Country Name	Product Name	Product Line Name	Sales Amount
						400
7	07/01/2019	Client 07	Spain	Prod2	Clothing	100
8	08/01/2019	Client 08	Spain	Prod3	Clothing	100
15	15/01/2019	Client 07	Spain	Prod5	Accessories	100
16	16/01/2019	Client 08	Spain	Prod1	Clothing	100

Products Sold
Prod1
Prod2
Prod3
Prod5

Products Unsold
Prod4
Prod6

Figure 15.18: The filter "Spain" applies everywhere, thanks to "full integration"

The only product that was unsold, in general, is Prod4. However, when selecting Spain, the report of Products Unsold dynamically changes to Prod4 and Prod6. This is because Prod6 was sold in general, but not in Spain. All the reports have simultaneously responded to the filter "Spain". This functionality is made possible by having all five reports come from one query.

Working with aggregates and details

Before concluding this chapter, we want to share an important thought about the concept of re-normalization and its potential usage with very large data sources.

Sometimes the business intelligence solution of an organization is not too large, and it can be entirely loaded into the RAM of a server, with all the existing detail at its finest granularity. This scenario is quite lucky, and it is still quite common today. Even very large organizations, regardless if they have a huge database, may be interested in analyzing only a small portion of their data. For example, they may be interested in analyzing sales, but not the history of the warehouse stock and the history of the pricing, which are usually very large data sets. When your "BI data domain" fits entirely in memory, life is easy: most likely, you will be able to fit your entire data set into one single integrated dashboard, with no issues of performance.

In all other cases, more and more frequently, the BI data domain is too large, and there is no hope that it will all fit into the RAM of a server. In this scenario, the BI solution for the end-users must be based on aggregates. This approach has been adopted for decades, and it works fine.

But what happens if an end-user, at some point, needs to see the detail? For example, they may need to investigate a particular case and drill down to the original transaction level. In most cases, today, the detail is still available through the ad-hoc approach. The end-user will need to ask a developer to write some query, specific for this particular requirement, and the detail will be available. But this is actually the ad-hoc approach that we are trying to eliminate.

With the USS approach, we want to expand the scope of self-service. We want to give the business users not only the access to aggregated data, but also the access to detailed data, and with no dependency on the developers.

Look at what we have done with Sales and Targets. We have been able to connect two fact tables to two dimensions, even if the granularities were not conformed. But then, if we have been able to do it with Sales and Targets, why can't we do it also with Sales and an aggregate of Sales?

Imagine that your Sales table has 100 billion rows—definitely too large to fit entirely in memory. Imagine that a developer creates a new table, called SalesAggr, where the transactions are grouped by date, country, and product line. This new aggregated table is much smaller, and it can entirely fit into the RAM of a server. So, with Sales and SalesAggr we can implement the same solution as the one that we have seen in this chapter: re-normalize Countries and ProductLines, build the derived keys, and treat Sales and SalesAggr as two independent tables, no matter if one is an aggregate of the other.

And then it's done! The end-users will start their analysis with the aggregates, at a high level. Then, at the moment when they need a drill down at the transactional level, the query will be extended to the original Sales table. Not all of the detail will be retrieved, of course, but just the filtered relevant part of it.

This is what Tableau does today with the live connection: starting from a drag and drop, Tableau generates a new query to the data source. The technology already exists, but it's a bit "blind": the end-users do not know in advance if drag and drop will generate a query of ten seconds or a query of ten hours.

The solution of "working with aggregates and details" will need to have a logic of warnings and limitations, aimed to avoid that a distracted end-user launches a query of 100 billion rows. This logic can be achieved by making smart usage of metadata. Before launching a query, the system will know the size and the exact number of rows of the requested detail because this information was collected during the process of aggregation.

We can even extend this thought and imagine the co-existence of multiple levels of aggregation of the same table.

With the USS approach, there is no need for conformed granularities. This is the key principle that can expand the scope of self-service to very large data sources.

CHAPTER 16

Northwind Case Study

In this chapter, witness how easy it is to detect the pitfalls of Northwind using the ODM convention. Verify that a join involving tables that form fan traps and chasm traps risks to produce incorrect totals. Become familiar with the concept of a "safe zone for a table", and that if we join all the tables together, not a single measure will have correct totals. Follow along with an implementation of the USS approach on the Northwind database with various BI tools. Understand that with the USS approach, all tables belong to a common safe zone: everything is compatible with everything.

Northwind is a sample database from Microsoft. Although it is very small and apparently simple, it is a perfect case study for this book because it shows in practice how to implement several of the conventions, methodologies, and solutions that were illustrated in this book.

Figure 16.1 shows the data model of Northwind. It is taken from the official Microsoft documentation. The database has only 13 tables and a total of 3308 rows. We can say with no doubt that it's a small database.

This data model gives us information about the relationships among these 13 tables. Each relationship is represented by a line that connects two tables.

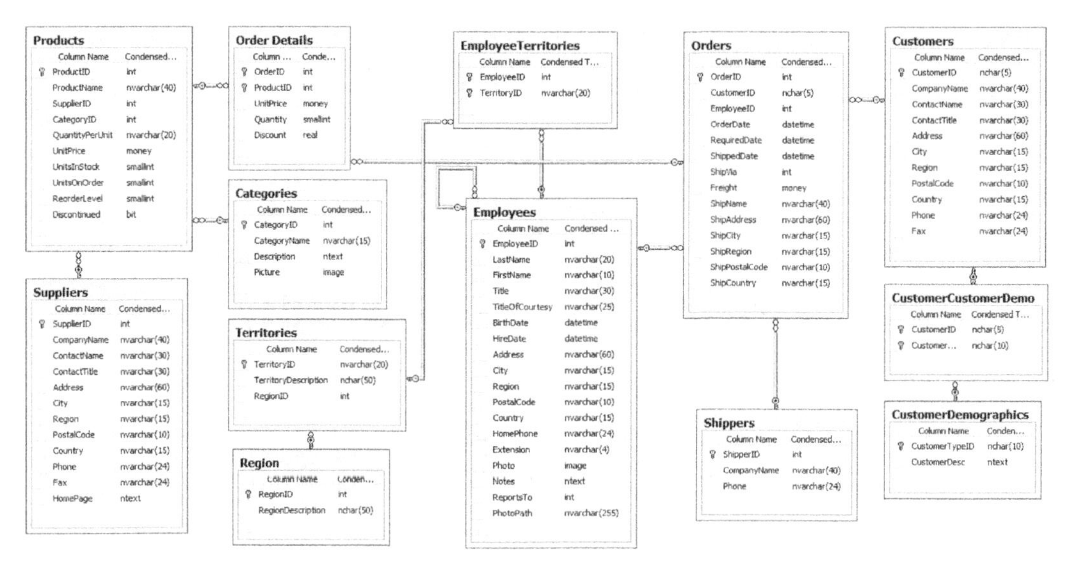

Figure 16.1: The data model of Northwind from the Microsoft documentation

Figure 16.2 shows one of the relationship lines. A line may end with a little infinity symbol or with a little key symbol. The infinity symbol represents a Foreign Key (FK), while the key symbol represents a Primary Key (PK).

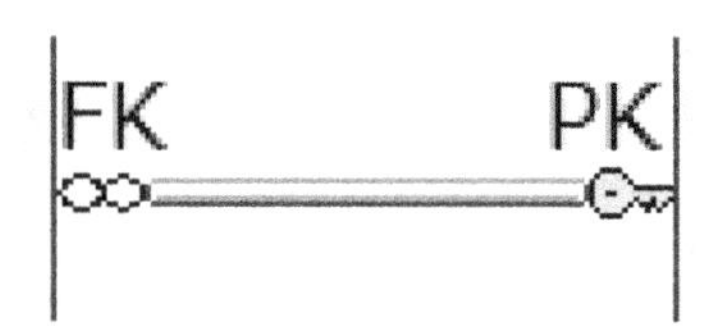

Figure 16.2: The line connecting two tables tells us about the cardinality

In this database, we can immediately notice that every relationship is one-to-many, because each line has a FK on one side and a PK on the other side.

If we look at the data model with more attention, we will notice that the database has no loops. In other words, you will never find any pair of tables A and B having multiple possible paths from A to B.

For example, let's try it with Shippers and Suppliers, as highlighted in Figure 16.3.

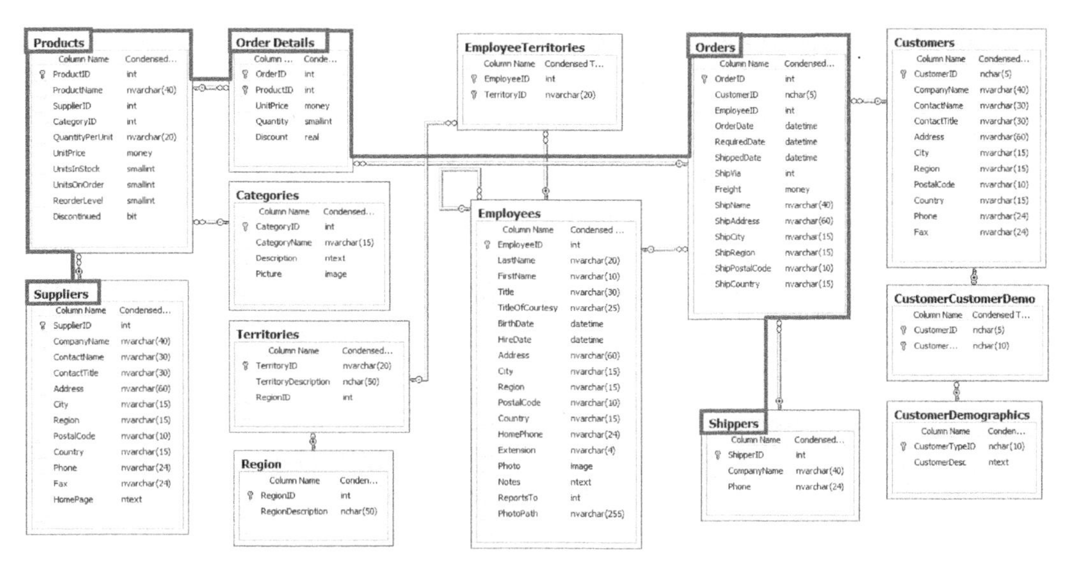

Figure 16.3: There are no loops in this model. There is only one possible path connecting Shippers to Suppliers

From Shippers to Suppliers, the only possible path is Shippers-Orders-OrderDetails-Products-Suppliers. There are no alternative paths. This is true for any other pair of tables.

Employees is a bit of an exception because it points to itself. This is a self-join and it will be resolved with an alias (probably named Managers) or with a hierarchy. Self-joins are very easy to handle, but they are not in the scope of this book.

This data model is useful, but it is actually not very easy to read. Your eyes risk getting lost while following the paths: they are similar to roads passing above each other, and this is not tidy. Rather than watching a data model, it feels like navigating a labyrinth. And if a data model appears difficult to read with just 13 tables, imagine how it will appear with 100 tables or more!

For this reason, as a first step, we need to tidy up the model. And we do it by applying the ODM convention.

Oriented Data Model for Northwind

So, let's tidy up and draw an Oriented Data Model (ODM). According to the ODM convention, for each pair of tables, the FK must be on the left, and the PK must be on the right. Every arrow points from left to right.

Let's pick, for example, Products and Suppliers. See Figure 16.4.

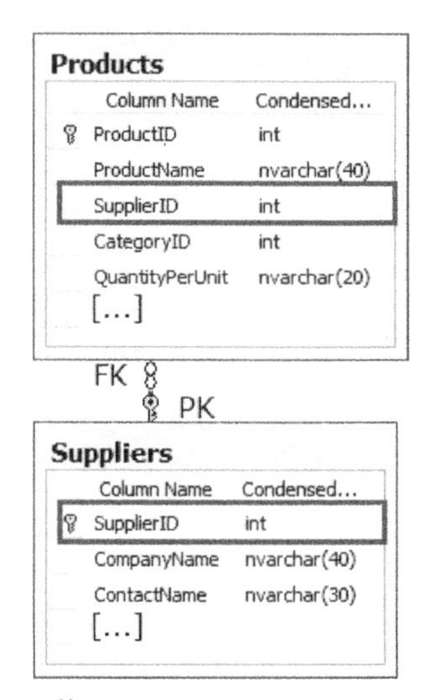

Figure 16.4: Products points to Suppliers

From the line connecting the two tables, we immediately see that Products points to Suppliers, and not vice versa. This is because the key symbol is on the side of Suppliers. We also see that the PK of Suppliers is "SupplierID", because there is another key symbol next to it. Unfortunately, the figure does not tell us which particular column in Products points to SupplierID. In this case, this is quite easy to guess because there is a column in Products called "SupplierID", and that column is clearly our FK.

The ideal process for detecting the correct FKs would be to read them from the database. If they are available, this is saving us some time. If not, a good alternative is to ask the database administrators, because they usually know how the tables need to be connected. If this is also not possible, then we have to do it on our own, based on names and common sense. Very often, we can use the process of thinking "by exclusion": knowing that one of the columns must be the FK, we look at all the existing columns and exclude the ones that cannot be. Among the remaining, we choose the "most probable". After that, it is good practice to validate our choice by verifying the existence of a "good correlation between the values of PK and FK". This is not a fully reliable validation, but it usually works quite well.

Back to our two tables. The Products table has the FK, and the Suppliers table has the PK. Products is the hunter, and Suppliers is the prey. According to the ODM convention, Products must be on the left, and Suppliers must be on the right, as we can see in Figure 16.5.

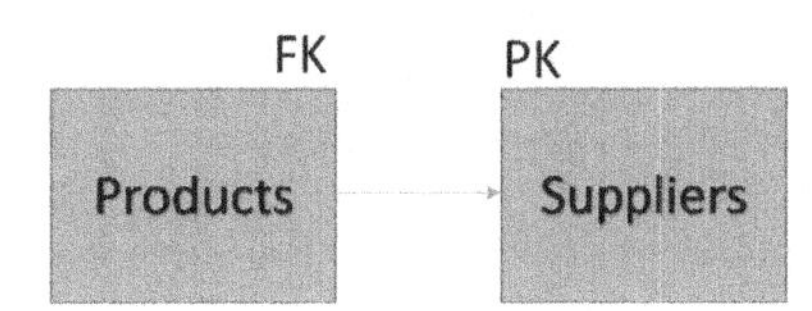

Figure 16.5: Products points to Suppliers from left to right

If we follow the ODM convention for all the other pairs of tables that are connected by a line, the Oriented Data Model of Northwind will look like in Figure 16.6.

This is the data model of Northwind based on the ODM convention. Please note, we have omitted two tables because these 11 tables are already sufficient to observe a lot of interesting things. When we look at the data model reorganized this way, it looks much clearer than before.

Notice that OrderDetails and EmployeeTerritories are the "lions": they are positioned on the very left of the data model, which means that they are "at the top of the food chain". OrderDetails is a proper fact table because each row represents an event and a measurement of a process. It is hunter and not prey. EmployeeTerritories is also hunter and not prey, but it is not a fact table because it does not represent any event or any measurement of a process. This is the classic "m-m table" that handles a pre-defined relationship between Employees and Territories.

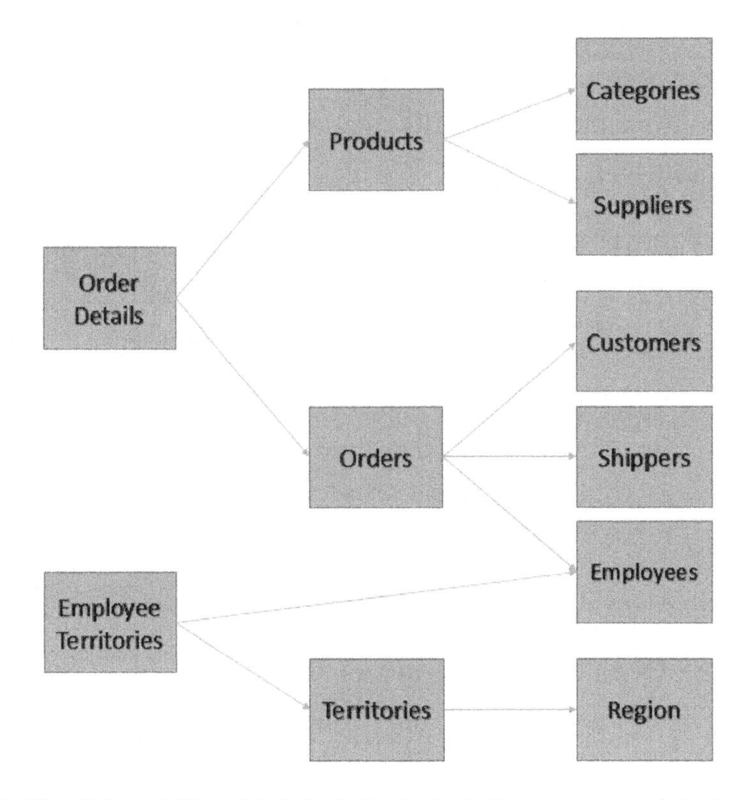

Figure 16.6: The Oriented Data Model of Northwind. Every arrow points from left to right, making everything much clearer.

As a rule of thumb, the tables on the left side of an Oriented Data Model usually have more rows and more columns than the other tables.

On the very opposite side of the data model, on the right, we can find six tables: Categories, Suppliers, Customers, Shippers, Employees, and Region. Each of these six tables is at the end of the food chain. Each of these six tables is prey and not hunter.

As a rule of thumb, the tables on the right side of an Oriented Data Model usually have fewer rows and fewer columns than the other tables. They are usually the easiest to understand because they contain a "list of something".

In the center of the data model we find Products, Orders, and Territories. Each of these tables is at the same time hunter and prey, as the leopard that we have seen in chapter 9.

Detecting the challenges

When tables are organized as an Oriented Data Model, it is much easier to detect the challenges. To do so, the first step is to identify all the tables that contain at least one measure. Why do we need to detect the measures? Because this way we can prevent the risk of their duplication, which can occur in the presence of fan traps, chasm traps, and many-to-many relationships. This will guarantee the correct totals in our reports.

As a reminder, the USS approach does not classify the tables as facts and dimensions: it only makes a distinction whether or not a table contains at least one measure. Any table can contain measures.

So, how do we identify the measures? In many databases, like Northwind, it is a straightforward exercise. But if we have a doubt, we can always try to get some help from end-users from the business departments, because they have a better knowledge of the processes of the organization.

So, let's start from the right, because the right side of the Oriented Data Model is always the easiest.

Figure 16.7 shows the Region table. This table has two columns and four rows. It is very small, just as we expected. The column RegionID is numeric, but it is clearly not a measure. We would never display an ID in the "Y" axis of a chart. Therefore, we can safely say that the Region table does not contain any measure.

RegionID	RegionDescription
1	Eastern
2	Western
3	Northern
4	Southern

Figure 16.7: The Region table has no measures

Note that many BI tools, today, do not make any difference between "numbers" and "measures". The truth is that a measure is always a number, but a number is not always a measure. Examples of "non-measure numbers" are column IDs, document numbers, Boolean flags, date-related columns (such as week, month, and year), and more.

Although artificial intelligence today is becoming more and more helpful in BI tools, the detection of measures today is still a prerogative of humans. We are the ones who must tell the BI tools, "do not make the sum of month numbers". So, it is a very good practice to "assess" all the numeric columns of our data sources, one by one. For each number that we recognize as a measure, we must decide the default aggregation function. In most cases, it will be the sum, but in other cases (such as unit price, rating, and score), it may be the average or some other aggregation. For all other "non-measure numbers", the aggregation function must be marked in the BI tool as "no aggregation". When a BI tool tries to "automatically generate insights", this preliminary assessment will make a difference because the software will be informed that the column IDs and driver license numbers should not be aggregated, and consequently, they should not be shown in charts.

Figure 16.8 shows the Shippers table, which clearly has no measures. The first column, again, is clearly an ID. The other two columns are text. No measures here.

ShipperID	CompanyName	Phone
1	Speedy Express	(503) 555-9831
2	United Package	(503) 555-3199
3	Federal Shipping	(503) 555-9931

Figure 16.8: The Shippers table has no measures

Then the analysis goes on. If you have the Northwind database available, you can try to do this exercise on your own. You will notice that several tables have a few numeric columns, but they are, in most cases, column IDs and ZIP codes. This is the case of Categories, Customers, Suppliers, Employees, and Territories. So, no measures in any of these tables.

Now, let's look at the Products table, shown in Figure 16.9.

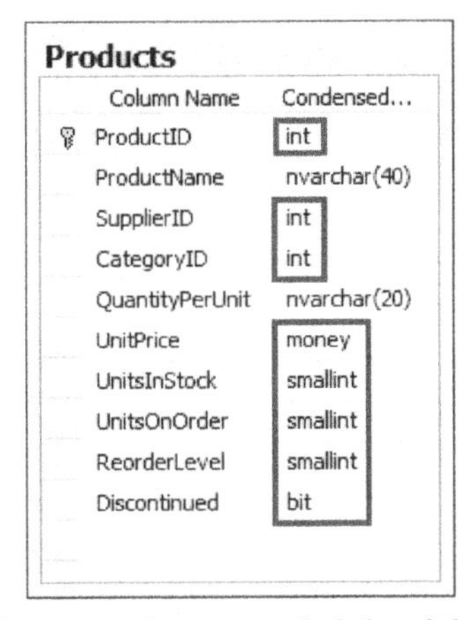

Products

Column Name	Condensed...
ProductID	int
ProductName	nvarchar(40)
SupplierID	int
CategoryID	int
QuantityPerUnit	nvarchar(20)
UnitPrice	money
UnitsInStock	smallint
UnitsOnOrder	smallint
ReorderLevel	smallint
Discontinued	bit

Figure 16.9: The Products table has ten columns, and eight of them are numeric

The Products table has eight numeric columns. The first three are clearly IDs, but for the last five, we need to see some values. See Figure 16.10.

The last five columns are a bit difficult to understand. If we look at the "Discontinued" column, we notice that the numbers seem to be always 1 or 0, which suggests that it is a Boolean flag representing true or false. This column is unlikely to be used as a measure. "ReorderLevel" is an example of a column that would require a bit of clarification from the end-users. But let's keep in mind, we are searching if the table contains "at least one measure". So, let's look at the other columns. Without a doubt, UnitsInStock and UnitsOnOrder are measures, so we can conclude that Products is a table that we must flag with the symbol "#", which means "containing at least one measure".

ProductID	ProductName	SupplierID	CategoryID	QuantityPerUnit	UnitPrice	UnitsInStock	UnitsOnOrder	ReorderLevel	Discontinued
1	Chai	1	1	10 boxes x 20 bags	18	39	0	10	0
2	Chang	1	1	24 - 12 oz bottles	19	17	40	25	0
3	Aniseed Syrup	1	2	12 - 550 ml bottles	10	13	70	25	0
4	Chef Anton's Cajun Seasoning	2	2	48 - 6 oz jars	22	53	0	0	0
5	Chef Anton's Gumbo Mix	2	2	36 boxes	21.35	0	0	0	1
6	Grandma's Boysenberry Spread	3	2	12 - 8 oz jars	25	120	0	25	0
7	Uncle Bob's Organic Dried Pears	3	7	12 - 1 lb pkgs.	30	15	0	10	0
8	Northwoods Cranberry Sauce	3	2	12 - 12 oz jars	40	6	0	0	0
9	Mishi Kobe Niku	4	6	18 - 500 g pkgs.	97	29	0	0	1
10	Ikura	4	8	12 - 200 ml jars	31	31	0	0	0
11	Queso Cabrales	5	4	1 kg pkg.	21	22	30	30	0
12	Queso Manchego La Pastora	5	4	10 - 500 g pkgs.	38	86	0	0	0
13	Konbu	6	8	2 kg box	6	24	0	5	0
14	Tofu	6	7	40 - 100 g pkgs.	23.25	35	0	0	0
15	Genen Shouyu	6	2	24 - 250 ml bottles	15.5	39	0	5	0
16	Pavlova	7	3	32 - 500 g boxes	17.45	29	0	10	0

Figure 16.10: The first few rows of Products: samples help understanding data

The OrderDetails table contains the unit price, the quantity, and the discount. These three columns will be used to produce the most important measure of the database: the gross revenue. Clearly, OrderDetails must be flagged with a "#". As a rule of thumb, the tables at the very left of the Oriented Data Model usually contain measures. This is not always true (EmployeeTerritories does not contain measures), but as a general trend, it is quite true.

The Orders table contains the freight, which is a measure. Very often, the Orders table, which represents the header of an order, does not contain any measures. But in this case it does, and that's going to be interesting.

Finally, EmployeeTerritories contains no measures, despite being on the left. This table has only two columns, and they are both IDs.

Figure 16.11 contains the Oriented Data Model of Northwind, enriched with the information about the measures.

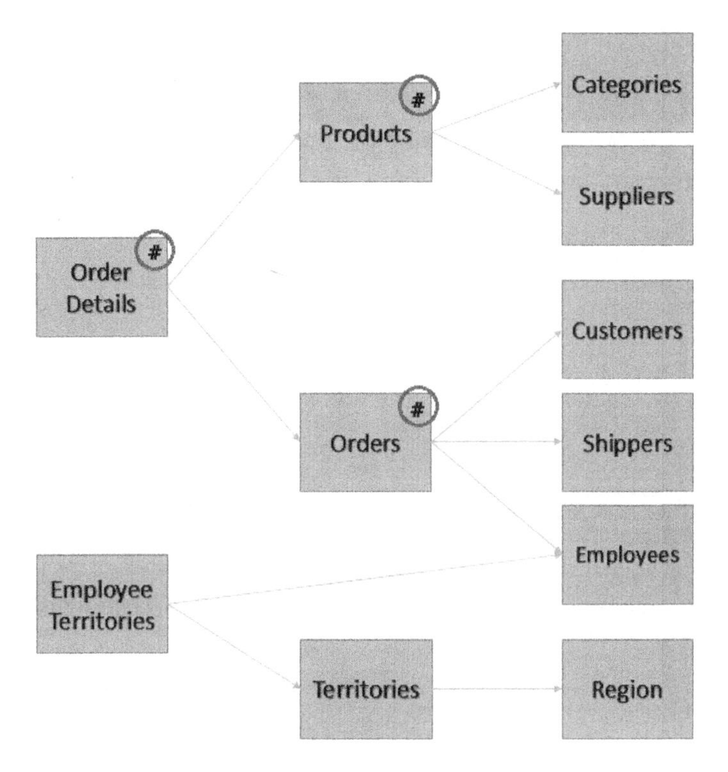

Figure 16.11: The data model of Northwind based on the ODM convention and with the "#" symbol, showing that three tables contain measures

After this exercise, we have found out that three tables contain at least one measure, while the other eight tables have no measures at all.

Now that we have all the information, we are ready to detect the challenges.

Based on the theory that we have seen in the past chapters, we can easily observe that the Northwind database has no loops, but it has two fan traps and one chasm trap, as shown in Figure 16.12.

OrderDetails and Products form a fan trap because the measures of Products will get exploded by OrderDetails, which is on the left. OrderDetails and Orders also form a fan trap because the measures of Orders will get exploded by OrderDetails, which is on the left. Employees, Orders, and EmployeeTerritories form a chasm trap, where Employees is the table "X", because it has two tables on the left. It is a chasm trap with measures because the measures of Orders will get exploded by EmployeeTerritories. Not only the measures of Orders but also the ones of OrderDetails will get exploded by EmployeeTerritories, as we will see later in this chapter. And we can say the same for the measures of Products.

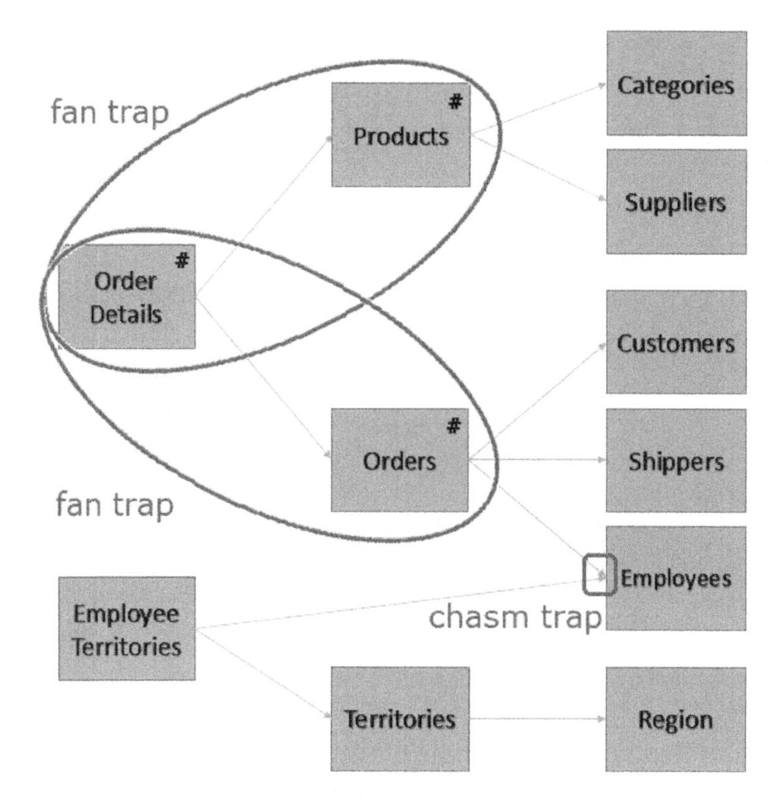

Figure 16.12: Thanks to the ODM convention we can immediately detect two fan traps and one chasm trap

---

In a chasm trap, the measures of one branch will get exploded by tables of the other branch (or branches).

So, now we have detected three traps. Great! The next question is, what shall we do with them? Why should we care about these three traps?

We must care because, by detecting the traps, we can avoid creating queries that deliver incorrect results. There is no need to test it. No need to join tables, run a query, look at the measures, and compare them with the ones in the source systems, hoping that they will match. They will not! We can already see, from the Oriented Data Model, that some queries will inevitably produce incorrect totals.

Understanding the effect of the traps

Let's verify the effect of the three traps that we have detected and understand why they are dangerous. The general method is to create two queries.

1. The first query must be based uniquely on the table that we want to analyze: this will give us the correct totals.
2. The second query must join that table with the other table(s) forming the trap. We want to test if it's true that the totals will become incorrect.

Figure 16.13 contains a query on the Products table on its own.

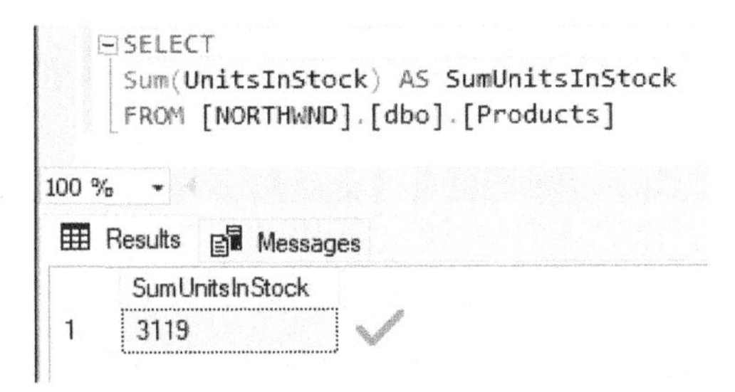

Figure 16.13: A query on Products on its own will show the correct total for the units in stock

The correct total for the units in stock is 3119. We need to keep this number in mind and compare it with the total of the second query.

Let's now run a query on Products joined with OrderDetails, shown in Figure 16.14. The total 85760 for the units in stock is clearly incorrect. The correct total is 3119. This error is due to the fan trap. The Products table gets exploded by OrderDetails, which is on the left.

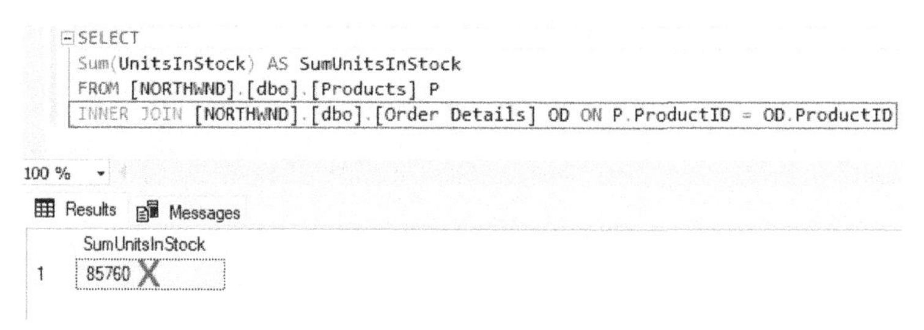

Figure 16.14: A query on Products joined with OrderDetails will show an incorrect total for the units in stock

Now, looking at the data model in Figure 16.12, we can see that there are two tables (Categories and Suppliers) on the right of Products. What happens if we join Products with Categories and Suppliers? See Figure 16.15.

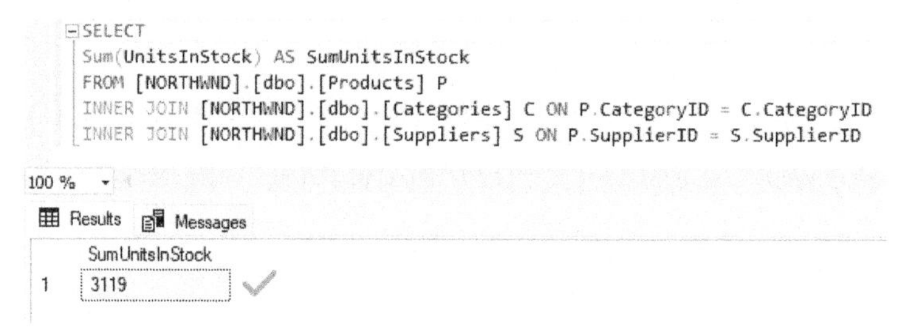

Figure 16.15: A query on Products joined with Categories and Suppliers will show the correct total for the units in stock

As we can see, this query is OK. After joining Products with the two tables, we still have the correct total for the units in stock. This is because Categories and Suppliers are on the right of Products. Please note that the query in Figure 16.15 does not retrieve any column from Categories, nor from Suppliers. During this testing phase, there is no need for adding columns: the join, alone, will tell us whether or not the measures will explode.

We can conclude the test by saying that some joins are allowed, and some are not. This introduces the concept of the "safe zone for a table".

The safe zone

In our test, we have seen that Products can be safely joined with Categories and Suppliers, because these two tables are on the right. On the other hand, when joining with OrderDetails, the totals of Products will get exploded, because OrderDetails is on the left.

The "safe zone for a table" is that subset of tables that can be safely joined with that table with no risk of duplicating the measures.

Figure 16.16 shows the "safe zone for Products", which is limited to the two tables on its right.

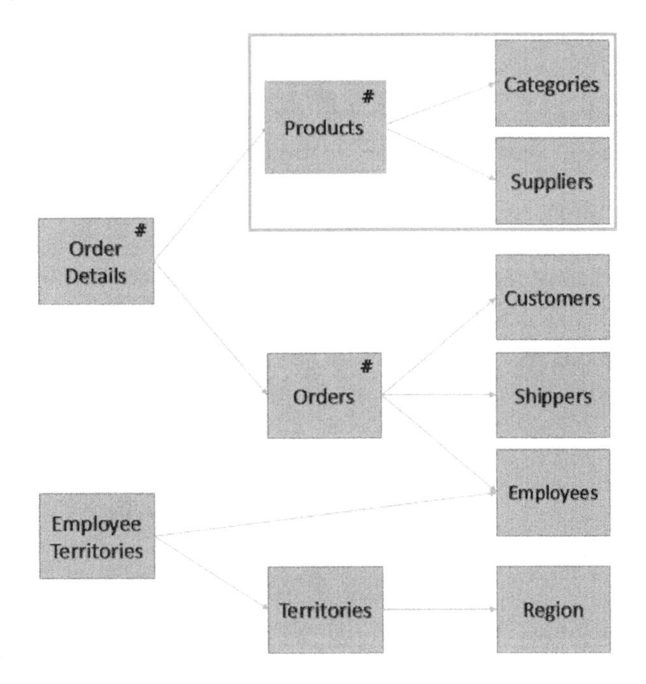

Figure 16.16: The safe zone for Products

If we want to display the measures of Products in a report or dashboard, we can safely join it with Categories and with Suppliers, because these two tables are on the right of Products. We cannot, however, safely join it with OrderDetails, because this table is on the left. Consequently, we cannot join Products with any other of the tables of this data model because the path to any other table would need to go through OrderDetails.

It is important to understand that a join between Products and OrderDetails, in general, is not wrong. If your focus is on the measures that come from OrderDetails, you can indeed join those two tables. However, you cannot include in the query the measures that come from Products.

Please note that we speak about the safe zone for a table only when that table contains at least one measure. The tables with no measures are never under threat. Our database has three tables containing measures, and for this reason, we can draw one safe zone for each of these three.

Let's have a look at the safe zone for Orders, shown in Figure 16.17.

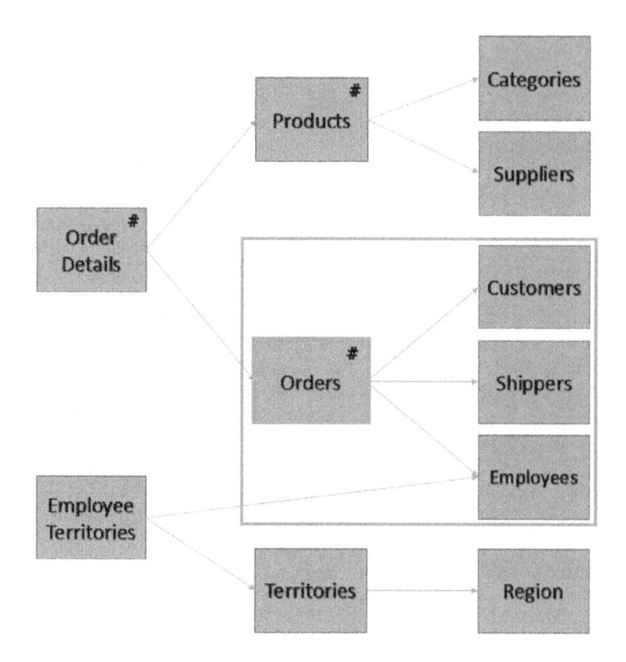

Figure 16.17: The safe zone for Orders

The safe zone for Orders consists of Customers, Shippers, and Employees because these three tables are on the right of Orders. If we add OrderDetails to our query, the totals of Orders will get exploded, because OrderDetails is on the left.

Consequently, Products, Categories, and Suppliers cannot be joined because the path would need to go through OrderDetails, which is outside of the safe zone for Orders.

EmployeeTerritories is also outside of the safe zone for Orders because it is on the left of Employees. Consequently, also Territories and Region cannot be joined, because the path would need to go through EmployeeTerritories.

The safe zone for a table is given by all those tables that can be reached by moving from left to right.

From Orders, you can safely go to Employees, because the movement is from left to right. However, from Employees, you cannot go to EmployeeTerritories, because the movement is from right to left.

In practical terms, if you disobey the rule, what happens? In this case, if you involve EmployeeTerritories in your query, some EmployeeID will get exploded by EmployeeTerritories. This will generate a duplicate of the entire row where the EmployeeID appears, and that row may also contain a measure, thereby creating a duplicate measure.

Please note that this whole concept of a safe zone for a table is based on the assumption that the PKs of all the tables are really unique. Sometimes they are supposed to be unique, but then in practice, they are not. This typically happens when your data source has been manipulated by a developer who has created duplicates by mistake, which is a very frequent scenario. For example, if the

Customers table has two different rows with the same customer ID, then you will inevitably have double measures for all the orders associated with that customer ID. We always recommend to verify the uniqueness of the PKs, both during the development phase and during the maintenance phase of your BI project.

Let's have a look at the safe zone for OrderDetails now, shown in Figure 16.18.

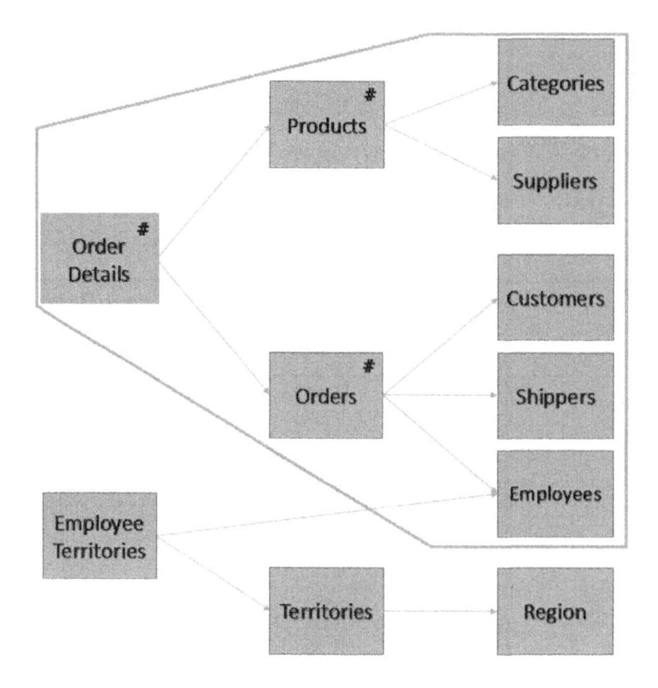

Figure 16.18: The safe zone for OrderDetails

When you are focusing on the measures of OrderDetails, the safe zone is quite big. All of the tables that are on the right of OrderDetails are safe because they will cause no explosion. Please note that this is the safe zone for OrderDetails, but it is totally unsafe for the measures of Products and Orders, as we have seen before. The only tables outside of the safe zone for OrderDetails are EmployeeTerritories, Territories, and Region. This is because EmployeeTerritories is on the left of Employees. Consequently, Territories and Region cannot be joined, because the path to those tables would require going through EmployeeTerritories. The measures from OrderDetails will get exploded if you add EmployeeTerritories to the query.

So, again, let's test if it's true!

First of all, we create a query on OrderDetails on its own, as shown in Figure 16.19.

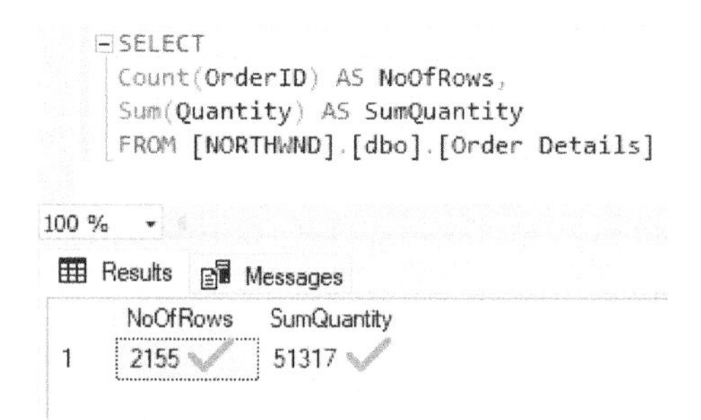

Figure 16.19: A query on OrderDetails on its own will show the correct total for the quantity

The correct total for the quantity is 51317. Please keep this number in mind.

The OrderDetails table has 2155 rows. A good developer always keeps the number of rows of a query under control. Ideally, before we launch a query, we should always know in advance how many rows we expect. For example, if we create a query from OrderDetails together with all the tables that are inside the safe zone for OrderDetails, connected with a left join, we expect to get 2155 rows again. Not one more, not one less. If this does not happen, then we need to investigate: we will probably find out that the PK of one of those tables is not unique.

Figure 16.20 shows the query extended to all the tables that are within the safe zone for OrderDetails.

The number of rows is still 2155, and the total quantity is still correct at 51317. All good.

```
SELECT
Count(OD.OrderID) AS NoOfRows,
Sum(OD.Quantity) AS SumQuantity
FROM [NORTHWND].[dbo].[Order Details] OD
LEFT JOIN [NORTHWND].[dbo].[Products] Prod ON OD.ProductID = Prod.ProductID
LEFT JOIN [NORTHWND].[dbo].[Categories] Cat ON Prod.CategoryID = Cat.CategoryID
LEFT JOIN [NORTHWND].[dbo].[Suppliers] Sup ON Prod.SupplierID = Sup.SupplierID
LEFT JOIN [NORTHWND].[dbo].[Orders] Ord ON OD.OrderID = Ord.OrderID
LEFT JOIN [NORTHWND].[dbo].[Customers] Cust ON Ord.CustomerID = Cust.CustomerID
LEFT JOIN [NORTHWND].[dbo].[Shippers] Ship ON Ord.ShipVia = Ship.ShipperID
LEFT JOIN [NORTHWND].[dbo].[Employees] Emp ON Ord.EmployeeID = Emp.EmployeeID
```

100 %

Results Messages

	NoOfRows	SumQuantity
1	2155	51317

Figure 16.20: A query within the safe zone for OrderDetails will show the correct totals for all the measures of OrderDetails

As we said before, this query is made only for the purpose of a technical test. Of course, there would be no business reason to create a query with many joined tables without retrieving columns from any of them: if you add tables to a query, it's usually because you want to retrieve some additional columns. This query has no business reason, but it has a very good technical reason: it provides a very quick integrity check.

Figure 16.21 shows an example of a query that has a proper business meaning. It shows the ordered quantity by product category.

If you sum all the eight quantities, you will obtain 51317, which is the correct total. And if you sum the eight row counters, you will obtain 2155, which is the correct total row count. Within the safe zone for OrderDetails, the totals of measures belonging to OrderDetails are always correct, because there is no explosion of rows.

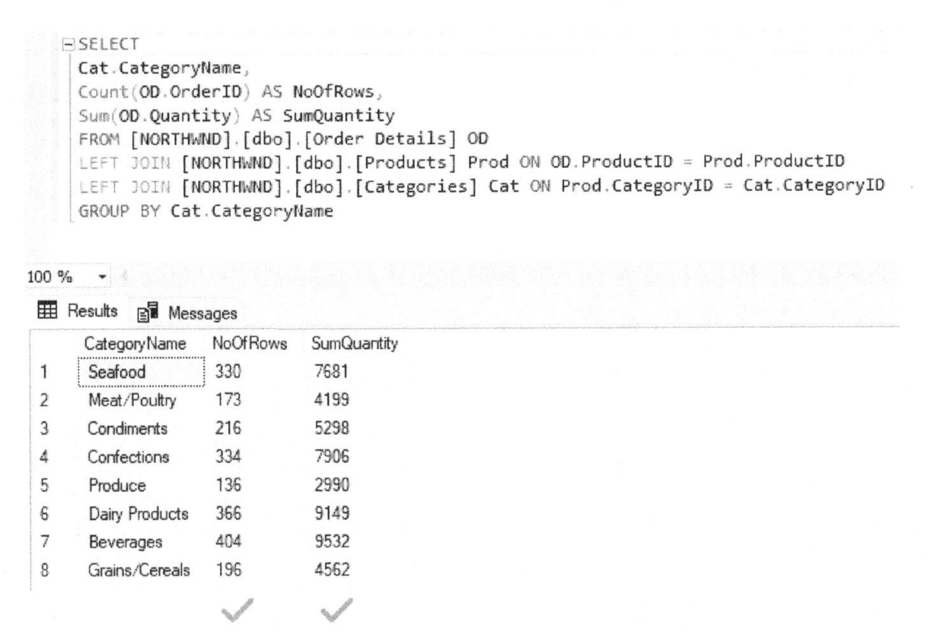

```
SELECT
Cat.CategoryName,
Count(OD.OrderID) AS NoOfRows,
Sum(OD.Quantity) AS SumQuantity
FROM [NORTHWND].[dbo].[Order Details] OD
LEFT JOIN [NORTHWND].[dbo].[Products] Prod ON OD.ProductID = Prod.ProductID
LEFT JOIN [NORTHWND].[dbo].[Categories] Cat ON Prod.CategoryID = Cat.CategoryID
GROUP BY Cat.CategoryName
```

100 %

Results Messages

	CategoryName	NoOfRows	SumQuantity
1	Seafood	330	7681
2	Meat/Poultry	173	4199
3	Condiments	216	5298
4	Confections	334	7906
5	Produce	136	2990
6	Dairy Products	366	9149
7	Beverages	404	9532
8	Grains/Cereals	196	4562

Figure 16.21: Example of a proper business query

Now let's create a new query that goes outside of the safe zone for OrderDetails and see what happens. We can see in Figure 16.22 that the EmployeeTerritories table has been added to our query.

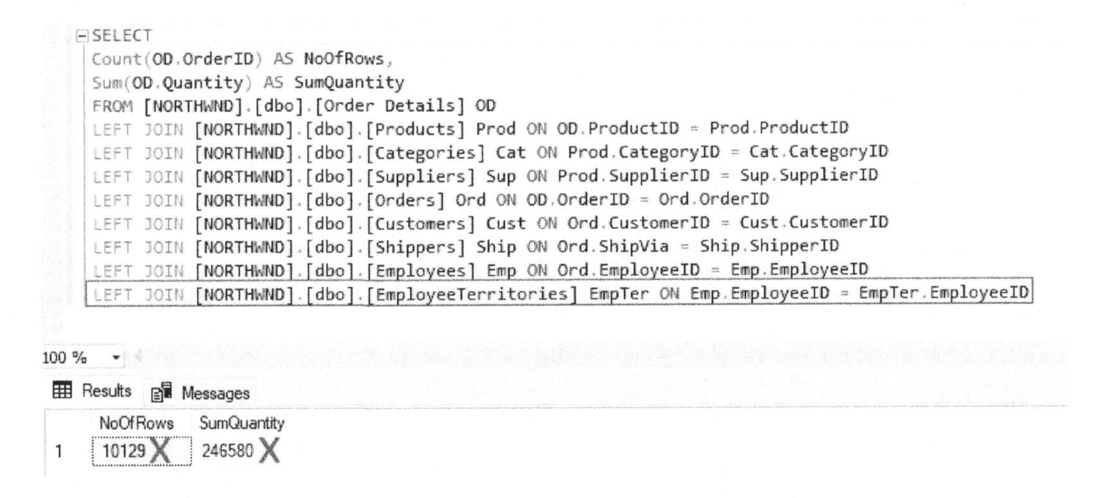

```
SELECT
Count(OD.OrderID) AS NoOfRows,
Sum(OD.Quantity) AS SumQuantity
FROM [NORTHWND].[dbo].[Order Details] OD
LEFT JOIN [NORTHWND].[dbo].[Products] Prod ON OD.ProductID = Prod.ProductID
LEFT JOIN [NORTHWND].[dbo].[Categories] Cat ON Prod.CategoryID = Cat.CategoryID
LEFT JOIN [NORTHWND].[dbo].[Suppliers] Sup ON Prod.SupplierID = Sup.SupplierID
LEFT JOIN [NORTHWND].[dbo].[Orders] Ord ON OD.OrderID = Ord.OrderID
LEFT JOIN [NORTHWND].[dbo].[Customers] Cust ON Ord.CustomerID = Cust.CustomerID
LEFT JOIN [NORTHWND].[dbo].[Shippers] Ship ON Ord.ShipVia = Ship.ShipperID
LEFT JOIN [NORTHWND].[dbo].[Employees] Emp ON Ord.EmployeeID = Emp.EmployeeID
LEFT JOIN [NORTHWND].[dbo].[EmployeeTerritories] EmpTer ON Emp.EmployeeID = EmpTer.EmployeeID
```

100 %

Results Messages

	NoOfRows	SumQuantity
1	10129 X	246580 X

Figure 16.22: A query involving any table that is outside of the safe zone for OrderDetails will produce duplicates and incorrect totals for the measures of OrderDetails

The query now has been exploded by EmployeeTerritories. The expected number of rows is 2155, while now they are 10129. And the total quantity, of course, is completely incorrect. This proves the concept: whenever your query goes outside of the safe zone for OrderDetails, the resulting totals for the measures of OrderDetails will be incorrect.

So, let's draw some conclusions.

Northwind is a very small database. However, the traditional SQL approach on Northwind has a high risk of having incorrect totals because the database has two fan traps and one chasm trap. If you create a standard SQL query that involves all the 11 tables of the database, all the totals of all the measures will be incorrect. This is certainly not due to a problem of size (the result has only 10129 rows), but rather to a principle that we have already mentioned: some particular combinations of tables cannot be joined together.

Have you ever been in a project where all the numbers were completely wrong? If yes, now you have a probable explanation.

From ad-hoc to self-service BI

Some particular combinations of tables cannot be joined together.

In many cases, developers are completely unaware of this. And this is not surprising because there is not much literature about fan traps, chasm traps, and many-to-many joins. And the existing literature is very often unclear or conflictive.

The most common practice today is "write a query, and see what happens". If some sample numbers are matching the data source, then the query is approved for production, and maybe only a few months later (or years), someone will realize that there are duplicates and incorrect numbers. Then the problem is very often solved by hacking the front end and using complex formulas that attempt to "de-duplicate" the numbers. This is not a good process.

In many other cases, however, the developer is aware that a combination of tables will produce duplicates. This is an interesting scenario. How do they solve this problem? The most common solution today is the "ad-hoc approach". For each new requirement, a new tailor-made query is created.

The ad-hoc approach works, but it is expensive. It's a small luxury, like wearing only tailor-made suits. We may want to buy an expensive suit for a special occasion, sure. But otherwise, we can simply go to a shop and buy a ready-to-wear suit (or, in French, prêt-à-porter). It will probably satisfy our needs, it will be cheaper, and we will have it immediately.

The Unified Star Schema is the "prêt-à-porter of data modeling".

With the USS approach, the tables are ready to be connected. The end-users do not need to be data experts, because the method is always the same: "take the tables that you need, and connect them to the Bridge by the KEY columns that have identical names". Each data element can be found in a table that has an appropriate and sensible name. The data about employees can be found in the Employees table. The data about sales can be found in the Sales table. The data about products can be found in the Products table. This is how the end-users expect data to be organized!

This is made possible by the fact that the USS approach uses normalized tables, and the USS naming convention makes it very easy to connect them together.

Self-service BI means that a business user can retrieve the needed information in a natural and intuitive way, with no need for help from data experts. This goal cannot be achieved by simply buying new software: it also requires data to be properly organized.

The best self-service BI experience can be achieved by combining a good technology with the Unified Star Schema.

In the next section, we will see how the Unified Star Schema can simplify a challenging business requirement.

Example of a challenging business requirement

Imagine that you have to implement this business requirement:

"Show the total ordered quantity and the product units in stock, by category name".

This requirement sounds easy, but it is actually quite challenging.

All the needed information comes from three tables: OrderDetails, Products, and Categories, highlighted in Figure 16.23.

So, can we simply create a query that joins these three tables together? Unfortunately, no, we cannot. Let's see why.

There is definitely no problem with Categories—this table has no measures. Tables with no measures are never under threat. There is also no problem with OrderDetails—this table has measures, but the other tables of the query are on its right.

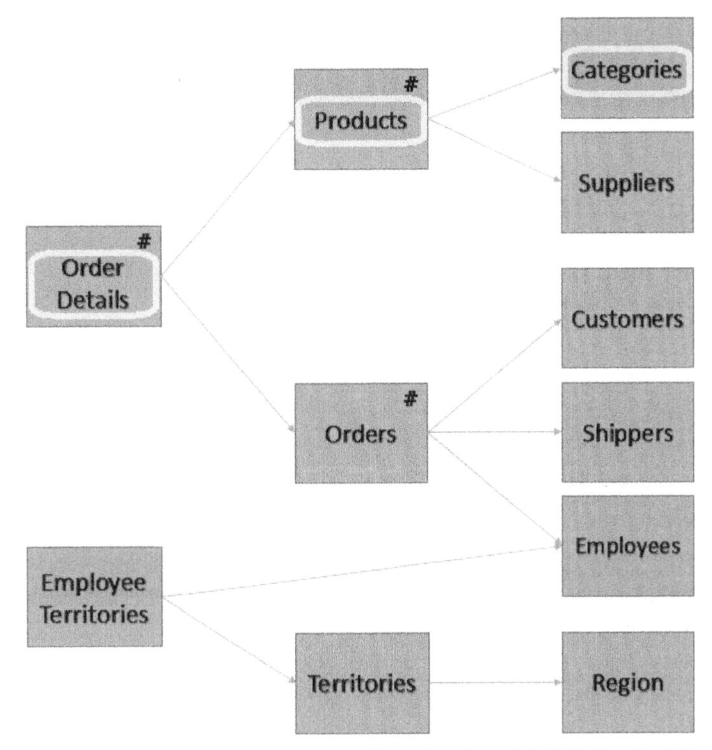

Figure 16.23: The business requirement is based on the three highlighted tables

The problem is with the Products table. It has a measure that is needed for this business requirement (the units in stock), and it is exploded by OrderDetails, which is on its left. If you create a standard join of these three tables, you will obtain incorrect totals for the units in stock.

Let's see in Figure 16.24 if this is true.

Despite looking very simple, this query is incorrect. The SQL engine gives the message "Query executed successfully", and for this reason, the SQL developer may probably think that everything is fine. But it is not.

The units in stock are 3119 in total, while the total resulting from this query is macroscopically bigger. This is because we have created a join with a fan trap.

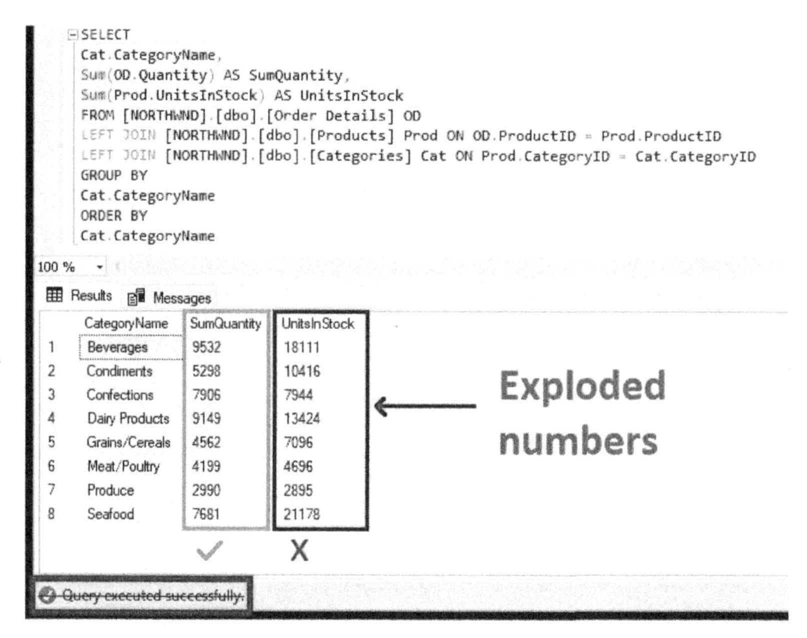

Figure 16.24: Example of an incorrect SQL query

The problem can be solved by creating a different query with multiple SELECT sub-queries, as shown in Figure 16.25.

This query is a bit more complex, but it is correct. If you make the sum of the displayed units in stock, you will obtain 3119, which is the correct total.

But there are a few problems here: this query is not easy to create, not easy to maintain, and it is hardly re-usable. This is actually the ad-hoc approach that we are trying to eliminate.

If we create a new ad-hoc query for every new business requirement, then every new business requirement will become a project on its own, and the business intelligence infrastructure will grow out of control.

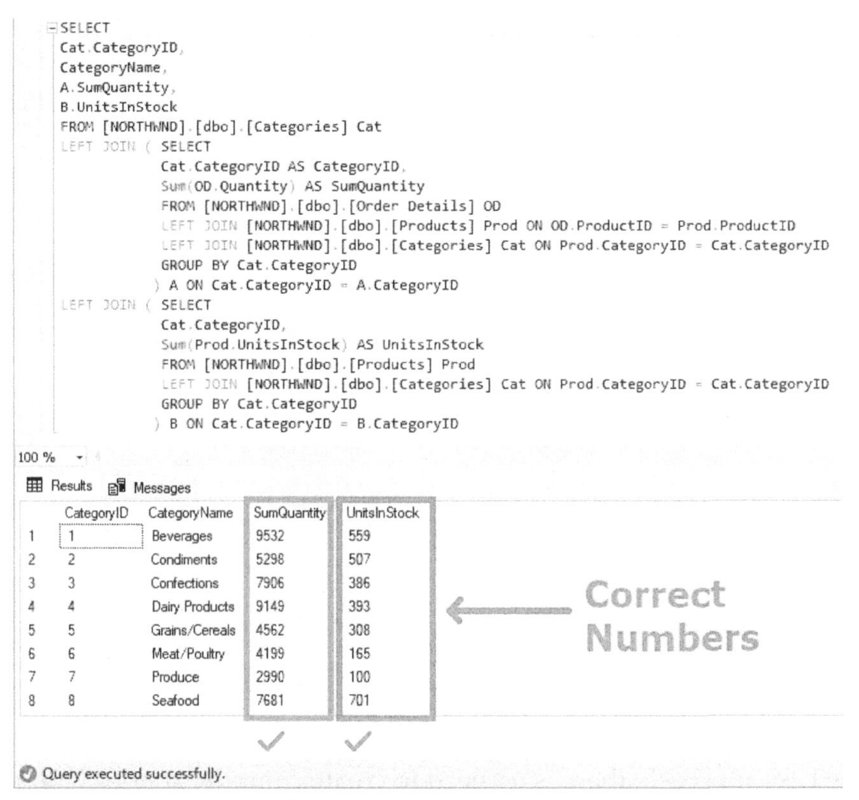

```
SELECT
Cat.CategoryID,
CategoryName,
A.SumQuantity,
B.UnitsInStock
FROM [NORTHWND].[dbo].[Categories] Cat
LEFT JOIN ( SELECT
            Cat.CategoryID AS CategoryID,
            Sum(OD.Quantity) AS SumQuantity
            FROM [NORTHWND].[dbo].[Order Details] OD
            LEFT JOIN [NORTHWND].[dbo].[Products] Prod ON OD.ProductID = Prod.ProductID
            LEFT JOIN [NORTHWND].[dbo].[Categories] Cat ON Prod.CategoryID = Cat.CategoryID
            GROUP BY Cat.CategoryID
          ) A ON Cat.CategoryID = A.CategoryID
LEFT JOIN ( SELECT
            Cat.CategoryID,
            Sum(Prod.UnitsInStock) AS UnitsInStock
            FROM [NORTHWND].[dbo].[Products] Prod
            LEFT JOIN [NORTHWND].[dbo].[Categories] Cat ON Prod.CategoryID = Cat.CategoryID
            GROUP BY Cat.CategoryID
          ) B ON Cat.CategoryID = B.CategoryID
```

	CategoryID	CategoryName	SumQuantity	UnitsInStock
1	1	Beverages	9532	559
2	2	Condiments	5298	507
3	3	Confections	7906	386
4	4	Dairy Products	9149	393
5	5	Grains/Cereals	4562	308
6	6	Meat/Poultry	4199	165
7	7	Produce	2990	100
8	8	Seafood	7681	701

Figure 16.25: Example of how to adjust the previous SQL query

If we create a new ad-hoc query for every new business requirement, every organization will end up having a multitude of queries, views, reports, dashboards, cubes, scripts, batches, processes, scheduled jobs, and more. All of these resources will increase the complexity of the business intelligence infrastructure and the effort to maintain it. Furthermore, when the organization will face a migration, it will be very hard to find reliable documentation about all these resources. Many of the existing reports and dashboards might be obsolete, but no one will want to take the responsibility to dismiss them. As a result, everything will get migrated, including obsolete resources. With this approach, the business intelligence infrastructure will grow out of control.

With the USS approach, the complexity of the business intelligence infrastructure is drastically reduced. Let's see how.

How the USS implements the Northwind database

With the USS approach, all of the tables belong to a common safe zone—everything is compatible with everything. See Figure 16.26.

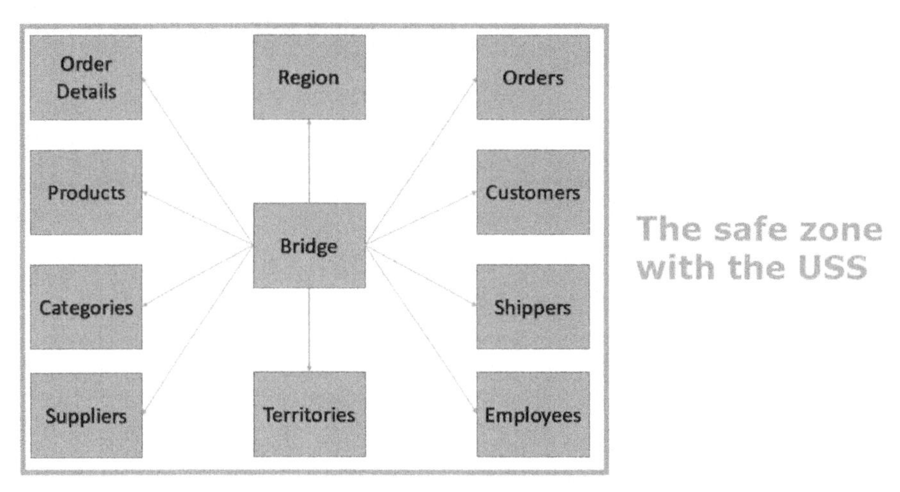

Figure 16.26: With the USS approach, all the tables belong to a common safe zone

With the USS approach, there is no need to create complex queries with multiple SELECT sub-queries. There is no need to create separate queries and then merge them inside a BI tool. There is no risk of having incorrect totals derived from fan traps. There is no risk of having duplicates derived from chasm traps and many-to-many relationships. There is no problem with loops. There is no problem when data is at different granularities. The way the structure is built does not depend on the business requirements.

With the USS approach, everything is easy.

The end-users simply need to load the Bridge, pick the tables that are useful to their need, connect them to the Bridge, make sure that joins are left joins (or associations, when possible), and then navigate in freedom within the BI tool. Let's see some practical implementations.

Implementations with various BI tools

This section contains sample implementations with different BI tools. The aim is to compare the traditional approach with the USS approach and to show that the Unified Star Schema is compatible with all the technologies of business intelligence.

For these implementations, we have chosen to save the tables in CSV format.

The choice of the physical format for the tables is totally up to the solution architect. In general, they can be produced as tables of a database, as well as in CSV files, XML, JSON, Avro, Parquet, or any other format that is capable of logically representing a table, either on-premises or in the cloud.

A set of CSV files has been prepared, as shown in Figure 16.27.

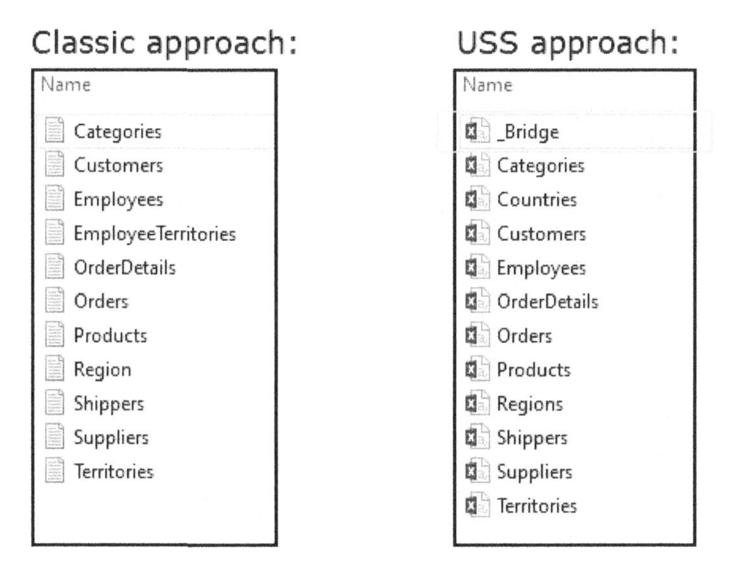

Figure 16.27: Preparing the CSV files based on the traditional approach and on the USS approach

For the sole purpose of differentiating the two approaches, the files following the traditional approach have the "txt" extension, while the ones following the

USS approach have the "csv" extension. This is also useful when using cloud environments because some of them tend to put all the files together, and the files with identical names and extensions would risk overriding each other.

Please note that the Bridge is named as _Bridge.csv, with a preceding underscore. By doing so, it will appear at the top of the list of files. This is a reminder to the end-users that they should always load the Bridge first.

Figure 16.28 shows an excerpt from the Bridge.

```
_Bridge.csv
1   Stage,_KEY_Countries,_KEY_Regions,_KEY_Territories,_KEY_EmpTer,_KEY_Emplo
    yees,_KEY_Suppliers,_KEY_Categories,_KEY_Shippers,_KEY_Customers,_KEY_Pro
    ducts,Product Unit Price,Product Units In Stock,Product Units On
    Order,Product Reorder Level,_KEY_Orders,Order Freight,_KEY_OrderDetails
2   Orders,FR,RE-1,,,EM-5,,,SH-3,CU-VINET,,,,,,OR-10248,32.38,
3   Orders,DE,RE-2,,,EM-6,,,SH-1,CU-TOMSP,,,,,,OR-10249,11.61,
4   Orders,BR,RE-1,,,EM-4,,,SH-2,CU-HANAR,,,,,,OR-10250,65.83,
5   Orders,FR,RE-4,,,EM-3,,,SH-1,CU-VICTE,,,,,,OR-10251,41.34,
6   Orders,BE,RE-1,,,EM-4,,,SH-2,CU-SUPRD,,,,,,OR-10252,51.3,
7   Orders,BR,RE-4,,,EM-3,,,SH-2,CU-HANAR,,,,,,OR-10253,58.17,
8   Orders,CH,RE-1,,,EM-5,,,SH-2,CU-CHOPS,,,,,,OR-10254,22.98,
9   Orders,CH,RE-3,,,EM-9,,,SH-3,CU-RICSU,,,,,,OR-10255,148.33,
10  Orders,BR,RE-4,,,EM-3,,,SH-2,CU-WELLI,,,,,,OR-10256,13.97,
11  Orders,VE,RE-1,,,EM-4,,,SH-3,CU-HILAA,,,,,,OR-10257,81.91,
12  Orders,AT,RE-1,,,EM-1,,,SH-1,CU-ERNSH,,,,,,OR-10258,140.51,
13  Orders,MX,RE-1,,,EM-4,,,SH-3,CU-CENTC,,,,,,OR-10259,3.25,
14  Orders,DE,RE-1,,,EM-4,,,SH-1,CU-OTTIK,,,,,,OR-10260,55.09,
15  Orders,BR,RE-1,,,EM-4,,,SH-2,CU-QUEDE,,,,,,OR-10261,3.05,
16  Orders,US,RE-3,,,EM-8,,,SH-3,CU-RATTC,,,,,,OR-10262,48.29,
```

Figure 16.28: The Bridge for Northwind

From this figure, we see that the Orders stage points to some tables but not to all of them. For example, _KEY_Countries and _KEY_Regions are populated, while _KEY_Territories is not: it means that Orders does not point to Territories. We can also notice a few columns containing measures: it means that for this implementation, we have chosen the technique of "moving all the measures to the Bridge". Then we can notice that the order freight in this stage is populated, while the other measures are not: this is because each measure must be positioned in the appropriate stage. The measures of Products can be found in the Products stage, while the measures of OrderDetails can be found in the OrderDetails stage. All as we would expect.

Now we will implement the challenging business requirement that we have seen earlier in this chapter. We will compare the traditional approach with the USS approach. We will also show how to append new requirements to the same query.

Implementation with Tibco Spotfire

We have to implement the business requirement: "show the total ordered quantity and the product units in stock, by category name". The information that we need for this requirement can be found in three tables: OrderDetails, Products, and Categories.

With Spotfire, we must start with a table, typically the most detailed, and then add the other tables with the command "Insert - Add Columns".

After loading these three tables, the resulting data model is shown in Figure 16.29.

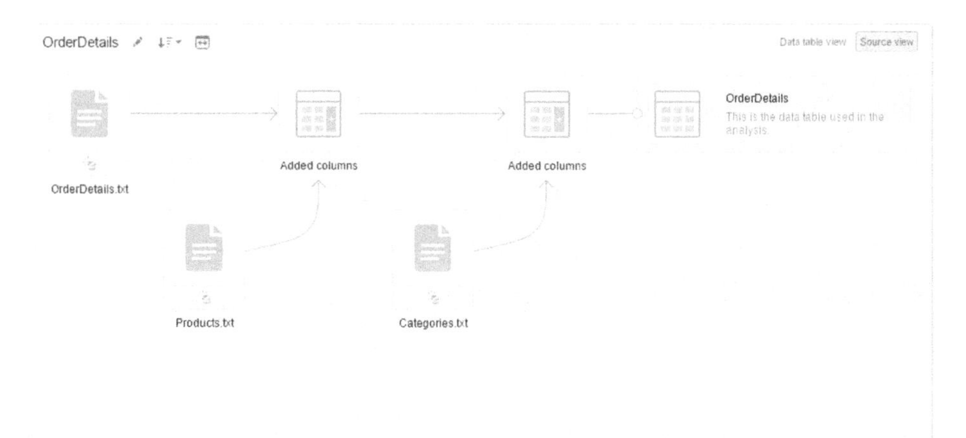

Figure 16.29: The Source view in Spotfire. With the traditional approach, columns are added to an initial detailed table

Spotfire creates one single denormalized table, as shown in Figure 16.30.

OrderDetails

Data table view | Source view

OrderID	ProductID	UnitPrice	Quantity	Discount	ProductName	SupplierID	CategoryID	QuantityPerUnit	UnitPrice (2)	UnitsInStock	UnitsOnOrder	ReorderLevel	Discontinued	CategoryName
10248	11	14.00	12	0.00	Queso Cabrales	5	4	1 kg pkg.	21.00	22	30	30	0	Dairy Products
10248	42	9.80	10	0.00	Singaporean Hokkien ...	20	5	32 - 1 kg pkgs.	14.00	26	0	0	1	Grains/Cereals
10248	72	34.80	5	0.00	Mozzarella di Giovanni	14	4	24 - 200 g pkgs.	34.80	14	0	0	0	Dairy Products
10249	14	18.60	9	0.00	Tofu	6	7	40 - 100 g pkgs.	23.25	35	0	0	0	Produce
10249	51	42.40	40	0.00	Manjimup Dried Apples	24	7	50 - 300 g pkgs.	53.00	20	0	10	0	Produce
10250	41	7.70	10	0.00	Jack's New England ...	19	8	12 - 12 oz cans	9.65	85	0	10	0	Seafood
10250	51	42.40	35	0.15	Manjimup Dried Apples	24	7	50 - 300 g pkgs.	53.00	20	0	10	0	Produce
10250	65	16.80	15	0.15	Louisiana Fiery Hot P...	2	2	32 - 8 oz bottles	21.05	76	0	0	0	Condiments
10251	22	16.80	6	0.05	Gustaf's Knäckebröd	9	5	24 - 500 g pkgs.	21.00	104	0	25	0	Grains/Cereals
10251	57	15.60	15	0.05	Ravioli Angelo	26	5	24 - 250 g pkgs.	19.50	36	0	20	0	Grains/Cereals
10251	65	16.80	20	0.00	Louisiana Fiery Hot P...	2	2	32 - 8 oz bottles	21.05	76	0	0	0	Condiments
10252	20	64.80	40	0.05	Sir Rodney's Marmal...	8	3	30 gift boxes	81.00	40	0	0	0	Confections
10252	33	2.00	25	0.05	Geitost	15	4	500 g	2.50	112	0	20	0	Dairy Products
10252	60	27.20	40	0.00	Camembert Pierrot	28	4	15 - 300 g rounds	34.00	19	0	0	0	Dairy Products
10253	31	10.00	20	0.00	Gorgonzola Telino	14	4	12 - 100 g pkgs	12.50	0	70	20	0	Dairy Products
10253	39	14.40	42	0.00	Chartreuse verte	18	1	750 cc per bottle	18.00	69	0	5	0	Beverages
10253	49	16.00	40	0.00	Maxilaku	23	3	24 - 50 g pkgs.	20.00	10	60	15	0	Confections
10254	24	3.60	15	0.15	Guaraná Fantástica	10	1	12 - 355 ml cans	4.50	20	0	0	1	Beverages
10254	55	19.20	21	0.15	Pâté chinois	25	6	24 boxes x 2 pies	24.00	115	0	20	0	Meat/Poultry
10254	74	8.00	21	0.00	Longlife Tofu	4	7	5 kg pkg.	10.00	4	20	5	0	Produce
10255	2	15.20	20	0.00	Chang	1	1	24 - 12 oz bottles	19.00	17	40	25	0	Beverages
10255	16	13.90	35	0.00	Pavlova	7	3	32 - 500 g boxes	17.45	29	0	10	0	Confections
10255	36	15.20	25	0.00	Inlagd Sill	17	8	24 - 250 g jars	19.00	112	0	20	0	Seafood
10255	59	44.00	30	0.00	Raclette Courdavault	28	4	5 kg pkg.	55.00	79	0	0	0	Dairy Products
10256	53	26.20	15	0.00	Perth Pasties	24	6	48 pieces	32.80	0	0	0	1	Meat/Poultry

Add rows

Figure 16.30: The Data Table view in Spotfire. The result obtained by using the traditional approach has duplicates

As we can see in this figure, multiple orders may include the same product. As a consequence, the units in stock are duplicated.

The resulting report is shown in Figure 16.31.

With Spotfire, we obtain the same results as we did with SQL, as shown earlier in Figure 16.24. The total for the ordered quantity is correct, but the total for the units in stock is not correct because the numbers have been exploded.

The column "Quantity" belongs to OrderDetails. The tables in this query are all from the safe zone for OrderDetails, and this is why the total for the quantity is correct. On the other hand, the column "UnitsInStock" comes from Products. In this query, we have OrderDetails, which is outside of the safe zone for Products, and this is why the total for the units in stock is not correct.

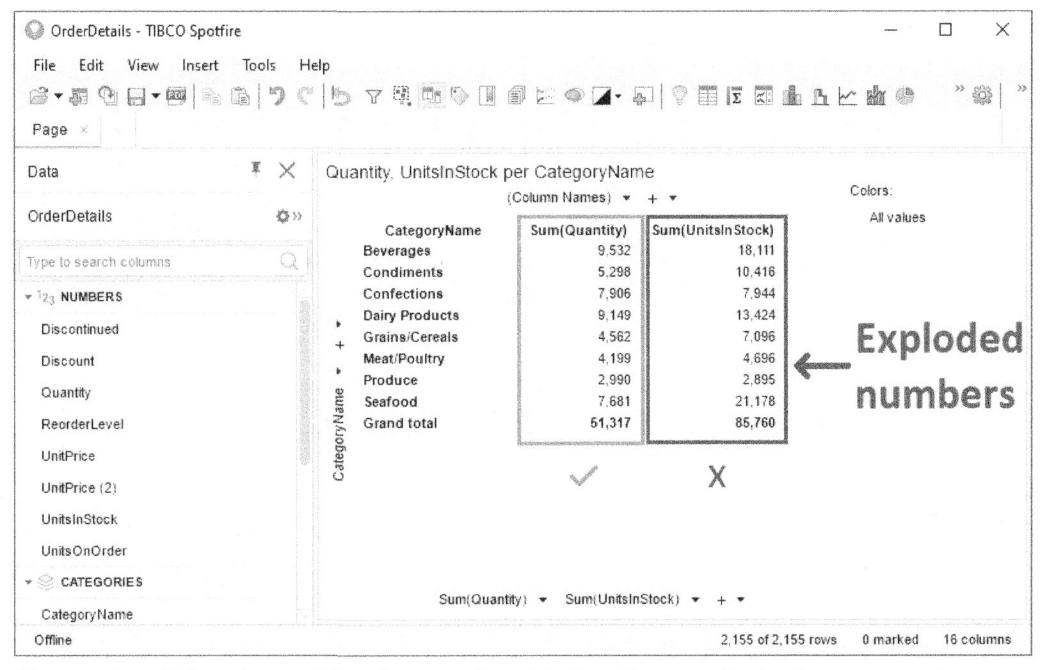

Figure 16.31: Using the traditional approach, with Spotfire, we obtain the same results as we did with SQL

This practical implementation proves that the definition of a safe zone for a table applies not only to SQL but also to the BI tools that create the join like SQL. We will see, in the next implementations, that the BI tools that create an association do not have this problem.

There is nothing wrong with SQL, and there is nothing wrong with the query created by Spotfire. The problem comes from a principle: some particular combinations of tables cannot be joined together. So, if we want to see the correct results with Spotfire, we need to change the approach.

Let's try now to implement the same requirement with the USS approach.

The first table to load is the Bridge, as always. See Figure 16.32.

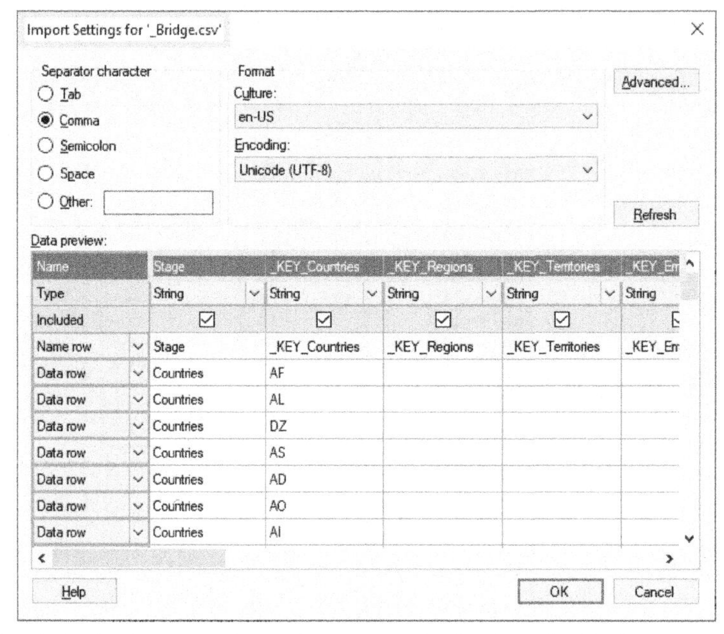

Figure 16.32: With the USS approach we always start by loading the Bridge

Then we can load the other tables. Figure 16.33 shows how to load OrderDetails.

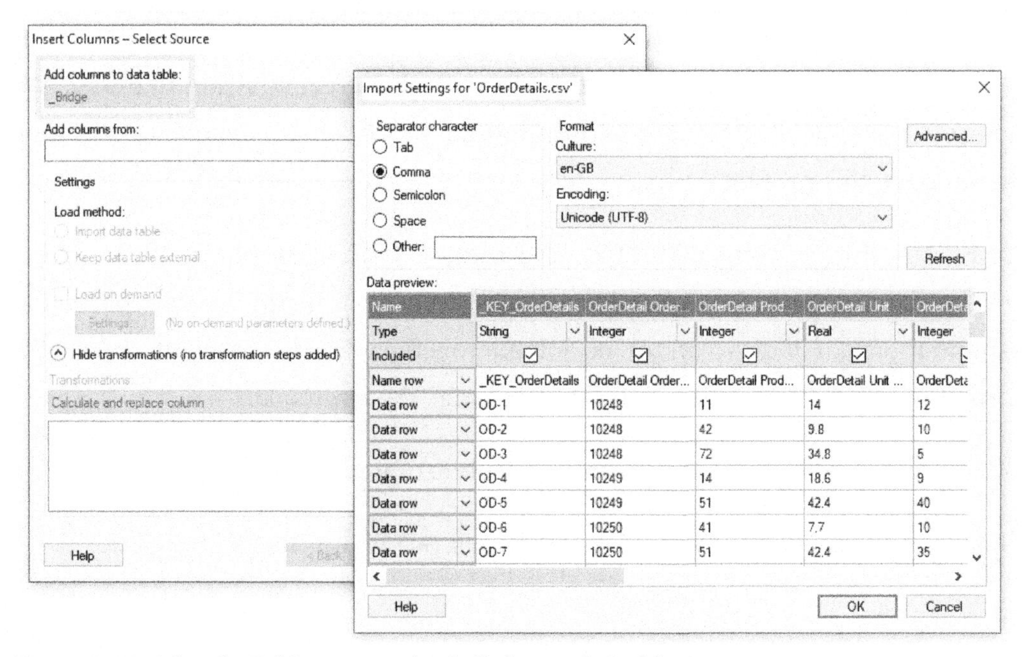

Figure 16.33: After the Bridge, we can load all the needed tables

After the Bridge, we can load all the needed tables. In this case, OrderDetails, Products, and Categories. See Figure 16.34.

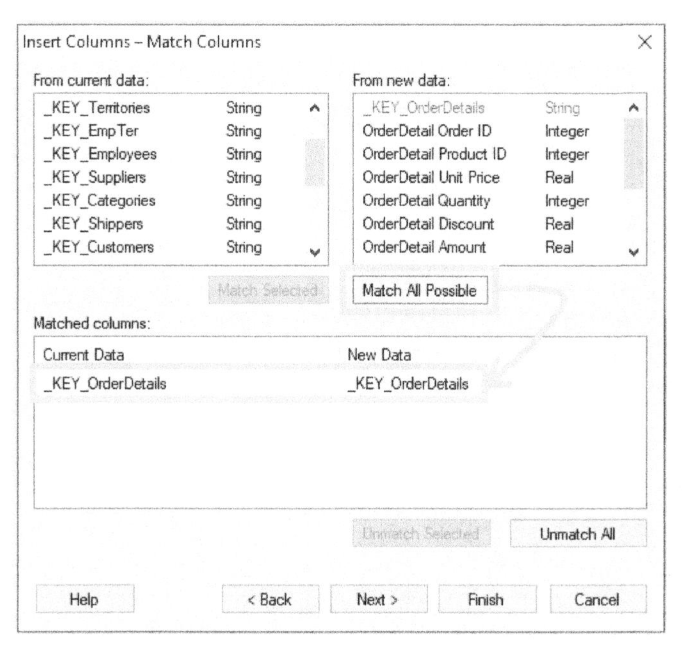

Figure 16.34: The USS naming convention makes it all much easier

While we load the tables, we can use the button "Match All Possible". This button automatically detects how to join the two tables, and thanks to the USS naming convention, we can fully trust it.

Make sure that the join is a left join, as shown in Figure 16.35.

And Figure 16.36 contains the report with the USS approach.

Now all totals are correct because the USS approach solves the fan trap.

But let's go a bit beyond now. Let's imagine that a new business requirement arises: "Order Freight by Shipper Company Name".

Insert Columns – Import

Columns to add from new data:

- [ ] OrderDetail Order ID
- [ ] OrderDetail Product ID
- [ ] OrderDetail Unit Price
- [ ] OrderDetail Quantity
- [ ] OrderDetail Discount
- [ ] OrderDetail Amount
- [ ] OrderDetail Category ID
- [ ] OrderDetail Supplier ID
- [ ] OrderDetail Customer ID
- [ ] OrderDetail Shipper ID

Select All | Clear All

Join method

- (●) Left outer (rows from current data only)
- ( ) Left single match (rows from current data only, single match from new)
- ( ) Full outer (all rows, from both current and new data)
- ( ) Inner (rows matching in both current and new data only)
- ( ) Right outer (rows from new data only)
- ( ) Right single match (rows from new data only, single match from current)

Options

- [ ] Treat empty values as equal

Help | < Back | Next > | Finish | Cancel

Figure 16.35: All joins must be left joins

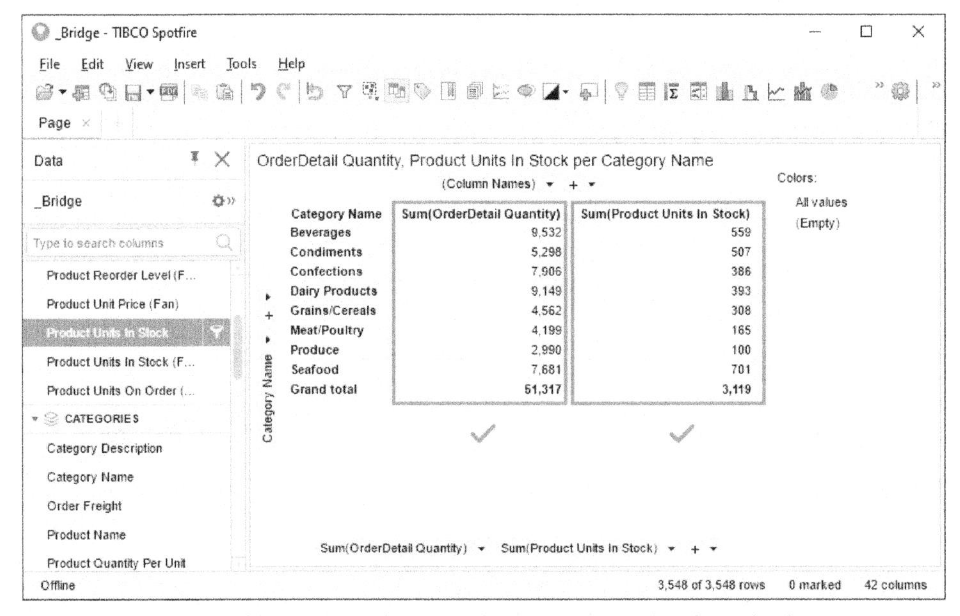

Figure 16.36: Now all totals are correct because the USS approach solves the fan trap

The information that we need can be found in two new tables: Orders and Shippers. With the traditional approach, these two new tables would not fit into the existing query because the query contains OrderDetails, which is outside of the safe zone for Orders: this would cause incorrect totals for the freight. As a consequence, the developer should create a separate query, most probably in a separate dashboard.

With the USS approach, instead, everything is compatible with everything. There is no need to create a new query for the new report. The new tables can be added to the existing query. Thanks to this, all the data will be fully integrated.

So, let's add the new tables. See Figure 16.37.

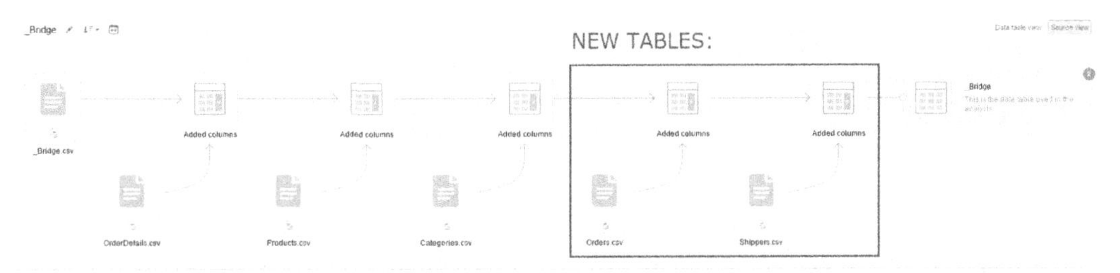

Figure 16.37: With the USS approach, we can always add new tables to an existing query

Now that we have loaded all the tables, we can show the two reports on the same page, as shown in Figure 16.38.

The reports are not only in the same place, but they are also fully integrated. A filter on the first report will propagate to the second report, and vice versa. This is happening automatically because all the data comes from one single query.

Now, with the USS approach, all of the tables are compatible with each other, and all of totals are correct.

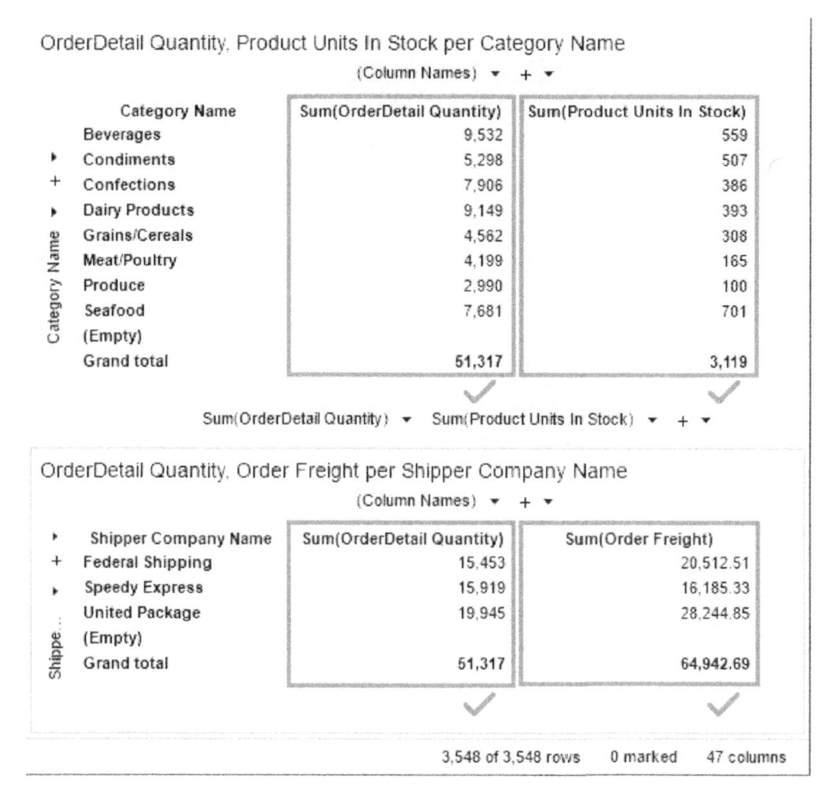

OrderDetail Quantity, Product Units In Stock per Category Name

Category Name	Sum(OrderDetail Quantity)	Sum(Product Units In Stock)
Beverages	9,532	559
Condiments	5,298	507
Confections	7,906	386
Dairy Products	9,149	393
Grains/Cereals	4,562	308
Meat/Poultry	4,199	165
Produce	2,990	100
Seafood	7,681	701
(Empty)		
Grand total	51,317	3,119

OrderDetail Quantity, Order Freight per Shipper Company Name

Shipper Company Name	Sum(OrderDetail Quantity)	Sum(Order Freight)
Federal Shipping	15,453	20,512.51
Speedy Express	15,919	16,185.33
United Package	19,945	28,244.85
(Empty)		
Grand total	51,317	64,942.69

3,548 of 3,548 rows 0 marked 47 columns

Figure 16.38: With the USS approach, we can always add new tables and new reports

Implementation with Tableau

Tableau is capable of association. For this reason, even with the traditional approach, the totals of the measures are always correct: as we have seen in chapter 11, the in-memory association is immune to the fan trap. The added value of the USS approach, in this case, is that the query is easier to create. Let's see it all in practice.

Let's start with the traditional approach. We will try to implement the same two reports as before. For these two reports, we need to create a query that loads OrderDetails, Products, Categories, Orders, and Shippers. Let's load them all at once.

We can start the query with any table, but we always recommend starting with the most detailed table, which in this case, is OrderDetails. See Figure 16.39.

Figure 16.39: Traditional approach using the "Data Source" page in Tableau—the query is not always easy to create

The main challenge, in this case, is that the end-user sometimes does not know how to connect the tables. For example, Shippers and Orders must connect through "Ship Via". If the end-user is not familiar with the underlying data model, this query will be too difficult to create. In other words, the end-user will need to ask for help from the IT department.

The resulting report is correct, as shown in Figure 16.40.

Let's try now the USS approach.

First of all, we must load the Bridge, and then we can add the other tables. This time, to try something different, we can add all the tables. Not only the five tables that are needed for the first two reports, but also the tables that may be needed for future reports. This is possible because, with the USS approach, every table is compatible with every other table.

Category Name	Quantity	Units In Stock
Beverages	9,532	559
Condiments	5,298	507
Confections	7,906	386
Dairy Products	9,149	393
Grains/Cereals	4,562	308
Meat/Poultry	4,199	165
Produce	2,990	100
Seafood	7,681	701
Grand Total	51,317	3,119

Figure 16.40: The report has correct totals because Tableau is capable of association

In a matter of seconds, and with no need to know the underlying data model, the end-user will be able to create the query in Figure 16.41.

The end-user does not need to know the underlying data model. Tableau has automatically connected the tables through the correct columns, and the end-users have no chance to make any mistake. This is thanks to the USS naming convention.

The resulting dashboard is shown in Figure 16.42.

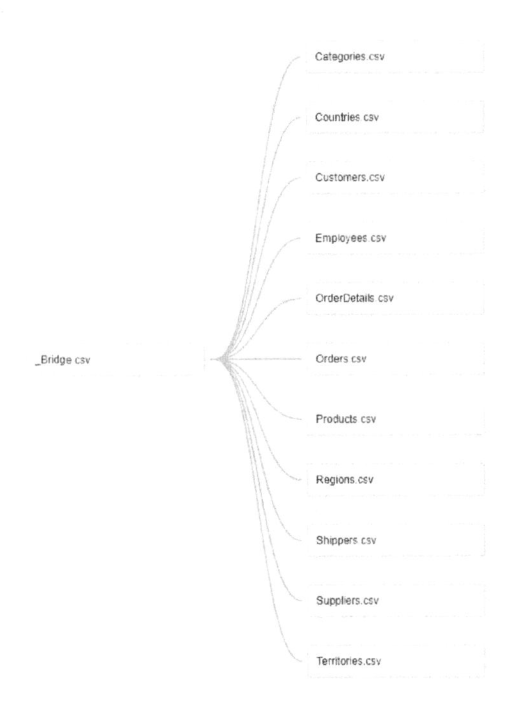

Figure 16.41: The "Data Source" page in Tableau. With the USS approach, the query is very easy to create

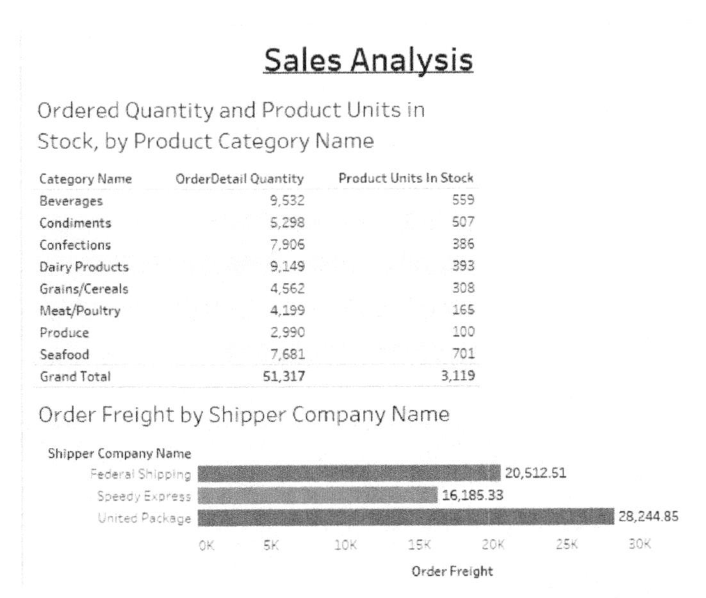

Category Name	OrderDetail Quantity	Product Units In Stock
Beverages	9,532	559
Condiments	5,298	507
Confections	7,906	386
Dairy Products	9,149	393
Grains/Cereals	4,562	308
Meat/Poultry	4,199	165
Produce	2,990	100
Seafood	7,681	701
Grand Total	51,317	3,119

Figure 16.42: One single dashboard integrates both reports. With the USS approach, everything is compatible with everything

The two reports are now integrated into one single dashboard. This does not mean that they are simply "in the same place". Much more than that, they are "fully integrated". A filter on the first report will propagate to the second report, and vice versa. This is happening automatically because all the data comes from one single query.

The USS approach allows the end-users to create their own reports, always starting from the same star schema. The new business requirements, in most cases, can be implemented directly inside the BI tools by the end-users, even if they are no data experts. For the majority of the new business requirements, there will be no need for any data transformation.

Any business user with a bit of training will be able to create a report from scratch. This is, in our opinion, the actual meaning of "self-service business intelligence".

Implementation with Microsoft Power BI

Let's now implement the USS approach with Microsoft Power BI. Figure 16.43 shows the data model with all the tables.

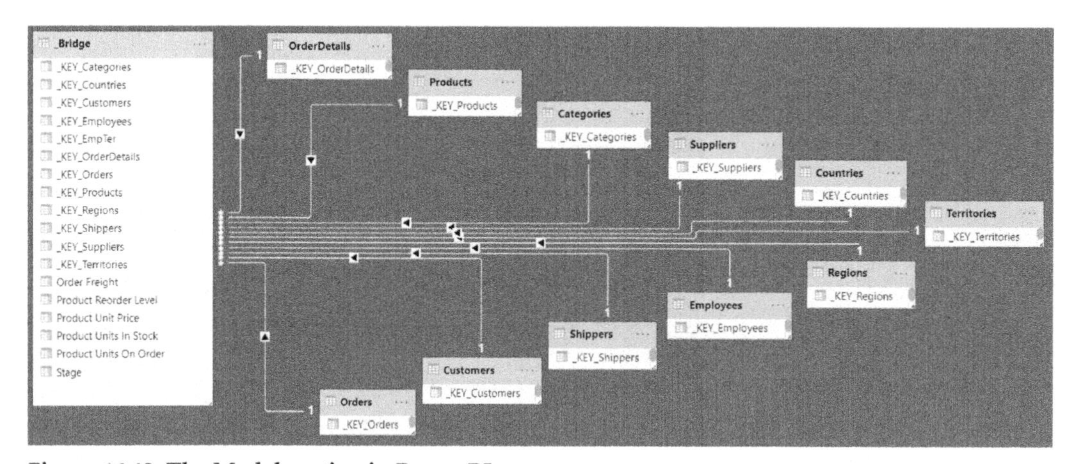

Figure 16.43: The Model section in Power BI

All of the connections are very easy to create, with no need to be a data expert.

Based on this data model, the end-users will be free to create all possible reports.

Implementation with Sisense

Let's try now with Sisense. See Figure 16.44.

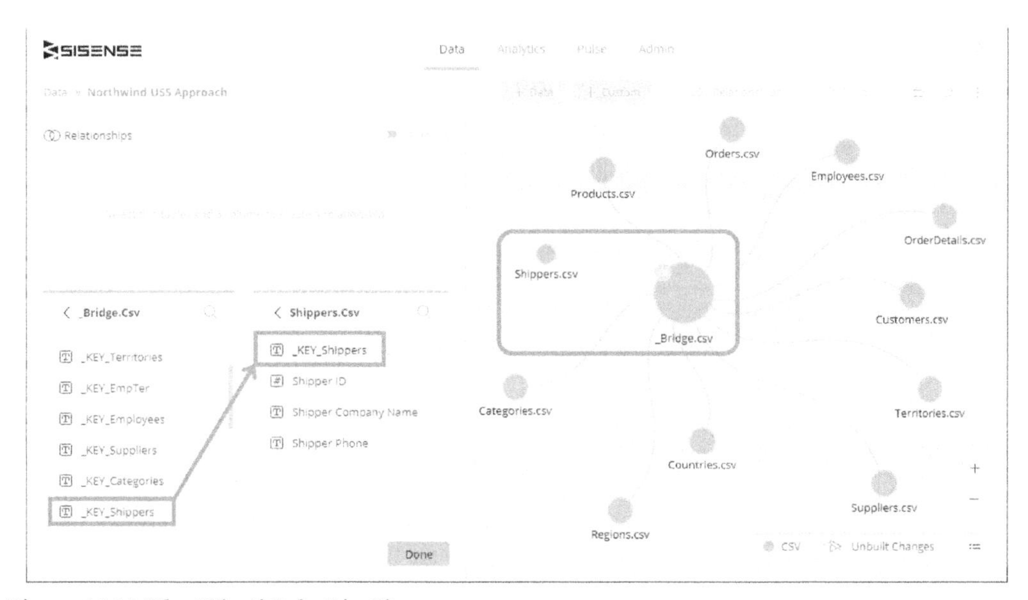

Figure 16.44: The "ElastiCube" in Sisense

Connections are very easy to create.

Based on this data model, the end-users will be free to create all possible reports.

Implementation with QlikView

Let's try now with QlikView. Figure 16.45 shows the data model.

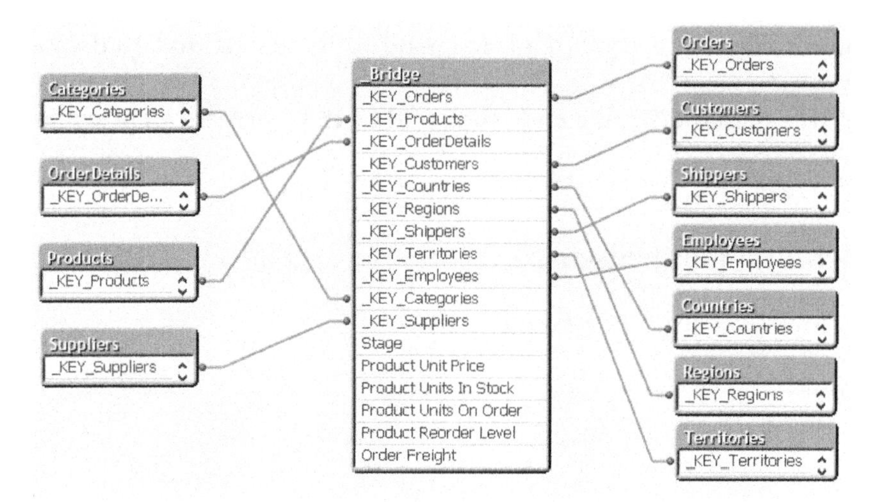

Figure 16.45: The Table Viewer in QlikView

Based on this data model, the end-users will be free to create all possible reports.

Implementation with Qlik Sense

Let's try now with Qlik Sense. See Figure 16.46.

Based on this data model, the end-users will be free to create all possible reports.

In particular, with Qlik Sense, the end-users can get insights by typing a request in natural language. See Figure 16.47.

Figure 16.46: The Data Manager in Qlik Sense

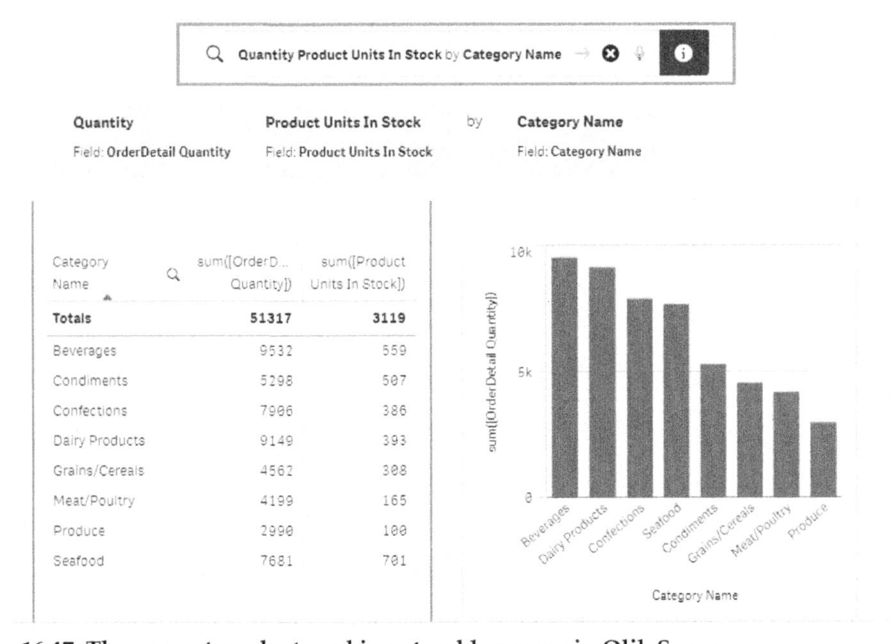

Category Name	sum([OrderD... Quantity])	sum([Product Units In Stock])
Totals	**51317**	**3119**
Beverages	9532	559
Condiments	5298	507
Confections	7906	386
Dairy Products	9149	393
Grains/Cereals	4562	308
Meat/Poultry	4199	165
Produce	2990	100
Seafood	7681	701

Figure 16.47: The request can be typed in natural language in Qlik Sense

Conclusions

The Unified Star Schema is easy.

Every business user can create reports and dashboards without being a data expert. It is impossible to create incorrect queries because the Bridge protects the end-users from the risks associated with loss of data, fan traps, chasm traps, multi-fact queries, loops, and non-conformed granularities. Basically, with the USS approach, numbers are always correct.

This solution must be implemented by a data expert. It is built entirely based on data, and it does not depend on the business requirements. One single star schema serves as a foundation for every present and future business requirement.

The key principle of the Unified Star Schema is that we need to watch and understand data before we start coding. We need to detect the risks and prevent them. This is what the USS approach does. Solving problems is great. Preventing them is even better.

Or, as Albert Einstein said:

"A clever person solves a problem. A wise person avoids it."

Index

Made in the USA
Coppell, TX
12 October 2021